THE VALE OF TEARS (EMEK HABACHA)

JOSEPH HACOHEN & THE ANONYMOUS CORRECTOR

THE VALE OF TEARS (EMEK HABACHA)

Translated plus critical commentary by

HARRY S. MAY

University of Tennessee

MARTINUS NIJHOFF / THE HAGUE / 1971

ISBN 90 247 1188 6

PRINTED IN THE NETHERLANDS

IN MEMORIAM

Professor Nelson Glueck,

my friend and mentor

INTRODUCTION

There were several compelling reasons which prompted me to undertake the work of translating and commenting upon the *Vale of Tears* by Joseph Hacohen, the sixteenth century physician and historian. First of all, those of us who have been teaching in the area of the Middle Ages have noticed over the past several years a distinct upsurge of interest in the field. Consequently, a number of Medieval Institutes, non-denominational in character and attached to major universitites, have sprung up all over the United States trying once more to relate themselves to that age which witnessed – among other things – the unparalleled struggle between two power complexes, the Church and the State. Scholars will also have to consider the Jewish Middle Ages, interconnected with the Christian Middle Ages, which lasted much longer and far beyond the Renaissance in Europe. Most of them tended to gloss over this aspect of Western Civilization which found the Jew in the juggernaut between these two powers. Students of all faiths, ecumenically oriented and truthful to the point of self-abasement are now ready, without a sense of embarrassment, to discuss this long bleak period in the history of European man, where greed, envy, suspicion and religious fanaticism had triumphed over reason and piety.

Yet, beyond all of this, there was another consideration which guided me in doing this tedious and often frustrating work: the knowledge of Hebrew has been on the decline in this country. Even Divinity Schools and Seminaries, where the study of the original Old and New Testaments ought to be of central importance, have no longer language requirements for their future teachers and preachers of religion. Many of them have become either skill oriented or defensively theological, whether this is out of grave concern for the Twenty-first Century man or out of subconsicous despair about organized religion in general. Be that as it may, the study of biblical languages has been neglected. Timid attempts to establish chairs in Judaic Studies, or to engage the services of part-time Hebrew Instructors, or fundamentalist Bible and Hebrew Literature critics, represent a token gesture toward a discarded tradition. Therefore, the translation of older Hebrew sources, heretofore inaccessible in the English language, has become a salutary almost dykeing device for our understanding of the centuries past. And more and more sources are being readied for the English reading audience, even in those countries which are not within the orbit of the English speaking world. Hacohen's work reflects the need for such a transmission into a modern sounding English prose. His stature will grow as the reader identifies himself with this unique and noble soul.

Joseph ben Joshua Hacohen's ancestors were long-time residents in Cuenca, Spain. They moved from there to Huete (85 and 55 miles East of Madrid, respectively). Later on, driven into exile, they and other refugees moved to Avignon, near the Franco-Italian border, synonymous for the Babylonian Captivity of the Roman Papacy which began in 1309 and which was not brought to an end until the Council of Constance, 1414-18. Hacohen's father, Joshua, married a certain Dolca (the Sweet one) in 1495. One year later Joseph was born. Four years after that event, his parents moved on to Genoa, Italy, where they resided from 1500 to 1516. In that year they were expelled from the city and moved about 30 miles northward to the small town of Novi. At the age of 23, Joseph married Paloma (little Dove), the daughter of a certain Rabbi Abraham Hacohen. When Joseph's father died in 1520, Paloma gave birth to a son whom the young couple named after the late father. Then, in 1538, Joseph and his family returned to Genoa where they lived until 1550. He worked there as a physician. During that period Paloma gave him three children. But he lost all of them prematurely. He also lost his adopted home again, and he and his co-religionists fled to their next domicile, Voltaggio, located in the Genoese Republic. Hacohen served his community as a physician until 1568. Then he and his family were on the move again, and settled down at last in Costoletto, in the Province of Montferrat. From what we can gather, Hacohen was welcomed there and held in high esteem. The date of his death is not accurately known. However, we may assume that he died around 1575 at the age of 79.

Joseph Hacohen's literary work consists of two major historical and other minor writings: *The Book of Chronicles of the Kings of France* and *The House of Ottoman* (Divré Hayamím L'málche Tzarfáth V'Ótoman) which describes the conflicts between Christianity and Islam during the time of the Crusades, although he begins his narrative with the demise of the Roman Empire. These Chronicles were first issued in Sabbioneta in 1554. (A second printing came out in Amsterdam in 1733). There are several factors that make this book interesting reading material, although it is in spots rather clumsy, going off on tangents and revealing, through repeated references, the suffering of the Jews in other countries outside Palestine. However, from his book we come to the conclusion that the Jews of Italy were not altogether hermetically sealed off from their Christian neighbors and that Hacohen knew perhaps even personally some of his more prominent contemporaries, the most famous of whom was Admiral Andreas Doria. He even had a detailed knowledge of the so-called Fiesco Conspiracy which pitted the aristocratic and emperialistic Doria (on the side of the French King Francis I) against the Tenth Century Ligurian first family of the Fiescos (brothers Girolamo, Verrina and Ottobueno, Counts of Lavagna) who were curiously enough Populists *and* on the side Pope Paul III.

The Chronicles have been translated into German and French. The original was in the possession of the Baron von Gemmingen family. Later on, several historians, such as Wilken, made ample use of Hacohen's accounts of his history of the Crusades. Also the Castilian scholar and diplomat Immanuel Aboab, Menasseh ben Israel (Rembrandt's friend), who was personally instrumental in the resettlement of the Jews in England during Cromwell's time, made use of Hacohen's work. Azariah de Rossi, another historian and physician tried to synthesize Judaism with Christianity, which prompted Joseph Caro[1] to declare him a heretic and apostat. Lastly, the Englishman Keightly incorporated Hacohen's narrative of the Second Crusade into his book *The History of the Crusades*. It was not until 1835 that Bialloblotzky[2] wrote a two-volume version of these Chronicles under the sponsorship of the Oriental Translation Fund, entitled *The Chronicles of Rabbi Joseph ben Joshua ben Meir, the Sephardi*.[3] However, this book was never widely distributed due to its unfortunate mistranslations and misinterpretations, which caused the indignation of Bialloblotzky's contemporaries - among them Dr. M. Wiener, Hannover-Germany, the German translator and commentator of Hacohen's major work, *Emek Habakha*.

Our work under consideration, *Emek Habakha, The Vale of Tears*, (some call it *The Vale of Weeping*) is a curious mixture of historiography and martyrology. From all indication, it seems that Hacohen had as his literary model (for style and approach) Samuel Usque's poem "Consolacam as Tribulacoens de Israel" (Counsel for the Sorrows of Israel), published in

---

[1] Talmudic scholar (1488-1575) who wrote the Shulhan Aruch (The Prepared Table), the authoritative compendium for the religious practices of the Jews. A sort of a "Mini-Talmud."

[2] Christian Hermann Bialloblotzky, 1799-1868, Jewish convert to Christianity.

[3] Jews of Spanish descent; mostly used for the exiles from Spain and Portugal. The Marranos can be included in this group. By contrast, we have the Ashkenazi Jews of Central and Eastern Europe. Modern Israel uses the Sephardi pronunciation of Hebrew in its daily language.

Ferrara in 1552. Usque's book contains a dialogue between three shepherds, Iacobo, Numeo and Zicareo. It was intended reading for Marranos (those unfortunate crypto-Christians, who under the watchful eyes of the Inquisition, practiced their former Jewish rites), which preached hope for a brighter future. Attacking the inquisition, Usque's book was put on the Index of the Church, and he was forced to flee. (Incidentally, the author became an ardent follower of David Reubeni, the false Messiah). The Christian scholar Mendes dos Remedios reissued these dialogues in 1907.

Hacohen began his work in Voltaggio around 1558, continued in 1563 and completed it by 1575. A "Corrector," writing anonymously at first but later on identified as the famous Samuel D. Luzzatto,[4] made his own chronological additions, picturing the tribulations of the Jews from 135 C. E. all the way up to 1065 C. E.

It seems that the original text of *Emek Habakha* is still in the former Royal Archives in Vienna-Austria, although three other copies are known to have been in the possession of Rabbi Samuel Luzzatto's family, Mordechai Samuel Ghirondi,[5] and the poet Joseph Almanzi.

A first attempt of an English translation of *Emek Habakha* was made by a certain Mr. Asher who had been commissioned by Dr. Max Letteris, the Polish Hebrew writer, in 1852 (Vienna & Cracow). However, Mr. Asher died in the process of doing this work.

It was not until 1858 that Dr. Meir Wiener translated the book from the Hebrew original into German where it was published by Oscar Leiner in Leipzig. I have consulted Wiener's footnotes and used them with discernment wherever advisable because Wiener was a first rate philologist and Bible expert. Readers of this German translation will be particularly grateful for the painstaking spadework Wiener has rendered in identifying the many biblical references and allusions which Hacohen used to embroider and beautify his Hebraic narrative.

While there are many anecdotal vignettes covering certain areas of Jewish live in Spain, France, Italy and other lands, Joseph Hacohen is the first known historian up to his time to write a comprehensive, chronological panorama of the last 1500 crowded years of Jewish History. This prompted the eminent historian of the 17th Century, Jacob Christian Bosnage, to exclaim that Joseph Hacohen is "the greatest historical writer since the days

---

[4] Abbreviation: ShaDal, 1800-1865, in Italy; founder of modern Jewish scholarship; defender of orthodoxy; rejected Cabalistic (mystic) Judaism, Maimonides and Spinoza. He maintained that the purpose of Religion is *goodness*, not truth. Foreshadower of Zionism.

[5] 1799-1852. Padua, Italy. Wrote a book on Ethics; also a Dictionary of Hebrew authors in Italy: Tól'doth G'dolè Yisraël. Professor of theology at Rabbinical College of Padua.

of Flavious Josephus" – an obvious reference to Hacohen's romanizing namesake and ancestor.[6]

In the eve of his life, Joseph Hacohen composed a few other books. Intrigued by the person of Columbus,[7] Hacohen published a smaller opus entitled *Who Sets The Boundaries of Nations* (*Matzív G'vulóth Ammím*) in 1557. It is the history of the conquest of Mexico appended by a complete recount of Columbus' journeys to the New World. In 1561, Hacohen composed a small dictionary of Hebrew nouns entitled *Péles Hashemóth*, and 1567 he wrote *Mekítz Nirdamín* (*The Awaker of Sleepers*), a Hebrew version of Meir Alguadez' *Spanish History Book*.

Hacohen wrote Jewish History from a very subjective point of view, as a Jew for his people in the Diaspora. He began his account where Josephus left off – with the beginning of the Via Dolorosa Judaica, from the ill-fated Bar Kochba Revolution in 135 C. E., all the way to the expulsion of the Jews from the Iberian Peninsula and their subsequent migrations until 1605. *The Vale of Tears* is the mirrored life of a people reflecting their suffering and almost unbearable agony. It is this heavy chain of pain which prompted Joseph Hacohen to write his historical narrative of events just as they occurred. To be sure, the writer suffers with his heroes, and he laments their fate in the lands of their migration and temporary domicile. However, he also interprets their fate sub specie Dei, as God-given and God-willed history.

What grips the reader is the brutality of man toward his fellow man, and the Jew who tries to bear his destiny with pride, dignity and prayerful submissiveness. And this same attitude of Hacohen shines through the pages of *The Vale of Tears* as he enumerates the multitude and the magnitude of his people's suffering. Thus we also experience moments of beauty, deeply felt pathos and temporary tranquility where our author turns poet and psalmist, longing for freedom and salvation, praying for an end to all injustice and all human barbarity.

Joseph Hacohen identifies himself and empathizes with his people. Therein lies the singular beauty of the book. He weaves his personal life and his own philosophy into his historical account, so much of which he witnessed and endured himself, so that he becomes an integral part of this unique history. Thus the reader follows him from Spain, all the way through Germany into Italy where he hoped to find rest, peace of mind, and a chance to work as a physician and writer. Hacohen leads us through the countries of oppression, recounting the Road-Stations of Disaster, but also the all too few moments of glorious peace and Jewish creativity.

---

[6] In *L'Histoire et la Religion des Juifs*.
[7] Presumably suspecting almost prophetically Columbus' alias Colon's Marrano origin.

His style is a mixture of medieval Hebrew and Biblical language, the flavor of which this translator and commentator can only try to preserve for the modern reader. However, it was necessary to eliminate many repetitive phrases and circumlocutions for the sake of clarity. Another great difficulty which presented itself was Hacohen's rather naive historiographical presuppositions primarily in the accounts leading up to his own century. Just to cite a few examples; many of the events leading up to the middle of the 11th Century contain a number of errors:

Bar Kokhba (Bar Kosiba) did not revolt during the reign of Domitian since the fort of Bethar fell in Hadrian's times. He is also quite hazy about early German and Italian poets and writers and antedates them. The reasons for this are chiefly that Hacohen learned about the fate of his people from secondary and tertiary sources, both Christian and Jewish, and from tendentious royal and clerical archives. As to his sources, the first and second crusades were from the Chronicles of Rabbi Eliezer ben Nathan and supplemented with data taken from the History of the German Kings. Such archives were written primarily to extoll either prince or pope. And the recording of events which involved the Jews were too often inaccurate, based on hearsay, or altered to suit the rulers. Therefore, this translator and commentator had to be the second "Corrector" in addition to the first, S. D. Luzzatto. Hence, the reader is asked to be patient with Hacohen and to follow carefully the over four-hundred and twenty added footnotes which are designed to give a clarification of historical data and to explain the many biblical allusions of *Emek Habacha*.

The present author has studied and compared the various Hebrew versions in writing this "free" modern translation and has supplemented them by adding his own commentary in the form of annotated footnotes to the text. The Hebrew scholar and specialist, who will look for a verbatim translation of this manuscript, will be diappointed. I shall brave his scorn and critique, because here is a late attempt to do adequate justice to the Hebrew text and at the same time to the contemporary reader (mostly non-Jewish) whom the Hebrew experts have neglected for all too long. The reason for this seems to be that as philologists they did perhaps not feel qualified to come to grips with Hacohen's many incorrect historical data, causing too much confusion and obvious difficulties. On the other hand, this translator is a historian who writes for historians, who uses the classical languages, be they Hebrew, Greek, Latin or Arabic as tools for the understanding of texts which ought to serve the student of history, who is entitled to also "witness" the events of the Jewish Middle Ages and to be able to identify with them.

This author is deeply indebted to his friend and colleague, Professor

Harold S. Fink of the University of Tennessee, who has given him unstinting support and made innumerable suggestions pertaining to a more elaborate extension of the footnotes which are especially geared to the non-Jewish reader. It is hoped that the "medievalist" will gain a better insight and understanding of Israel's unparalleled travail in the Diaspora.

Thus says Joseph ben Yehoshua, the son of Meir, son of Yehuda, son of Yehoshua, son of Yehuda, son of David, son of Mosheh of the priestly stock who went forth from Huete in Castile. Since the misfortunes which befell us from the day of Judah's exile from its land of his which was destroyed (as is here and there referred to), I undertook the task of putting them together in a small book which contains all that I have found in the booklets of writers who wrote before my time in Hebrew and in their books. I have entitled the work *Emek Habacha* because that title corresponds to its very content. Everyone who reads in it will be astounded and will gasp,[1] with tears welling down from his eyes; and putting his hands to his loins, he will ask; "How long, Oh God?" God, may the days of our mourning come to an end and may He send us the Just Messiah, and he will redeem us, soon, for His Mercy's sake. Amen, Amen.[2]

After Jerusalem had lost all its glory, Titus, the Roman Emperor, (79-81 A. D.), left a Jewish remnant in Bethar, Usha and their daughter communities and, as long as he lived, Rabbi Yochanan ben Zakkai was their head and guide. And it happened that the Romans killed Rabbi Shimeon ben Gamliel and Rabbi Ishmael ben Elisha, both of whom had stemmed from a noble and priestly family, and there was no deliverer for them on the day of God's anger. Titus also intended to murder Rabbi Gamliel, son of Shimeon, but Rabbi Yochanan ben Zakkai petitioned before him and Gamliel ben Shimeon was pardoned. The rest of the Israelites, also saved, lived and multiplied after that in the cities of Bethar, and from there they spread afar. After Titus had reigned two years, he died and Domitian succeeded to the throne. Then

---

[1] Isaiah 42:14

[2] Amen, Amen; i. e., so be it. This is the regular liturgical response of the worshipper, Jewish and non-Jewish. The phrase was often doubled at the end of a prayer or psalm. Said the Rabbis: Who soever says Amen with all his strength, to him the gates of Paradise shall be opened.

Kosiba (bar Kochba)[3] arose in Bethar and spoke: "I am the Messiah, the son of David." And he rebelled against the Emperor Domitian and killed the Roman general who was in the Land of Judea. And Domitian was powerless to do anything against him because he (Domitian) was still young. After that, Kosiba ruled in Bethar in the fifty-second year after the destruction of our Temple[4] (68 A. D.) When bar Kochba died, his son, Rufus (the Red), ruled; and after Rufus died, his son, Romulus, reigned in his stead. Many Israelites in the different locations in which they lived scattered sided with Kosiba and his sons: after Kosiba had gathered many foot soldiers and equestrians, he rose up against the Emperor; their call spread throughout the lands; he fought with the peoples who surrounded him, and even attained great power in Egypt. And Kosiba reigned, with his son and grandson, over Bethar and its surroundings until the time of Hadrian; and the nations obeyed them. After Domitian had ruled fifteen years, a plot built up against him, he was slain, and his corpse was thrown to the dogs. Then Nerva reigned in his stead for one year,[5] and when he died, Trajan followed him on the Imperial Throne (98-117 A. D.)

In those days many Jews could be found in the land of Cyrene in eastern Africa.[6] These people arose and with the sharpness of the sword they slaughtered Romans and Greeks who lived there. The Jews of Egypt also arose in that time, and those who dwelt on the Isle of Cyprus deserted the Romans and slew them. The number of the dead amounted to two hundred thousand. Therefore, the Emperor decreed that each Cypriot Jew who could be found shoud forfeit his life, and even those whom the waves of the sea had spilled upon the land were also to be killed. Trajan then sent a mighty army to Cyrene which killed all the Jews living there; and not one soul was left alive. The number of those killed in the bloodbath amounted to four hundred thousand. After Trajan's death, Hadrian ascended to the throne.

Romulus, the son of bar Kochba, happy in his heart, spoke thus: "I am

---

[3] Hacohen here follows the historical account of Rabbi Abraham ben David in his book, *Sepher ha-Kabbala.* (Abraham ibn Daud, Cracow 1820)

[4] At first, Kosiba ruled without Roman interference. Later matters changed: Hadrian passed through Judea and noticed that Jerusalem had not been rebuilt since the destruction by Titus. He founded on its site Aelia Capitolina, a Roman colony and placed a Temple of Jupiter on the spot where the ancient temple stood. Under Bar Cosiba, the Jews began a savage rebellion. It ended with the death of five hundred eighty thousand "rebels"; the utter depopulation of Palestine and a law allowed Jews only once a year admission to their Holy City. But in spite of their rebellion, the surviving Jews still enjoyed freedom of worship.

[5] The text reads Nirosta, an abvious misspelling meaning Nerva. Actually he ruled from 96-98 A. D.

[6] Today's Cyrenaica on the northeast tip of Lybia.

the Annointed of God." But when many accepted him, Hadrian's fire flamed up he moved against them with a mighty and powerfully equipped army. He besieged Bethar for three long years, and on the ninth day of the fifth month in the seventy-third year after the expulsion of Judah from the land, the city was captured.[7] Much blood was spilled therein, the aged were not spared, mothers were dashed near their children[8] on that day of God's grimness, and the blood of the slain splashed almost to the bellies of the horses in the streets. The streams changed into blood and their stench reached into the Heavens. As the blood flowed into the sea, it washed away with it the large stones which can be found at Jericho.[9] The number of the dead was forty-five thousand, and among these was Romulus, the son of Kosiba.[10] Those who remained alive, Hadrian led as captives to Spain, and these are the exiles of Jerusalem who live in Spain still to this very day.

In these hopeless days, the Romans had Rabbi Akiba flayed with iron cudgels, they burned Rabbi Hanina ben Teradion while he held the scrolls of the Law in his hands; and they expedited from life to death Rabbi Jeshbab, secretary of the Sanhedrin, and Rabbi Hutzpit, who was an interpreter. On the order of the Roman Emperor an official announcement was made: any city was to be destroyed in which Teachers of the Law had been given licence through the ceremony of ordination (S'micha);[11] the ordained were to be killed, and the ordainer was to be throttled. At that time, Rabbi Yehuda, son of Baba, went forth and settled between the big city of Usha and Shefar-aam; and as he was about to ordain Rabbis Meir, Jose, Simeon, and El'azar ben Shamua, the Romans fell upon him suddenly and gouged him with swords and lances, and he died. Thus he fulfilled the word of the Lord which He had prophesied through his servant Daniel: "And those among the people who are wise shall make many understand, though for some days they shall fall by sword and flame, by captivity and plunder."[12] After this vicious Hadrian had ruled for nineteen years, he died, and Bubanus reigned in his stead for some time; and after he, too, had passed on, Hadrian II, to whom many nations were subject, came to power.[13] This Hadrian gave orders to rebuild the ruins of Jerusalem, and Jews hastened to obey him, although God had not commanded it. Hadrian gave the city the cognomen Capitolina and

---

[7] Bethar was captured in A. D. 135, not 134 as is indicated by the text.
[8] Hosea 10:14
[9] Joshua 4:5-7
[10] Kosiba himself was also among the dead.
[11] Placing of the hands on the ordained.
[12] Daniel 11:33
[13] At this point the text is incorrect: there was no Roman Emperor Bubanus nor was there a Hadrian II. Hadrian was succeeded by Antoninus Pius in 138 A. D.

forbade that it should ever be called Jerusalem again. The Jews were very gladdened but it was not pleasant in God's eyes. Many non-Jews lived there also, and everyone worshipped his own gods, and altars were erected to these gods. However, the Jews were not permitted to serve the Lord their God according to their will. This saddened them and made them arise against the Romans, and they chased the Legions from the Land of Judea and afflicted a great defeat upon them. After that, Hadrian II sent out his general, Julius Severus, who warred against the Jews and defeated them.[14] The armies of Severus also destroyed all fertile fields, razed fifty large and beautiful watch towers besides numerous fortifications, and burned down nine hundred eighty-five towns whose smoke rose to the skies in this wretched time. And the number of those who fell in this war was great: Fifty thousand warring men died besides those others who also died as a consequence of the hunger and other deprivations which God had decreed for them. The remaining Jews were expelled from Jerusalem and these Dispersed lived then in the lands of their enemies and remain there to this days. After Hadrian had ruled twenty-one years, he died – Oh God, repay him for his meanness! Meanwhile, God remembered his Covenant into which he had entered with our Fathers, and in which He spoke: "Yet for all that when they are in the land of their enemies, I will not spurn them, neither will I abhor them."[15] And God reflected upon possible harm (to the Jews) in the fulness of His mercy, for it came to pass that Antoninus Pius became Emperor, and our Holy Teacher[16] found mercy in his eyes and extended it to him for his entire life span. After the death of Antoninus, Commodus, who also loved our Holy Teacher very much, reigned in his stead.[17] The Teacher redacted the Mishnah in the year 3949, that is, one hundred twenty years after the expulsion of Judah from his Land. Later on, about two hundred years after the dispersion, Rabbi Yochanan redacted the Jerusalemite Talmud.[18]

In the year 4134 (374), the King of the Persians[19] showed himself inimical toward the Jews and ordered Amemar, son of Mar Jenuka, Rabbi Meshar-shiya, and the Prince of the Exiles, Mar Huna, to be jailed and then killed.

---

[14] In A. D. 132, Hadrian sent Julius Severus to take Bethar which he did in 135. The battle here is the same as that referred to on page 3.

[15] Leviticus 26:44

[16] Rabbi Jehuda ha-Nassi (?)

[17] Antoninus Pius was not succeeded by Commodus, but by Marcus and Lucius Aurelius the two being joint emperors from A. D. 161-169 at which time Lucius died. Marcus ruled alone until A. D. 180. In that year he was succeeded by Commodus who ruled until 192.

[18] Zunz, *Gottesdienstliche Vorträge*, 1892, p. 53. Frankfurt a/M J. Kauffmann.

[19] The Sassanian King Shapur II

He also laid hands on Israelite youths and forcibly led them astray from the Lord, the God of Israel.

After some time, God allowed Rav Ashi to rise. He began to write down the Talmud before the eyes of all Israel, but he took ill before he completed it and died in the year 4187 (417). The holy work was completed after his death in the days of Rabba bar Joseph (in the year 427), and all Israel accepted it forever. The memory of Rav Ashi will not vanish from posterity.

Rabba Tosphaa died in 4233 (473), during the time when the Persian Kings dealt cruelly with the Jews with the intent to turn them away from Judaism. They thus ordained suffering for the Israelites, and their life took a turn for the worse.

The Emperor Heraclius reigned in Constantinople in 613, that is in the year 4373 since the creation; and about the same time (in 616), Sisebut, from the tribe of the Visigoths, ruled in Spain.[20] Sisebut most emphatically ordered the Jews of his realm to convert to his faith, for it was his intention to make them renege on their Judaism. This caused the Jews, like hunted gazelles,[21] to stumble, and indeed, many of them fell then.

In these days Mohammedanism came to Spain (711 A. D.). As Isidore the Holy wished to capture them (the Moors), the forced apostate Jews informed them thus, and they fled from Isidore.[22] As many of the converts then returned to their faith, the Spaniards rebelled against them, but God redirected the heart of the King[23] so that he no longer plotted against their lives, but merely chased them from his land. After an eight year rule, he was poisoned, and his son reigned for only seven months after him. After he had died his son, Chintila, followed him to the royal throne. Chintila recalled the exiled Jews and many of them returned to their ancient faith.[24] After this, the Emperor Heraclius (ca. 575-642) fought against the Persian King, Cosroes, for some time and finally returned to his land after he had killed Cosroes.[25] It then happed in the twenty-first year of his reign, that is, in the

[20] See note 22
[21] Isaiah 13:14
[22] Presumably a reference to Isidor, Archbishop of Seville (d. 636).
[23] One of the Sisebuts, father of Chintila.
[24] Jews fared rather well under Visigothic rule. They protected the Pyrenees against Gaullic (Frankish and Burgundian) invasions and were even allowed to hold slaves and convert heathens to Judaism. Catholic ascendency in Spain changed all that. Under pressure from nobles and clergy, King Reccared restricted both Jews and Arians. King Sisebut, a Westgoth and contemporary of Heraclius, infected by the anti-Jewish laws of the Christian rulers of Spain, put the same alternative before the Jews: either conversion or emigration. Some Jews converted, others fled. Siomtila, who succeeded Sisebut, allowed the forcibly converted Jews to return to the land and to their religion. Generally, the succeeding Visigoth kings were fair toward the Jews.
[25] Cosroes was actually killed by his own son, Siroes.

year 4393 (633),[26] and after Heraclius had obtained a knowledge of Astrology, that he saw through the eyes of that science that the Roman Empire in his days was to fall into the hands of the circumcised (Moslems). It was then that this miserable creature thought that God wished the Jews to share in this honor, since they were also circumcised. Hence, his ire erupted against them, and he ordered that all Jews in his realm, who refused baptism, be killed. He also sent delegates to Dagobert, the King of France, with instructions to behave in the same vicious manner. Dagobert proceeded likewise, and many Jews in France changed their religion, while many others succumbed to the sword. But the nefarious Heraclius did not know that this matter referred to the Arabs who are circumcised like us.

At this time appeared Omar ben Alkataf[27] (634-44) who conquered Syria, Philistia, Damascus, Egypt, and the whole of Palestine, including Jerusalem. He inquired about the Temple where the name of the Lord was called upon and, being answered, he brought a huge amount of silver and gold to the place in order to restore it to its previous splendor, prostrated himself upon the ground and prayed to God. He also fought against Yazdegerd, King of the Persians, captured his entire country, and carried off his wives and children into captivity. And Omar gave one of Yazdegerd's[28] daughters to the Exilarch Bustanai for a wife,[29] and when she was married, she left her people and her faith, and he loved her exceedingly.

Much suffering and disorder occurred also in Germany and Italy in the year 4405 (645) and the fortune of the Jews sank as they drank from the cup of God's wrath. In the year 4450 (690) a brutal war between the Arabs and the Persians occurred,[30] and the Persians were beaten and subjugated. Con-

---

[26] The text is incorrect here: Heraclius came to power in 610 A. D. :twenty-one years later would be A. D. 631.

[27] Omar (Umar ibn-al-Khattab in Arabic transliteration) was the second orthodox Moslem caliph. He found the Temple in ruins; it was never rebuilt, although it was a holy site in the eyes of a Moslem.

[28] Yazdegerd ("Made by God") is the name of three Sassanid Kings of Persia. In our story we are dealing most likely with Yazd. III, a grandson of Chosroes II who had been murdered by his son Kavadh II in 628. He never "enjoyed" his throne and fled from one district to the other, until he too was murdered at Mero in 651. It is of interest to note that the Parsees, who use the old Persian calendar, count to this day the years from Yazdeg. III's accession (June 16, 632).

[29] Bustanai was the first Exilarch under Arabian (Persian) rule.

[30] After the Arab conquest, the greater part of Persia was divided into four provinces: persian Iraque, Khuzistan, Khurasan and Seistan. The Arabs interfered very little with the Persians. There was even intermarriage between the two ethnic groups (Modern Persian is the result). However, fiscal pressures of the Ommayyads caused malcontent between the two. Also Moslem missionary zeal spread conflicts. Hacohen seems to allude to these acts of occasional warfare.

sequently, many Jews, living until then in Persia fled before the swords and migrated from people to people and from one country to another until finally they came to Russia, Germany, and Switzerland, where they found many of their own people living. And some migrated even as far as Halle, in Germany, where Mar Sutra[31] lay buried, and there they erected academies in order to cling to God's Torah. Rabbi Benjamin ben Serach was their chief; and these are the names of men who judged Israel after him until that terrible day, on which the stars in their courses warred[32] to test the princes: Rabbi Amitai, Rabbi Solomon the Babylonian, who died in Spain and is buried there, Rabbi David from Muenzburg, Rabbi Ephraim from Bonn, Rabbi Menachem and Rabbi Shabatai.

Roderic from the tribe of the Visigoths reigned in Spain in the year 4471 (711). He had sent his servant, Count Julian,[33] to Africa, but during his absence Roderic went to the Count's daughter and raped her. Hearing this, Count Julian became very irate against his master, gathered a force of brave Arabs and returned to Spain, which he conquered with his mighty force in 4478 (718). Roderic died without leaving behind an heir.[34] The Arabs then laid siege to Toledo for a long time. On the Sunday before Passover, as the citizens of Toledo feared that the King[35] might be angered, so they declared: the Jews were our traducers in that they betrayed us to the Arabs. Thereupon, the King extended his wrath against the Jews in his realm, and the people stormed against them and pounced upon them like bears and wolves, as if they intended to swallow them alive. But God had mercy upon the Jews and permitted them to find grace in the eyes of the King who would not permit that any further suffering come over them, saying, "Why are these people to die who now live amongst us, and in what way have they committed a crime?"

After Toledo had been conquered, a band of Arabs came from the desert and entered like night-robbers into the city of Medinat al Nabi[36] where

---

[31] Mar Sutra (Zutra) was one of the most famous Talmudic scholars and redactors (Amora) of the exile in the Academy of Pumpeditha. He submitted to the authority of Rav Ashi of Sors (Sura), one of the other luminaries in Babylon.

[32] Judges 5:20

[33] Julian was the commander of Ceuta, the ancient Septum.

[34] Roderic, the last Visigoth King of Spain, was defeated in the battle of Rio Barbate by the Arab Tariq; he died in that battle which took place in 711.

[35] The Arab and Berber revolt in and their withdrawal from Spain led to the new Kingdom of Alphonso I (739-57). The Spanish nobility – always anti-foreign – was hostile toward the Jews as "collaborators" with the former Moslem occupying powers. Hence Hacohen's remark.

[36] Medinat al Nabi is Medina, city of the Prophet Mohammed. It is problematic whether this incident refers to the actual Medina or a town in Spain by that name held by the Moslems.

Mohammed's grave was, stole the holy garments and the percious stone which was near Mohammed's sarcophagus, and then went their way. The guards asked, "Who can we blame for this infamy?" And thereupon they put it upon the Jews. Thus, in those days, a poor and needy Jew by the name of Abraham della Cappa, together with other Jews who were in his retinue, moved out of Toledo in order to settle down in a place which they found opportune. And these Jews were accused, that they had been sent out to steal the coffin which had been despoiled. When the rumor was heard in the Arab regions, they arose against the Jews, killed many, and destroyed forty synagogues of which one of the first to fall was located in Toledo. It was this time which was one of want and lamentation for all Jews who lived in the Barbary and the Orient; and the Arab kings were angry toward them and thought to convert them by force. And in their great anxiety the Jews prayed to God, and He showed compassion for them and did not leave them completely to perdition in this hopeless time.

In the year 4570 (810) Christians and Moors fought against each other and many men of outstanding physical stature were struck down. And this was also for Israel a time of suffering: many Jews fled before the sword from Germany to Spain and England and many communities which had hesitated to flee, sanctified the name of the God of Israel with their death, for they spurned to yield to their enemies. Thus hardly a remnant of refugees remained in Germany on that day of God's ire. However, God did show mercy on the escaped remnant for He sent to Germany Charlemagne, the Emperor of France, to whom the nations submitted.[37] Charlemagne brought Kalonymus who was born in Lucca, from his home in Rome to lead the surviving Israelites back to Germany. And Charlemagne gathered up the scattered of Judah and entered into a covenant with them: Academies of the kind that had existed before were then founded in Germany for the teaching of God's Torah, and Rabbi Kalonymus was their head. May God remember them for good. Also, at that time, the Jews of Italy despaired of their lives and Charlemagne came to their aid. Oh Lord, remember him for these good deeds, and champion their cause.

[37] Charlemagne who actually became literate in old age, attracted to his Palace School in Aachen quite a number of scholars. Amongst them the famous Alcuin, a disciple of the Venerable Bede, who introduced the study of Greek, Latin and even Hebrew. Alcuin had a decisive influence on Charlemagne and became not only the King's closest advisor but also his "regulator" vis a vis the Pope's behavior and was responsible for the intellectual revival that "nourished learning throughout the Frankish Empire". (Joseph Dahmus, *Seven Medieval Kings*, Doubleday, N. Y. 1967, p. 133/34.) As a matter of fact, Alcuin conducted "dramatic Bible sessions" with the King who became very enamoured with the Bible and who took King David as his own model for rulership. Hence his love for the People of the Book.

In the year 4824 (1064), a certain Jew by the name of Joseph Halevi, son of the Nagid Rabbi Samuel, lived in Granada. It was this Nagid (Prince) who did much good for the Jews of Spain, the Magreb,[38] Africa and Egypt, for Joseph walked in the ways of his father in any way, except, that, because he did not have to suffer in his youth, he was not as modest as his father had been. Thus, he became proud to his own undoing, and the nobility of Granada envied him and spoke to him in terms that were none too friendly. Indeed, they arose against him on the Sabbath, the ninth day of the tenth month (Teveth) and killed him together with the whole congregation, including those Jews who had come from distant lands to see his Torah (erudition) and greatness.[39] The mourning over their death spread over all the lands in which this terrible news became known. Mark it, Oh Lord, see it, and champion their cause. After that, Rabbi Alfasi came to Spain and settled in Cordoba in the year 4848 (1088).

During the time of Philip (1060-1108), the son of Henry I (1031-1060), King of France, Peter the Hermit had gone to Jerusalem and he saw the sad burden of the uncircumcised (Christians) who lived there. Upon his return in 4956 (1096),[40] he reported this news to Philip. The Christian rulers then offered to go there in order to conquer Palestine, and Jerusalem in particular, and they gathered up from all countries an innumerable multitude of people, men and women, who offered to go on this march. And that horrible year was a time of trouble for Jacob in the lands of the uncircumcised and in all places in which they lived scattered: and they despaired with their lives as manifold and terrible sufferings were inflicted upon them, for these irresponsible ones, the French and Germans who joined the armed forces, and imprudent nation who gave no respect for the aged nor showed favor toward the lads.[41]

[38] Magreb, Arabic for West, usually identified with Algiers and Marocco, North Africa. It is a lose term to signify the land from which the Moors came.

[39] More than 1500 Jewish families are said to have lost their lives (c. f., M. Wiener, *Shevet Jehuda*, Ch. 5). Viscount Berengar protected the Jews in his country, Narbonne, against the fury of the Christians and received for this a letter of commendation from Pope Alexander II. (*Shevet Jehuda* by Solomon ibn Verga) (Warsaw 1822)

[40] Peter the Hermit is a legendary figure. He is regarded as the originator of the First Crusade (1095-1099). Actually it was Pope Urban I who conceived the plan. Peter was popular with the masses. It is therefore not surprising that Hacohen reflects this popular view and fictional record. Peter actually returned before 1096, because Pope Urban preached his Crusade at Clermont in 1095.

[41] Deuteromony 28:50. These outrages took place in 1096 when the First Crusade got started. Most of these massacres were by the rabble who followed irresponsible and irrepressible popular leaders like Peter the Hermit, Eric of Leisingen, Volkmar and Gottschalk who started ahead of the Crusades. See Steven Runciman, *A History of the Crusades*, I (Cambridge U Press, 1951, pp 121-23; 134-41). Runciman has used Solomon bar Simeon, Eliezar bar Nathan and other sources.

And they said, "For the Savior's sake, let us take vengeance first upon the Jews and wipe them out of the family of nations, and the name of Israel shall not be remembered unless they accept another faith and become Christians as we are. Afterwards we shall go on." As the Jews in Germany heard this terrible news, their hearts melted and turned to water,[42] panic gripped them, and birth pangs as in pregnant women came to them; and they raised their eyes toward the Heavens, decreed fasts and cried to God in their plight. And He covered himself into a cloud so that the prayer could not penetrate. The enemies then rose against the holy congregation of Speyer on the fifth of Iyar (May third), which was the Sabbath, and then people were killed by the mouth of the sword, because they had refused to be unfaithful to their God. The first to die was a pious woman who preferred death to life: she grabbed a knife to commit suicide, because she scorned to abjure her faith. (Verbatim: she refused to exchange her glory for something of no worth.) She said, "God is my portion, therefore I abide in Him." The remainder of the Jews were saved by Bishop John for his eye had pity on them and he saved them from the hands of the enemy; and Eliezer ben Nathan Halevi composed an elegy at that time.

On the twenty-third day of the same month (Sunday, May 18th), the rabble arose like hungry wolves against the community of Worms and many Jews fled to the Palace of Bishop Allebrandus, fearful that misfortune might fall upon them also. The riff-raff broke into the houses of the Jews, murdered those whom they found there, and spared neither women nor men. After that they destroyed the houses, tore down the watch-towers and reached out to plunder; and no salvation came to the Israelites on that day of God's wrath. The Torah Scrolls were thrown to the ground, cut to pieces, and trampled upon; and they created much noise in the House of the Lord, as if it were a holiday. They devoured Israel with a full mouth and left over only a small remnant whom they forcibly converted from the God of Israel. These, however, after the storm had subsided, returned to the Lord, the God of their forefathers. But those, who were killed, had sanctified the Name of the God of Israel before all the world by preferring death to life because they did not wish to become unfaithful to their God. Many of them had killed themselves, or their brothers, or friends, or their dear wives and children; yes, even merciful mothers slaughtered their own children with fortitude and courage reciting the Shema (the Watchword of Israel) as their children gave up their souls at their mothors' bosoms.

After seven days, on the first of Sivan (Sunday, May 25th), the scum

---

[42] Joshua 7:5

proceeded in the same way with those who had fled into the Bishop's palace. They mocked them and slew many as they had done to the others before. But these also did as their brothers had done, for they slew one another: and only a few escaped on this disastrous day. The number killed on these two terrible days were eight hundred. Amongst them was a young man by the name of Simcha Hacohen whom they had dragged to the church to baptize him by force. But he took a knife from his pocket and gored one of the city-councilmen, a relative of the Bishop, whereupon he, too, was struck with a pike so that he died. For all these I mourn and clamour: I lament like jackals and grieve like ostriches. For these also Eliezer composed an elegy.

When the holy Congregation of Mainz heard the terrible news, they all fled into the Bishop's palace in which they assumed their lives could be protected in the face of perdition. But their enemies arose against them on the third of Sivan (May 27th) and slew them: even the old men were not spared: and as the enemies charged toward them, they uttered in a loud voice the Shema Yisrael, and stretched out their hands towards those who were the delight of their eyes. And they, too, butchered their own wives and children; yes, even the women carried out the work of the slaughterer on this fateful day. Some of the old men had wrapped themselves into their prayer shawls, and they recited the prayer: "The Rock, perfect are His deeds, for by them He teaches the daughters of Israel to mourn and a woman to intune lamentations."[43] For lo, the Higher Powers also sob in the streets and Messengers of Peace are weeping over this holy community against whom the Spoilers have decended with their axes like cutters of wood. Therefore do I cry and lament, walk about wild and bare, because of the thirteen-hundred souls who became prey and booty on that fateful day. Will You ever refrain, Oh Lord?

Sixty helpless people had hidden themselves in the Treasury, and the Bishop had disbursed them to the villages to save them,[44] but their enemies pursued and killed them. In all the places to which they had fled, even the stones cried out after them from the walls,[45] to ruin them and bring them to naught, for the Despoiler was given license to destroy in this wretched time. Only two men, who had been forcibly converted, saved themselves. The name of one was Uri, and the other, who was the head of the congregation and whose two daughters were with him, was Isaac ben David, and

[43] Jerem 9:19
[44] The Archbishop's name was Rothardt. According to some, he was not really innocent in his pretense to hide the Jews from the wrath of the populace: he too, had his eyes on the wealth of the Jews (c.f., Wilken, *Geschichte der Kreuzzüge*, p. 98).
[45] Habakkuk 2:11

these two returned to the God of their fathers. But on the day (May 29th) preceeding the Festival of Weeks (Shavuoth), Isaac killed his daughters, ignited his house, and offered God the sacrifice of himself and his friend Uri as they stood before the Ark of the Covenant in the burning Synagogue. The flames engulfed them and their souls ascended to the Heavens. My heart is troubled over the slain, and those who died in the flames, and my soul rejects all consolation. Champion, Oh Lord, the flight of their souls and judge their righteous cause.

This terrible news reached Cologne on the fifth of Sivan (May 29th), and the Jews hid in the homes of their friends. But on the following day much noise and terror came, when their enemies arose, destroyed their homes, tore down the watch-towers, and took much booty; and to aid them was impossible. After that, the populace broke into Synagogues, ripped out the Torah Scrolls and made them the objects of mockery. And on the holiday of the Lord, which commemorates the Giving of the Torah,[46] they trampled upon the Scrolls in the streets, and the blasphemers tore them to shreds and stepped upon them. Finally the culprits dishonored and burned them. Will God not avenge this? Oh Lord Zebaoth, do justice; to You I commend this case.

After that, they apprehended the learned sage, Rabbi Isaac, who had refused to flee, and they dragged him to their church, where he spat before their statues, abused and insulted them. Then he was killed and a woman was also murdered there. On the tenth day of the same month (June 3rd), when the storm had subsided, the Bishop sent those, who had been hiding in the homes of their acquaintances, to the villages and distributed them in seven localities in order to save them. There they remained until the fourth month (Tammuz), fasted daily, promised donations for holy works and prayed to God. On the morning after the New Moon (Wednesday, June 25th)[47] the enemies moved to the little village of Neuss and were followed by much scum. They rose against the Jew, Samuel ben Asher, killed him together with his two sons, trampled on them with their feet, as if they were street manure, and hung the sons from the door posts of their house. And they made merry over them by reviling the people of the living God.

On the following day the enemies of Israel arose against the poor Jews in the small village of Wevelinghoven, to take their lives in quick order. Rabbi Levi ben Samuel lived there with his daughter, an old woman named Rachel,

[46] Shavuoth or Feast of Weeks

[47] In that year, the birthday of John, the Baptist, was celebrated with great pomp and utilized by the Crusaders for Pogroms to avenge the death of him who had baptized the Christian savior.

Rabbi Solomon Hacohen, and with the other Jews whom he had led there to save them. When castastrophy befell them, they sacrificed themselves so that the Name of the God of Israel would be hallowed through them. They killed each other in the watery trenches surrounding Bacharach so that the Christians could not mock them. And there children and women, brides and grooms, old men and women fell as they sacrificed themselves to their God; and their pure souls rose to Heaven. Among those who had been there was a very old man whose name was Rabbi Samuel ben Yechiel. This was a simple, pious, and God-fearing man avoiding evil who had only one son, a young lad, who was slender like a cedar.[48] This lad had fled with his father into the water-trench. The old man, after the younger had stuck his head out of the water, grabbed his knife, and, pronouncing the traditional benediction for slaughter, killed him. The young man had added "Amen", and those who stood there joined in by saying "Shema Yisrael." Look and see, all you Wanderers, does there exist any pain like theirs, any strength and fortitude like theirs, which prompted them to do as they did, have you ever heard anything like this since God created man on earth? Woe unto the eyes who have beheld this!

There was also present in this place another God-fearing young man by the name of Menachem, the sexton of the Synagogue. The old man, Rabbi Samuel ben Yechiel, said to him, "Take my knife and kill me next to my son." At this the young man took heart, killed him, and then found his own death also. There were many who preferred death to life and who sanctified the Name of the Holy God of Israel in bright daylight as they scoffed at changing their faith and remained true to their God: some of them drowned in the water and sank into the deep like stones. And only a few remained, at most two or three berries at the top of the bough.[49]

On the third day of this terrible month (June 27th), the rabble killed the Jews of Ilinda:[50] only a few remained alive and they, too, offered themselves as a supreme sacrifice. The enemies apprehended Rabbi Isaac Halevi, beat him mercilessly, tore his flesh, and baptized him while he was unconscious and near death. After three days, when he came to, he walked to the Rhine, plunged into the river, and died. Of him it is said, "I shall bring back from the depth of the Sea . . ."[51]

On the fourth day of this month, the enemies gathered a second time

[48] Song of Songs 5:15
[49] Isaiah 17:6
[50] Historians are unclear where to place this town. It is believed to have been in the neighborhood of Ulm, Germany.
[51] Psalm 68:22

against the Vineyard of the Lord in Ilinda in order to torture and taunt the Jews until they gave in, became Christians and turned away from their faith. When the Jews learned the terrible news, and before their enemies came, they all gathered together, about three hundred of them, and voiced their woe to God with a sad heart. At this, the heads of the congregation, Rabbi Gershon, Mar Yehuda and his brother, Mar Joseph, both the sons of Abraham, Rabbi Peter, and Rabbi Yehuda ben Samuel Halevi, offered to kill them. And these men stood up, took their swords, closed the door (of the Synagogue), and killed them as one man. After that, Rabbi Peter killed these other four also, ascended a watch-tower, plunged to the ground and gave up his soul before the Lord. From the whole of the holy congregation only two young men and two children remained alive, and when they were found alive, their throats were cut.

On the evening of that terrible day, the Jews of Xanten also emptied the cup of suffering. A few of them were reciting the Kiddush (the Sanctification of the Wine) when the wild beasts fell upon them, but they sacrificed themselves like their brothers, and the Holy God of Israel was sanctified through them. Rabbi J . . .[52] of France dug a grave in the ground, pronounced the traditional blessing over those to be slaughtered, cut his own throat, and gave up the ghost while the whole congregation cried out the "Shema Yisrael." Nobody escaped on that day of God's ire except a few who were afterwards found writhing under the corpses.

On the seventh day of the fourth month (July 1st), the Crusaders arose against the poor unhappy community of Meurs, and they besieged the town. As its inhabitants lifted up their eyes, they saw a multitude of people, as numerous as the sand of the sea. The Crusaders demanded to do with the Jews according to their will, as they had done in all the other cities through which they had marched. But the mayor of the city walked out to them and addressed himself to the commander of the army thus: "What do we stand to gain by this, when we kill our Jewish co-citizens who live here amongst us and conceal their blood?[53] Remain outside first, and I shall talk to them and give you a report of their reaction. Perhaps they will mind our wishes, be baptized and turn Christian as we are. At least we will have avoided the shedding of blood." They liked his words and he returned to the town where he called all the Jews together and made them this proposition: "You know, how I have treated you from the time when I first became mayor until now, and how I have protected you according to my pledge against injustice and oppression, so that not even a dog could stick out the tip of his tongue

---

[52] The rest of the name of the Rabbi is missing in the original.
[53] Genesis 37:26

against you and so, that nobody has stolen so much as a shoe-lace from you. You are witness to all this to this very day. But now you can see for yourselves, the children have reached the mother's mouth[54] and she has no strength to give birth. Today is a day of plight and calamity, a day of gruesomeness and shudder, a day of ire and punishment. I am incapable of withstanding the power of the glowing ire and smoldering firebrand of the Crusaders, for they could easily kill me, my wife and child, also. Therefore, make your choice: either you accept Christianity willingly to be like us, or to be handed over to them so that they can do to you as they have done in the other parts of the country through which they have marched. The choice is yours; I shall be free from all guilt." And all answered as one man: "It is better to die in fear of God than to do a thing like this and to sin against God. See here, Sire, we are now in your hands; do with us as it seems right to you. Now that the catastrophe has come, it is because of us that this grave threat of harm has come to you." When the Mayor realized that he could not accomplish anything with them, he thought of a trick: he sent a number of Jews out of the city in the company of his servants and ordered that the latter should return when they had smeared their swords with the blood of the animals of the fields.

When these servants came back into the city, they showed their swords to the other Jews, saying, "Behold, this is what happened with your brothers; thus it will happen to you also, if you refuse to accept our wish that you should become Christians like us." But all the remaining Jews countered by saying as one man: "We shall not accept your religion, nor your God. Do with us as you like, for the Eternal, our God, is One. We wish to adhere to Him, serve Him, and swear by His name forever. From the teaching which Moses, God's servant, has commanded, we will not deviate, neither to the right, nor to the left." The mayor then permitted the Jews, whom he had sent out of the city to return, and he imprisoned them, each one to a cell, so that they could not kill one another as they had done in other cities.

There were two women, one whose name was Gentila, the other, Rebecca. One of them knelt down in her cell and gave birth to a son as the birthpangs surprised her. With them was only one girl, who was very beautiful to behold. Now, as they saw that their enemies came toward them, they grabbed the child, wrapped it in garments, for they had pity on it, and flung it down from the tower, in which they were incarcerated, to the ground. After the Crusaders saw what she had done, they came up to the tower, on the following morning, dragged her by force to a mount and abused her according to their caprice. And nobody ordered a halt to it.

[54] Isaiah 37:3; i.e., the bottom of her womb.

Some Jews were killed by the sword on this terrible day, others converted and turned their backs on God. Among the latter was a Jew, by the name of Shemaryah. The Bishop's treasurer said to him, "Shemaryah, Shemaryah, don't be afraid. Stay with me, and I shall save you from their power." Shemaryah agreed to stay on and gave him what money he had with him. The treasurer then took him, his wife, and his three children to the forest and left them there until the ninth day of the month of Ab (July 31st). And this no-good pressured Shemaryah to send to his sons in Speyer to get silver or pieces of gold. After they returned with a part of the available money, the treasurer took it away from them, and immediately handed them over to the power of their enemies. The villagers had great sport with Shemaryah, for they knew him all too well. They agreed that he could adjure his Faith on the morrow, and thus his family was not forced to eat any forbidden food during the whole day,[55] for he had said with cunning, "Today we still want to live according to our Law, and then tomorrow we shall be all Gentiles." They retreated then to their chamber, for they were sad and exhausted, and they spent that night behind closed doors.

As morning had scarcely approached, the sleep had already escaped Shemaryah's eyes, and he arose even before one could recognize the other, brought a knife, butchered his wife and sons, then gathered all his strength and cut his own throat. But he was unable to make the wound deep enough and did not die, but got only a cramp and fainted. After day broke, his enemies came to him, and when they saw what he had done, they became agitated and asked of him, "Why did you do this nefarious thing? You have forfeited your life, you have sealed your own doom, and we are innocent. But through it you may atone for your sin, for when you become one of us, you will have turned and become a new person, and your life will have been saved. But if you will not be baptized, we shall do worse to you than happened with the others: you will be buried alive with them." And he answered them, "Far be it from me to do so! Do as you wish, for I shall never sin against God." Then they dug a grave, and he was forced to walk with them on foot and was buried there. They laid his wife to the right and his sons to the left, shovelled earth on them, and admonished him several times: "Turn to our teachings and you shall live and not die." But he did not listen to their voices. They even shovelled the soil from off him twice or thrice to see if he could still be won over, but since he did not want to listen, they covered him

---

[55] Jews observe Dietary Laws. It was the practice of Jew-baiters to force Jews to eat non-kosher foods, mostly pork as a sign of contempt. Historically, this kind of psychological torture was used already during Hellenistic times.

over with earth altogether. His cries could be heard all day, but they scoffed at him. Can You restrain Yourself, Oh Lord on High?

In the city of Kerpen they dealt with the Jews as they pleased, maltreated them and led them astray from their God. And the Jews of Geldern[56] also had to empty the cup of God's wrath: they were handed over to plunder and destruction, and on that day of God's ire there was no escape nor survivor.

Those whom I have nurtured and reared, my enemy has destroyed[57] It is for their sake that I weep and my eyes are flooded with tears. Daughters of Israel: Weep for them! Do not clothe yourselves in silken garments; may no jewelled edge embroider your raiment. Because of our sinfulness the splendor of Israel has fallen away. Her enemies surrounded and pursued her whenever she found rest, captured and gleaned her in the streets. And Israel declined dearly!

And as they dealt perniciously and frivolously with the Jews in the places already named, thus they also dealt with them in Trier, Metz, Regensburg, and Prague. In these places the Jews sanctified the Name of the Holy One of Israel and would not leave His path. All these tragedies took place between the months Iyar and Ab, which is the fifth. In those times they sanctified themselves in order to ascend to God. And they were potters, dwellers of the plantings, who assisted the King of all Kings in His work. They stood by His side as they gave their lives for Him and poured out their blood like water. He will reward them according to their deeds and the work of their hands, and their souls will be bound up in the bond of life[58] in the Temple of the Lord of Hosts. May their merit- (-orious conduct) as well as their piety inspire us forever. Amen, Amen.[59]

And in Italy, the Jews were also weary of their lives.

This is spoken by Joseph Hacohen: the above related incidents, which took place during the time of Philip I, King of France, I have taken from the report of Rabbi Eliezer, as well as from the Chronicles of the Kings of Germany.

After these events, the roguish Pilgrims i. e. (the Crusaders) marched to the Orient where they suffered such manifold pain and calamity that only a few of them remained alive. This is related in my Chronicles of the Kings of France and the House of Ottoman.[60]

[56] Kerpen and Geldern are two towns in the Netherlands.

[57] Lamentations 2:22

[58] This phrase is used during the Jewish funeral rites. It can also be seen in abbreviated from on Jewish tombstones in Hebrew lettering.

[59] Hacohen used, up to this point, the historic report of Rabbi Eliezer ben Nathan Halevi (according to M. Wiener).

[60] This translator has been unable to locate the above mentioned Chronicles. Hacohen

On the eleventh of July, 1099 (which was the fifth month of the year, 4859), the Pilgrims conquered Jerusalem and they slew her inhabitants with the sword.[61] About ten thousand people had fled to the court of the temple, but they were also slain, and not a single person escaped. And in this time, God's prophecy, which he had revealed through his servant, Moses, was fulfilled: ". . . your enemies who settle in it, shall be astonished at it."[62] After the Christians had dwelt there for eighty-eight years, they also succumbed to the power of those who were after their lives, namely, the Kings of Persia and Egypt;[63] and hundreds and thousands of them fell during the war through pestilence, the sword, and hunger.

During the reign of King Henry I,[64] ten mean people accused a certain French Jew as follows: he had cooked a Host[65] in a large pot of oil and water, and a child was seen swimming on the surface. As these people were about to kill him, he escaped their power. But they arose again in order to devour him alive. After he had been caught, judges had him apprehended and embittered his life; however, he admitted nothing. Yet when his wife and children were tortured, they confessed, which he had not expected; whereupon he was burned alive, holding the Talmud in his hands. But his wife and sons were forced into apostasy from the Lord, the God Israel. At the news of this incident, all the inhabitants of the land arose against the Jews, who lived in distant parts of the realm, slew many of them, and confiscated their property.

They also intended to destroy the Jews in Normandy, and therefore, one of them consulted a magician and executioner,[66] who said, "You will see

himself authored same; they are most likely not extant. Dibrei Hayamim Le' malkei Tzarfath Ve'Otoman (Sabionetta 1554)

[61] Jerusalem was taken on July 15, 1099. There was a most disgraceful massacre, primarily against the Arabs, but also against many Jews that could be found there. The Temple area, then and now, is the site of the Moslem shrine, The Dome of the Rock, reputed to be the place where Mohammed ascended Heaven.

[62] Leviticus 26:32

[63] Presumably, Hacohen refers here to Khwarizm-Shah Takash who ruled a large part of the former Persian Empire from 1172 until 1199; and to Saladin who founded the Abbasid Caliphate in 1171 (which lasted until 1252). The Crusaders surrendered Jerusalem to Saladin on October 2, 1187. Saladin held Syria and Egypt. He represented orthodox Islam in Baghdad. Hence, he seems Persian to our Chronicler.

[64] Hacohen refers here to Henry I of France who ruled from 1031-1060.

[65] The desecration of the Host is one of the most well-known and sinister accusations levelled against the Jews during the Middle Ages. Many Jews fell victim to this alleged crime and were murdered in cold blood, often in connivance with corruptible priests. In much later years, the Church condemned these allegations.

[66] After the words ". . . consulted a magician . . ." the phrase ". . . and investigator of the city . . ." was left out of the Jerusalem Edition as an unclear reference. Perhaps an "Executioner" is meant here.

how I play with them today." He then consulted a hangman and buried magic formulas under the heart of a pig. At that, many pigs gathered and fought among themselves so that they died, and not one remained alive. And, as many people were astounded at this incident and asked after the cause of this happenstance, the executioner reported in the presence of the Lord-Mayor[67] that the Jews had craved to obtain from him the heart of a human being, whom he had killed according to his judgment and right, but that instead, he had given them the heart of a pig, which they had then buried. "Who knows," he asked, "whether they have not done so, with the aid of their magical art, in order to kill us? We must prove this most diligently one way or the other." Other most unworthy people also testified that they had seen how the Jews had buried something, although they really did not know what it was, and that certainly the Jews desired a human heart in order to kill the Christians. These people then arose suddenly against the Jews like hungry wolves, killed many, and took their belongings.

They also desired to destroy the Jews in Navarre, in Spain, and they met them with drawn swords so that the Jews retreated into their homes before sundown, because they feared for their lives. There was a Jew, a smith by trade, who had broken a civil law, yet whose transgression was certainly not a capital crime. Still he was sentenced to death. Although his father had grave misgivings about his son, he finally took ill and lost his mind, yet the ire of the Christians did not cease, and they fell suddenly upon them and killed many Jews. Only a handful escaped in this fateful moment. When the King[68] learned of this, he was told by the cunning inhabitants of his country: this Jew has posed as a maniac for a long time to take vengeance for his son. He had also manufactured foot-traps, iron thorns and prongs to throw into the city's streets in order to waylay our steps and burn us during the night. It is because of that that we have slain them. And after the King had heard this, he forgave them their guilt. And even the judges were enemies of the Jews. Behold this, Oh Lord; look down on us; avenge the mischiefmaker for his meanness, and help us, for Thy Name's sake.

It was in the year 4902 (1142), after death had removed the pious Rabbi Joseph Halevi in Spain, that the Academies of Israel ceased to function. And the study of the Law was dearly missed. After his death, the Moslem, ben Tumart,[69] arose in the Arab lands as an enemy of the Jews. He redacted an

---

[67] The name of the city in Normandy is not mentioned in any of the manuscripts.

[68] I.e. the King of Navarre.

[69] Ben Tumart (abu-Abdullah Muhammad ibn Tumart in the Arabic transliteration) was a great religious leader and reformer of Islam (a Mahdi) from around 1121 until his death in 1130.

urgent decree in all the cities of his realm which diverted the Jews from their God, and which forced them to move away from their domiciles: that which belonged to Death, fell to Death; that which was the sword's, fell to it; that which was to Hunger, fell to Hunger; and that which was to Captivity, fell to Captivity. Many Jews also left the Covenant because of ben Tumart's sword, since he had forbidden them to live according to the Law of Moses, God's servant, and he said, "Lo, we wish to exterminate them from amongst the nations, so that Israel's name may no longer be remembered." And he left them nameless in his whole empire and in all the provinces, which he had conquered, from one end of the earth to Amahadia, so that Israel declined.[70]

The power of King Alphonse,[71] the son of Reymond, also weighed heavily over the Moslems of Spain during this time. When his dominion was firmly established, he took Calatrava in Southern Spain away from there, as it was on the border of the path which one took to travel from the land of the Moslems to his country. The mutineers[72] from the land of the African Saracens,[73] after they had not left a single remnant of Israel from Tangier to Amahadia, crossed the Straits into Spain. They intended to do likewise in all the cities of Spain which were under the rule of the Moors, but when the Jews learned that the rebels came to traduce them from the Lord, the God of Israel, they fled for their lives. And the fathers were hardly able to look after the children because of their agony. Some allowed themselves to be captured by the Christians and others sold themselves, so that they would be allowed to flee from the land of the Moslems; some fled on foot unclothed, their children asking for bread and no one breaking it for them. Yet, as they cried, their imploring reached Him who prompted King Alphonse to appoint Rabbi Yehuda Hanassi, son of Rabbi Joseph ben Ezra, as royal administrator in Calatrava. And his fame spread throughout the land. His ancestors belonged to the noblest of Granada, among whom power and dominion were inherited from one generation to the next and who were said to be descended from the inhabitants of Jerusalem who had been exiled to Spain.

As he now had been appointed to rule over Calatrava and the refugee-exiles, he unwound their chains, and the homeless and those expulsed from the land of the Moors joined him. He freed the oppressed, and the hungry

---

[70] The Almohades conquered southern Spain ca. 1149-1174. In their missionary zeal they forced all non-Moslems into their faith. Although the Jews in North Africa (the original starting point of the Almohades) recovered from the blow, the Spanish Jews either fled to Christian (North) Spain or saved their lives by converting to Islam.

[71] King Alphonso II of Aragon (1162-96) was the son of Raymond, Count of Barcelona.

[72] Mutineers or rebels against the Caliph of Cordoba is here a euphemism for butchering any missionary Moslems.

[73] The Almohades, Moorish fanatics, who were invited over to Spain in 1146.

and thirsty received gifts at his table: he broke bread with them and gave them clothes. He led the tired on horses and mules in honor to Toledo, they called Tolitula.[74] He met them with respect and decency, friendliness and mild manner, and he enjoyed great respect among the Gentiles who accompanied them. He had no use for money, and he did not enrich himself with gold during his royal service, but pursued solely the Justice of the Lord and His commands with respect to Israel.[75] He shared his bread with the poor and brought the needy and homeless into his house, for God had sent him in advance for the sustenance of the exiles, and he was a guiding light for them. After that, the Emperor, Conrad III, and Louis VII of France decided to march to Jerusalem with a huge and powerful army.[76] They affixed the Cross to their raiments as a symbol and prepared for their departure in May, that is, the second[77] month of the year 4906 (1146).

This was also to become for the House of Jacob a year of pain and suffering, a time when all was emptied out and vacated, when the knees trembled and the loins were anguished, when faces grew pale.[78] It was the monk Rudolph[79] who had come to Germany to gather those who wished to go to Jerusalem and to put them under the Cross. And he talked against the vileness of the Jews, the remaining remnant of previous suffering, thinking it was an opportune time to appear and to agitate against the not altogether widowed nation[80] in order to kill, destroy and annihilate it. He made a habit of summoning followers in the name of his Lord to march to Jerusalem, and he subverted the people in all the places through which he travelled, saying, "Avenge our Lord on his enemies who are with us, and let us move on afterwards."

When the Jews, who stood before the wrath of an oppressor, who planned only their doom, heard this, they were gripped by panic, their hearts melted and no fortitude remained in them. They implored God, and said, "Oh Lord God, hardly fifty years, the time between Jubilees,[81] have passed since we

---

[74] Zunz, *Zeitschrift des wissenschaftlichen Judentums*, Berlin, 1823, I, p. 148.

[75] Deuteronomy 33:21

[76] The author refers to the Second Crusade.

[77] The Jewish month of Iyar.

[78] Nahum 2:10

[79] The monk Rudolph was a fanatical Cistercian, a follower of St. Bernard of Clairvaux who preached this crusade (see S. Runciman, *Crusades II*, p. 254)

[80] Jeremiah 51:5

[81] It was celebrated every seven times seventh year as described in Leviticus 25:8-18. It commenced on the Day of Atonement (Yom Ha-kippurim) and was ushered in by the blowing of the trumpets (shofarim) throughout the Land. The Jubilee Year restored individuals to their former economic and "civil" rights. Hebrew servants were set free and even inheritances returned to their original owners. People who refused their newly won

shed our blood like water for Your holy, great, and mighty Name on the day of the Great Pogrom.[82] Will You be irate against us eternally? And what will You do for Your own Great Name? Will time and again tribulation arise?" Then God heard their entreaties, remembered His covenant, turned toward them and, in the fulness of His mercy, had pity on them. For He sent after this terrible man, St. Bernard of the city of Clairvaux in France, who challenged their attitude. And Bernard said to the Crusaders: "Onward! Let us go to Zion, to the grave of our Messiah. But be careful to speak to the Jews in a manner which is friendly: he, who molests them, acts like one who touches the eye of Jesus, for they are His flesh and blood. Rudolph, my disciple, did not speak justly of them for, as it is said, 'Kill them not, so that my people will not forget them!'"[83]

And they obeyed his voice: for he was much respected amongst them; the heat of their ire eased, and they desisted from their decision to harm the Jews. Yet this man did not take any ransom from the Jews, but out of the pure heart[84] had he spoken only good of Israel. Therefore, I say, "I praise Thee, Oh Lord, though Thou hast been irate against me, for now Thy wrath hath turned from me, and Thou hast given me solace: Thou hast left of us a remnant upon the earth and hast preserved life amongst many refugees on that day." For, had not God's mercy sent this priest, not one of the saved and escaped would live today. Praised be He who brings salvation and rescue. Amen. And in other locales, Jews sacrificed their gold and silver only to save their lives from perdition, but they did not renounce even one part of their faith as it had been demanded of them. Thus, God saved them.

But the following occurred in the month of Elul when the monk, Rudolph (may God pursue and destroy him) came to Cologne. Rabbi Simeon walked out of the city to return to his home in Trier. He happened to run into a few rogues who were among the Crusaders, and they cajoled him to be spotted with baptismal water; but when he would not listen to them, this fresh-miened folk spared him not and decapitated him. They stuck his head upon the gable of a roof and his corpse was left lying in a field as if it were dung, and there was no one to bury him. When the Jews heard this, much grief and

freedom had their ears pierced (this was also done at the end of the Sabbatical Year) by wearing a splint through their earlobes for all to see. The Jubilee was a truly unique festival considering the times where slavery was common and freedom a not universally cherished tradition.

[82] I.e. during the First Crusade

[83] Psalm 59:12

[84] St. Bernard is often described as a friend of the Jews. Actually he opposed the murder of the Jews prior to their possible conversion. Besides, converted Jews could have, out of gratitude for having been spared death, contributed heavily to the successful financing of the Crusades.

fear came over them and they said, "The days of Judgment have arrived; God's wrath has come forth; the Plague has set in; our time has come; the end is near. We believe we are finished." And the people wept beyond description. Thereupon, the elders of the Congregation went to the Mayor of the City and gave him a petition, the result of which was that the head and body of this pious man were returned to them. And they buried them in their cemetary and mourned over him: Woe, Oh Lord!

About this time also, the rogues apprehended the Jewess, Minna, as she travelled from Speyer; and they cut off her ears and the thumbs of her hands. But she bowed down her shoulder to bear it[85] for the sake of her holy Creator. And Judah declined much in these most horrible days.

After that the Jews lifted up their eyes and, behold! a whole army of those who had dedicated themselves to the Cross marched behind them; and they became very frightened. The Jews focused their eyes upon the mountains and ramparts, and each one who had acquaintances, who possessed a castle, or fortified citadel to give shelter in the cracks of rocks and the clefts of stone, sought out his friends and hid himself there until the storm had blown over. The Jews left their houses after the festival of Succoth (Feast of Booths) in the year 4907 (1146) and moved to the Castles and mountain fortifications where they lived until the men of war had moved on. After that, they returned to their homes.

Then the Jews of Cologne gave the Bishop all he demanded, he turned over to them the Castle Wolkenburg[86] which was heavily fortified. He even ordered the guards of the castle to move out, so that no stranger would be living among them. The Jews had pawned all of their houses and possessions to the Bishop, and when this became known, they were no longer presecuted. And other Jews who also lived in strongholds have, since that day, no longer been molested. Praised be the Lord forever. Amen, Amen.

Elieser Halevi, who was amongst those in the Castle who were related to him on his mother's side, has recorded all this. He was thirteen years of age then. And all the other Jews who lived in the countries of the realm of the French King saved themselves, each man the best way he could: into the house of an acquaintance or up to the Castles and Towers with his relatives and friends: and they remained there until the storm was over. Thus the Lord saved them.

In those days, when the Jews lived at Wolkenburg Castle, an old Jewish man lived in the foothills. He had two sons, one named Abraham and the other Samuel. Misguided by their own youth, they ascended the mountain

---

[85] Genenesis 49:15
[86] Near Koenigswinter by Cologne

and met a dispicable man who slew them and then walked away. Two other young men came downhill, and as they saw the dead dying there, they rent their clothes, went further down and reported it to the father who becried his sons and mourned over them for a long time. After the case had been investigated, the murderer was apprehended, and when the Bishop had been given presents, he had the man's eyes cut out. He died three days later. May thus all Your enemies perish, Oh Lord.

During the time of the grape harvest, two Jews, one called Isaac, the other Yehuda, had travelled from Mainz. A Christian with a fresh mien arose against them, killed them, walked away from his crime and did not return home. The Prince confiscated all that had belonged to this man. And in Mainz also lived a strong and courageous man called Samuel ben Isaac. As he was travelling, the Christians befell him, between Worms and Mainz, and killed him. But he was valiant: before he died, he killed three of those who had attacked him.

Three Jewish men living in Bacharach had fled to the Castle[87] with their wives and children. After they had lived there for quite some time, on the fifth day of the third month (May 6, 1147), they came down from the Citadel. And the Crusaders fell upon them and pressed them hard with these words, "Come over to us, so that we will be one People." But they did not listen to them and neither did they turn from their God. The names of these three were Alexander ben Mosheh, Abraham ben Samuel, and Kalonymus ben Mordechai. When Kalonymus spit upon their idol,[88] they slew him; and the other two, who had hidden themselves under some beds, were also stuck by the sword so that they died. They were buried in Mainz. May the Lord see and judge it.

In these therrible days no King meted out justice to the Israelites, for the Emperor Conrad was among the Crusaders and on his way to Jerusalem. Still, many Jews were forcefully turned away from the Lord, the God of Israel, yet they returned afterwards to the Holy One of Israel and served the Lord as before. A Jewess, by the name of Guthalda, was caught in Augsburg, and when she refused to change her faith, she was drowned for the Holy One, her Creator. Remember her forever, Oh God, and champion her Cause.

---

[87] A reference to the mountain castle Stalecke, the residence of the Count of Pfalz.

[88] Judaism forbids the worship of "other Gods" and idols. Hence, the depicting of saints and religious figures was alien to the Jews. Any form or mode of "representative worship," be they statuettes of Christ, the Madonna with Child or other central figures of Christianity were to the Jews an abomination. The act of spitting out before a Cross or God-symbol was quite common, perhaps even tied to superstition, and still in use until deep into the 20th Century; particularly in Eastern Europe where the Greek Church predominated.

In those days all the Jews of Germany fled, the one here and the other there, to Rocks and Castles, to save their lives. Only the Congregation of Wuerzburg did not think it necessary to flee and reminded in their homes. On the twenty-second day of the twelfth month in the year 4907 (February 24, 1147), the most abominable accusation was voiced against them in order to give the Christians pretense to fall upon them. It was said, "We have found a Christian in the river whom you killed and have thrown into the water, but through it he has become sanctified, and behold! he performs miracles." Thereupon the misbelievers rose, together with the riff-raff, and they killed the Jews without leaving a gleaning. There Rabbi Isaac[89] was slain while studying, and with him twenty-one others. With him also was a disciple[90] upon whom they inflicted twenty wounds, and he died only after he had lived for a year. They led his sister to a church, and when she spat on their idol, they beat her with their fists and wounded her with stones until she fainted; and there was only one step between her and death. After they had beaten her, they sprinkled water on her[91] and laid her down on a marble stone. But she did not awaken from her swoon, lifted neither her hand nor her foot, and pretended until nighttime so that they believed that they had killed her by their hand. However, around midnight a Christian woman came, took her home, for she had pity on the Jewess, and hid her to save her and to be able to return her to her brother. The other Jews saved themselves in the homes of their acquaintances and, on the following day, they fled to the Castle Zuelpich where they stayed until the storm had blown over. And God saved them.

On the following day, the Bishop ordered that all the corpses of the slain during that plague be gathered up. And they laid upon the carts all the precious limbs, thighs and shoulders,[92] fingers of the hands and all else that could be found of the dead, and they were buried in the Bishop's garden. Thereafter Rabbi Rechakiah and his wife, Judith, purchased this garden for him, and it serves to this day as a burial place.

Also, in Bohemia some one hundred fifty people were slain with the sword; many were also killed in Silesia because they refused to turn away from their God. When in Kaernthen these criminals also arose against them, the Jews gathered in a courtyard. Two brave young men, sons of a man who had sided with the Jews all his life, beat down upon the enemies so that they could do not the least harm. And the reputation of these two was heard afar. But,

---

[89] Rabbi Isaac ben Rabbi Elyakim
[90] Shimeon ben Isaac
[91] To see if she were dead; not to be regarded as an act of baptism.
[92] Ezekiel 24:4

during this fight, some of the enemy came up from behind into the courtyard and slew the Jews there so that not one of them remained alive. And they slew the great learned man, Rabbi Peter, a disciple of Rabbi Samuel and Rabbi Jacob of Rameru, as he went out to bury the head of the Congregation. May God observe this and judge.

On the seventh day of the third month (May 8, 1147), the Crusaders assembled in Rameru, in France, broke into the house of Rabbi Jacob, stole everything he owned, and tore up the Torah Scroll of our Lord into pieces before his very eyes. Then they seized him, led him into a field where they spoke harshly to him and counselled among themselves whether they ought to kill him. They beat him over the head and said, "You are a very prominent man in Israel and, therefore, we will take vengeance on you today for our Lord: the same way you treated Him, we will treat you." The Rabbi's soul then dwelt near the Land of Silence,[93] but the good Lord willed it that a very renowned Prince should pass by. The Rabbi, recognizing him, cried to him for help; and the Prince helped him on his horse, and liberated him from the power of the Crusaders. He then turned to them with the words, "Leave him to me. I will try to persuade him; perhaps he can be won over, and if not, I'll give him back to you on the morrow." The Crusaders listened to his voice, and thus the Rabbi was saved through God's mercy from their clutches. Praised be His Name forever, Amen, Amen.

From the rest of the cities in France, we have not heard similar incidents; yet God's people came down to the gates,[94] for King Louis VII's edict was announced in all the cities of his realm: that anyone, who had the inclination to march with him to Jerusalem, was to be free from all the debts which he owed the Jews. Thus, Israel's fortune sank very much in those days.

But the rest of His people God helped through King Henry in England[95] – for the heart of a King is in God's hands – and not even a shoelace was taken from them. The Name of the Lord be praised, Amen, Amen. Also to those Jews who had become apostates in those days, God extended His mercy through a priest who took them to France, yet not for money or gain. There they remained, until the rage of the Crusaders against them had subsided, and then returned to their God. May God remember him for his good.

Most all of the men of war, who had dedicated themselves to the Cross and who had marched away, died on their way in the water, through pesti-

[93] Psalm 94:16
[94] Judges 5:11; i.e. here: their fortunes deteriorated.
[95] Since Hacohen was writing about atrocities spawned by the Second Crusade, he must have been referring to King Stephen (1135-54) of England, although he refers in error to King Henry, presumably Henry I (1100-35) or more probably Henry II (1154-89).

lence, or the sword, through famine or thirst or want of all necessities, so that they never again saw their homelands. But the Jews of Germany again reached their desired haven.[96] They were permitted, on the fifteenth day of the fifth month in the year 4907 (July 14, 1147) to make their homes again in their cities as heretofore; and they live there on this very day.

The remaining happenings of the war, which I shall set down, have been described in the Book of Chronicles of the Kings of France and the House of Ottoman.

Rabbi Abraham ben Meir Ibn Ezra wrote his commentary to the works of the twelve minor Prophets on the Isle of Rhodes in Greece, and he completed his work on the first day of the twelfth month in the year 4917 (December 16, 1156). Rabbi Abraham David Halevi wrote his opus, Sefer ha-Kabbalah, in 4921 (1161).

In Persia, namely in the city of Amadia[97] situated by Mount Khaphtan, there lived a Jew named David el Rai[98] around the year 4923 (1163). In Amadia there also lived at that time about one thousand Jewish heads of families whose language was Chaldaean (Aramaic) and who had to pay to the King an annual head-tax of one Guider on anyone above the age of fourteen. Now this David had been studying in Baghdad under the direction of Rabbi Hasdai and Rabbi Jacob, and he had obtained proficiency in the Talmudic and profane sciences and even in the arts of alchemy. He became very haughty so that he ordered quite a number of those Jews who lived on the mountain Khaphtan to visit him in order to convince them to emigrate and to war against Jerusalem, for he had told them that he was the Messiah. Indeed, many believed him, saying, "Verily, he is our Messiah." And they revolted against the King of Persia[99] and slew many of his people with the sword.

When the King saw that he could not cope with him, he spoke to David in a friendly manner, and David went to him without suspicion. But when the King of Persia discussed with him his own dreams, David countered by saying "I am the annointed of God; therefore, extend to me all honor that is mine." At this, the King again became irate and ordered him to be jailed in the city of Daghestan by the river Gosan. And his foot was cast in chains. After three days, at a moment when the King was counselling with his

---

[96] Psalm 107:30

[97] In the northern part of the former Kurdistan (upper Tigris region)

[98] David Reubeni, King of the Jews, the pseudo-Messiah.

[99] Presumably Hacohen refers here to the Seljuk Sultan (Military Commander) for the Abbassid Sultan of Baghdad. The Caliph in 1163 was al-Mustanjid (1160-70). See Hitti, The Arabs, p. 479. The Sultan was probably Sanjar who ruled for a long time (1097-1156) in this area (see also the Encyclop. Britannica; article on Seljuks).

princes and advisors regarding the Jews who had sinned against him, David entered the room, for he had broken the copper doors with his science. The courtiers were all very astonished at this, and when the King asked, "Who in the world has brought you here," David replied, "I have come here with the help of my own talents, and I will not fear you or your servants from now on." And when the King commanded his servants to apprehend him, they asked, "But where is he?" Then David spoke to them, but they could not see him; and they were amazed. Thereafter, David went to the Palace and said this to the King: "You can do me no harm. You will see with your very eyes, how I shall walk out of here." Then he walked away, took the turban from his head, spread it out over the river Gosan, and walked upon it across the river to the utter amazement of the King and all his princes. Then, on the King's order, many chased after him in boats, but they could not harm him. And on that very same day, he covered the distance of a ten-day-travel by using the Tetragrammaton[100] and reported these happenings to his fellow Jews. And they, too, were left awed.

After that, the King sent a letter to Emir Almumenin, the Caliph of Baghdad, with the following content: "Please confer with the Exilarch and the leaders of the Israelite community, to persuade David to desist from his evil practices; if not, I shall have to kill them." It was then for the House of Jacob a time of anxiety: The Jews of Persia were gripped by great fear; panic and horror got the best of them, and they wrote to David: "Far be it from you to do so, for the days of salvation have not yet come and we have not seen a sign;[101] through might alone man shall not prevail."[102] They sent to him Zakkai, the Prince, and Rabbi Joseph Borhan with his own addenda, but David did not listen to them. And the Jews began to suffer with great pain. After this, they castigated themselves and implored God. And He listened to their prayer and made arise a Turkish Prince, Seifeddin by name,[103] who was about to take his annual tribute to the King. He invited the son-in-law of David el Rai, who lived in his land, and said to him, "I will give you these ten thousand pieces of gold, if you will assassinate David or hand him over to me." And when this man saw the terrible plight of the Jews in Persia, he killed David during the night while he slept. Thus, the

---

[100] The Tetragrammaton consists of the four letters of God's ineffable name (Y H W H). Each of these letters has in the language of the Cabbalists unheard of mystical powers. The abuse of any of them is frought with great danger and punishment ("Thou shalt not take the name of Thy Lord in vain", is the basis for this extraordinary belief).

[101] Psalm 74:9

[102] Samuel I, 2:9

[103] Seifaddin-el Adil Sa'if-ed-Din (to mean: the just sword of Religion) is a brother of the famous Saladin. He ruled in Damascus after his brother had died.

Persian Jews went from darkness to light, and thanked God for it. And the King of Persia was very happy in his heart, made peace with those who had adhered to David, and forgave them their guilt after they had given him one hundred talents of gold, since they were rich and numerous. With that, the wrath of the King was assuaged. Maimonides,[104] of blessed memory, wrote about the man David[105] in his well-known epistle.[106] However, he may not have heard all the facts as they really happened.

Joseph Hacohen speaks: Woe unto me, and to my mother for having born me. A catastrophy loomed out of France, and a great tragedy appeared in Blois.[107] Upon Your fruit and harvest the battle-shout has fallen.[108]

It happened in the year 4931 (1171) that a Jew went out at eventide to water his horse, and he met a Christian. The Jew became fearful and frightened, and the end-piece of a fur hide, which he wore under his garments, slipped from his bosom. As the horse of the Christian saw this in the darkness, it became equally fearful, stepped backwards, and refused to go to the water. The Christian became angry, returned to his master, and told the following story: "I saw a Jew, who threw a little boy, who had been killed by the Jews, into the water. I feared, he might also kill me, and the horse became frightened by the noise of the water. I came to report this to you." On the following day this man saddled his horse and went to see the Count of the city,[109] a miserable man, to tell him about this matter. The Count got very angry and ordered all the Jews, about forty in number, to be arrested and thrown in jail.

Yet in Blois there lived a Jewess by the name of Pulcellina, a decent woman, but one who had been hated by her master for some time.[110] This Pulcellina inspired the incarcerated Jews with courage because she trusted the Count, who liked her because she was a decent woman. But to no avail: the Count's wife misled him through much talk and all sorts of accusations against the

---

[104] Maimonides, the famous physician, philosopher and talmudic scholar, who was also in the service of Saladin in Cairo, Egypt. (see Hitti, *The Arabs*, p. 584 and others)

[105] It is to be noted that Maimonides refers to a different "Messiah" active in his time of the Arabian Peninsula. Hacohen is therefore mistaken, although it is unimportant because most of the pseudo-Messiahs did come from one of the oriental lands.

[106] "Iggereth Teman" (*Histadruth of America* Vol. XXXIV, transl. by Salomon Goldmann, N.Y. 1950

[107] Jeremiah, 6:1

[108] Isaiah 16:9

[109] Count Tibaud (L: Theobaldus Blesensis), or Theobald V.

[110] The sentence beginning "Yet in Blois there lived a Jewess. ." has been moved to the beginning of this paragraph from its original position, and the sentence beginning "On the following day. . ." at the end of the preceeding paragraph, as it seemed to be more in place here.

Jews. Consequently, Pulcellina did not find favor in his eyes, and he even hated her much more in his own heart for this reason. He therefore ordered his guards not to permit her entry to talk to him, and she was the only Israelite who had not been jailed. The Count then conspired to cast the guilt upon the Jews, but he was unable to do so as witnesses were not found to corroborate the killing of which the Jews were accused. But a monk came and said to the Count, "I'll give you some advice about what you should do, Sire, to shed light on this matter, only don't take money of expiation from the Jews. Let the servant come who was witnessed this matter and make him descend into a tank filled with the water in which the monks sprinkle themselves. Now, if his testimony is correct, he will swim on the surface of the water; if it is untrue, he will sink."[111] This plot was approved by the Count, and thus he did. They brought in the servant, let him swim in the water, pulled him out, freed the guilty ones, and declared guilty the innocent. And the whole town was in an uproar.

After that, the Count sent out a Jew to inquire of his brothers, how high a price of ransom they would impose upon themselves to remain alive. They discussed it among themselves and declared their willingness to give him one hundred Livres and thus admit their guilt and forfeit to the demands against them which amounted to about one hundred eighty Livres. But during their discussion, the monk countered obstructingly and said to the Count, "Ignore their present," and thus he changed his mind and would not listen to their voices.

At the command of the Tyrant, they were taken to a wooden house which was surrounded with chopped wood and brush. After they had been un-fettered, people called out, "Save yourselves and become like us; then you shall live and not die." But when they refused to let go of their God, they were beaten and tortured to see if, perhaps, they could be turned away from their Lord, the God of Israel. But again they refused and said to each other, "Let us be brave and strong for our God, for we are His people and the flock of His pasture. May God do what is right in His sight, for beside Him there is no God." And at the order of the Tyrant, the Christians laid hands on Rabbi Yechiel ben David and Rabbi Yekutiel ben Jehuda, both from the family of Priests (Cohanim), and both disciples of Rabbi Samuel, and also Rabbi Yehuda ben Aaron.[112] They tied them up with rope and ignited the lumber. Now as the flames had caught the rope around their hands afire, they tore loose; the three men stepped out of the fire, and said to the servants

---

[111] Trial of ordeal in reverse, Hacohen misunderstood the real procedure!

[112] The following is, of course, a poetic fantasy and wishful thinking, based on the Daniel stories from the Apocrypha.

of the Tyrant, "Lo, the fire has no power over us; why should we not step out?" But the servants replied, "By our lives, you are not to get out of here," and they stormed against the Rabbis a second time and drove them back into the inferno. Yet they walked out again, got hold of a Christian, and dragged him along on to the burning stake for they were very strong. The Christians, however, snatched him out of their hands, slew them with the sword, and tossed them into the fire. But neither they, nor the remaining Jews, about thirty-one persons, burned: they only gave up their spirits and died before their Lord. When the Christians saw this, they were astounded and said, "Verily, these were holy people, for they became sanctified. The finger of God is in this."

Rabbi David Hacohen, who resided in one of the Tyrant's cities, witnessed all of this; he pleaded for them, but in vain, for it was God's design, unfathomable in our eyes. The other Jews of the land were forced to surrender one thousand Livres to the Tyrant, but salvaged at least the holy Scrolls of the Law from the power of the Christians. This plague took place on Wednesday, the twentieth of the third month (May 27th), during the reign of King Louis the Younger.[113] These incidents were reported to Rabbi Jacob of Orleans, near the place where they had died for God. And it was further written to him that, as the flames leaped upwards, they raised their voices together and sang, and that the Christians had said, "We heard a song whose meaning we did not understand. We have never heard a more beautiful song." And it became known that this song, which the Christians heard on that horrible day was the hymn Alénu l'shabéach (It is for us to praise the Lord).

Daughters of Israel, weep over these pure souls who were beloved and respected during their lifetimes as in death; do not clothe yourselves in silken garments, do not walk about in embroidered dresses, for the glory is gone from Israel; may your brothers, the whole House of Israel, mourn this conflagration which God's enemies have caused.

And after several days, other Jews came, interred the bones of those who were burned, and grieved heavily, as their pain was great. And the Jews of France and of the Islands[114] took it upon themselves to commemorate this disastrous day as a Day of Mourning and Fasting so that their memory should not cease among their descendents. So it was ordered by the Gaon Rabbi Jacob ben Meir who also wrote: May this Fast Day be more important than the Fast day in the seventh month,[115] since it is a Day of Atonement. And the Jews began to do so, and accepted this forever.

[113] King Louis the Younger, is Louis VII (1137-80).
[114] Perhaps a reference to England.
[115] A reference to the Fast of Gedalyah.

In that year, Rabbi Benjamin, the Philanthropist, came to Cologne, and also Rabbi Abraham, the writer of Torah Scrolls. As they were walking through the streets of the city, a money changer incited a woman against them who was of the city's populace. And she said, "See here! These Jews have brought us counterfeit money to deceive us, and they have given me this piece of false coinage." But she had lied, for the money-changer had given it to her so that she could utter this untruth. Immediately, mean people gathered by the thousands, tied and tortured the Rabbis, and cast their legs in chains. The sons of Jacob, when they heard this, went to the nobles and promised them presents, but they did not heed them; and this saddened the Jews. Thereafter, they went to the Bishop, but he was rough with them, kept them in suspense, and would not talk forthrightly with them. On the third day, the Rabbis were brought to Court where they said, "Give us a defense counsel." But no one wished to listen to them, and it was ordered that their hands should be cut off. In the meantime, the citizenry had surrounded the Court to witness the event. When the Jews heard that, they rent their clothes, rushed into the Synagogue, and young and old fasted, cried out and wept. They took the Torah Scrolls from the Ark and pledged gifts to holy causes, which they deposited with tears flowing in streams, and they prayed to God. And God listened to their entreaties, and inspired the judge with the good sense to accept a bribe and not to shed innocent blood. Thereupon, the Congregation, together with the Jews of the surrounding territory, gave up one hundred eighty Crownpieces[116] for the salvation of the two, and the Rabbis themselves gave thirty. Sing unto the Lord, for He has done great things. Now it is known all over the land that, whoever enters, the court in Cologne, man or woman, as soon as a judge finds him guilty, he is killed without delay, and neither gold nor precious stones can save him. Indeed, these Christians had already blown into the trumpets, the church itself had already given out alarms,[117] and the bells had been rung with ropes of falsehood.[118] Rabbi Benjamin had already been surrounded and pursued. Rabbi Abraham had also been left outside and had been given hardly any rest. And it was at this moment that God saved them. For such a thing had not happened since Israel became a Nation. Praised be the Lord, who did not turn them out to the teeth of the robbers, Amen, Amen. After they had been set free, they blessed the people and thanked God, and the whole people

---

[116] The word "magen" or "shield" indicates that a crown-piece showed a shield or scudo on one of its sides as a mark of identification.

[117] In Hosea 5:8 we read: "Blow ye the horn of Gibeah, and the trumpet in Ramah, sound an alarm in Beth-Avon. . ." This phrase implies the ringing of church bells.

[118] Isaiah 5:18

answered: Amen. Oh Lord, remember the members of the Congregation of Cologne for good, and champion their cause. Ephraim ben Jacob wrote all this down in those days, and I took it upon myself to copy his words.

In the year 4940 (1180), several Jews left Cologne, in Germany, by ship and some of them disembarked. When they reached the city of Boppard, another ship followed them whose crew had found a Christian girl dead by the shore of the Rhine river. No one knew who had slain her, but they screamed at the Jews, "Why did you murder this girl?" Thus they shouted after them, until they came to the city where they beat them up and threw them into the water alive, and all those who were still on the ship, jumped in after them when the Christians tried vainly to persuade them to change their faith. With that they sanctified the Name of the Holy One of Israel and did not leave their faith. Hereafter, the Emperor, Fredric Barbarossa (1152-1190), the Red-Beard, punished the Congregation with a fine of five hundred Guilders; and the Bishop also laid a heavy fine of forty-two hundred Guilders upon the Jews of his realm. And if God had not stood by our side, we would have experienced almost another Sodom, as the tortures grew ever more intense. Rabbi Yehuda ben Menachem by name, one of those murdered, they dragged by the feet through the water and the dry land, from place to place, from city to city; even in Cologne they ground him down[119] from one city gate to the other. And all the Jews were almost swallowed up alive: if God had not assisted them who gave up for the Jews their own treasure. Praised be His name forever and ever!

In the year 4942 (1182), [120] Saladin came to Jerusalem and conquered her. On the second day of the month of Bul,[121] that is, the eighty month (October 13th), a great confusion took place in Germany and it was decided to go to Jerusalem and take her away by force.[122] The Christians arose against God's People to hand them over to perdition, but the good Lord showed them mercy in the actions of Emperor Fredric Barbarossa who ordered his clergy not to do any harm to the Jews who have given him presents. Thus God saved them. The other details of the war are written down in the Book of Chronicles of the Kings of France and the House of Ottoman.

[119] Ground down, implies a body torn to pieces by dragging it over the cobble-stones.

[120] After the Christian Crusaders held it for about eighty-eight years, Saladin conquered it (Jerusalem) in 1187.

[121] The month of rain; c.f. Kings I 6:38. It is an extinct Canaanite word which appears on a Phoenician inscription on the Eshmunazar tablet in Cyprus, Bul Heshvan. This word was adopted by Israel after its entry into Canaan together with the other names of months: Ziv, Abib and Etanim. The eighth month is an approximation since the Canaanites used the solar calendar. The etymology of the name is disputed. The correct date is October 2, 1187.

[122] The Germans actually did not get started until 1188 (see Runciman, *Crusades II*, p. 10).

During the reign of the Emperor Fredric, three young Christian boys went out onto the ice in Vienna to play. When the ice cracked under their feet, they fell into the water, and nobody knew about it. But the Jews were accused in their death as was, of course, customary; and witnesses testified that they had seen the boys walk into the houses of the Jews who were supposed to have committed this deed.

To the story they added this: this is their custom and habit, they offer sacrifices to their God; and even this: sometime back a certain woman had given them a Host, which they abused. With that, they created a bad name for the Jews in the eyes of the population. After the Emperor had learned this, all of the Jews of the cities of his realm were taken into protective custody, and it was a time of anxiety for Jacob. About three hundred were burnt, though they had committed no evil; the others saved themselves from disaster, for God had mercy on them. A short time later, when the waters had returned to their river-bed, they found the boys under the ice. The judges had all red faces and were much ashamed.

The Jews of Paris and it environ had multiplied much and had become very powerful through their wealth and possessions. They had hired servants and maids and chose them, as was their right, from among people who did not belong to their religion. Because of this the Frenchmen became very envious and accused them as follows: You accept as pawn the silver vessels and chalices which can be found in churches, and you permit your sons and daughters to drink from them in order to desecrate them. As the hatred of the French against them became ever more intense, other accusations were raised against them, and it was said that they crucified every year a Christian in the caves. Thus, the Christians embittered their lives and burnt eighty of them. King Philip heard this, and since he was still a young lad[123] during the liftime of his father Louis, he remembered this incident.

In the year 4946 (1186),[124] Philip had all the Jews of his empire apprehended, robbed them of their silver and gold, and expelled them from his country. Many of them changed their religion. Those who did, had their money and other possessions returned to them, and they mingled with the Christians and lived like them. Philip converted the Synagogues into Churches for his God and from that which he had stolen from the Jews, he had many edifices erected such as the Hotel de Ville, the wall around the Forest of Vincennes, near Paris, and the Champeaux[125] where the open market in

[123] Philip Augustus II was crowned while a child and followed his father, Louis VII, to the throne on the latter's death on September 18, 1180. He was a mere fifteen years old. He ruled from 1180-1223.

[124] Actually, this incident took place five years earlier, i.e. in 1181.

[125] *Zeitung des Judentums*, 1857, p. 105

Paris takes place. The number of Jews in France was double that which had left Egypt.[126] Now they moved out of this cursed land on seven roads,[127] and Israel's fortunes declined. About this exile[128] the author of Even Bochan had this to say: "I listened to the Mountains, saying: Cover us: and to the hills: Plunge down on us. I was bent down when I heard about this disaster which happened to my people, and aghast when I saw the destruction of my generation. My soul was weakened by the suffering of Israel when, seventeen years ago, the will of the Emperor rose against us to drive out my people who were the first of those to go into exile;[129] over the Hosts of the Holy One he stretched out the plummet of confusion,[130] destroyed them in his ire and exiled them from the land with his powerful hand."

After King Henry II of England had died, his son, Richard, came to the throne in 4950 (1190).[131] When numerous people from France and the Islands gathered there, some of the Jews, the heads of Congregations, were amongst the strangers who brought gifts to the King. The populace of the land murmured against them, saying, "The Jews are unfit to watch this coronation which is performed by the clergy." And they pushed them aside and maltreated them. The King, however, did not know what was happening. Meanwhile, a rumor was heard in the city according to which the King was supposed to have ordered the extermination of all Jews. Suddenly, they were fallen upon: their homes and houses were quickly destroyed and about thirty persons were killed by the sword. And there were some who killed themselves and their children in order to remain faithful to their God. On that fateful day, Rabbi Jacob of Orleans was also murdered. Still, the King did not know about all this, but when he heard the clamour of the people and inquired after its cause, the guard of the city gates replied, "There is nothing to it, only some young people were in a happy and gay mood; they were joking with each other." But when the King, later on, learned about this terrible crime, he ordered the guard to be dragged through the streets and market places by the horse's tail until he gave up his ghost and died.

In the same year, a Christian stood up against a Jew in the city of Bray, in France, and killed him, for he had hated him for a long time. But when

---

[126] A large, but indefinite number.

[127] Hyperbole; c.f., Deuteronomy 28:7

[128] Hacohen is here mistaken: Kalonymus' elegy deals with the expulsion of 1306.

[129] Amos 6:7

[130] Isaiah 34:11

[131] Richard was crowned in 1189. This is Richard, the Lionhearted, a glamorous character in legend; able, cruel in war – but no statesman (he spent only six years of his reign, or even less, in England. He compares poorly with Saladin in chivalry and statesmanship. He was indeed an "unholy" crusader.

thereafter the relatives of the murdered man protested to the Duchess of the city, she ordered that the murderer be apprehended and thrown in jail. On the Feast of Purim[132] he was arrested and hanged. When King Philip learned this, he became very angry, had his carriage prepared, and took his guards with him[133] to Bray. After he had arrived in that city, some eighty Jews were burned to death upon his command. No savior arose for them on that day of Divine anger. They were all rich, prudent, intelligent, and educated men who did not wish to choose a new religion and turn from their Lord. On that horrible day Rabbi Yomtov took heart and slaughtered many of them so that they did not have to change their faith. But the others were cremated alive. Upon the order of King Philip, those under thirteen years of age, were spared so that they did not have to sacrifice their lives.

In 4951 (1191) the Crusaders rose against God's people in the city of Eboracum (York), in England, on the Sabbath ha-Gadol.[134] In their great fear, the Jews fled into the Synagogue. Rabbi Yomtov took his place and slaughtered some sixty people, and he was joined by other men in this gruesome task on that fateful day. One man was among them with his only son, the soles of whose feet had yet to touch the ground,[135] and he, too, was killed. The number of those killed in this tragedy was one hundred fifty men, women and children. Those whom I have nurtured and brought to adolescence, my enemy has destroyed. They tore down houses, turned over the watch-towers, and stole many riches and precious Torah Scrolls and brought them to Cologne where they sold them back to the Jews. Thusly behaved our enemies in other places. Also, in another city, where there were only about twenty Jews, the Christians arose against them and slew them because they had refused to turn from their religion. Behold this, Oh Lord; see it and champion their cause.

In 4956 (1196) there lived a man in Austria by the name of Solomon. He was a God-fearing man, always charitable and abstaining from evil. The Duke[136] employed him as an overseer of his domain and all his belongings;

[132] This event took place almost symbolically on the day of Purim. Pur means lot, (see Esther 3:6, 7 & 9:24-32). Tradition has it that the Jews were saved on that day in Persia by the two Jewish folkheroes, Esther and Mordechai (Ashtarah + Marduk). They and their fellow-Jews were to be victimized by Haman, the symbol of all future Jew-baiters. In modern Israel this festival has taken on the form of a Middle-Eastern Mardi Gras where over-seize puppets of present day Jewish enemies are carried about, including of course those as proscribed by tradition.

[133] Exodus 14:6

[134] I.e. the sabbath before Passover.

[135] Deuteronomy 28:56

[136] The text does not name the Duke although it may have been Frederic I (1195-98). His father Leopold V (1177-94) had died in 1194. He was a lenient ruler as far as the Jews were concerned.

and this Solomon had servants and maids, both Jewish and Christian, and large herds. The Christians had planned to go to Jerusalem that year. Many thousands and myriads of them gathered until it was well nigh impossible to count them. Among those who were to leave was one of Solomon's servants who had stolen twenty-four Guilders from him. This embittered Solomon, and he had him thrown in Jail. After that, his wife went to the Church, when the Christians conducted their holiday services, and screamed out loud because of her husband whom the Jew had thrown into jail. Whereupon the Crusaders rose in Vienna, broke into Solomon's house and slew him and some fifteen other persons with him. When the Duke learned this, he got very angry and ordered that two of the ringleaders of the people who had committed this crime be apprehended and put to death. But he did not do anything to the other people since they were Crusaders: because of this, he did not concentrate[137] on them.

In 4957 (1197) on the seventh day of Adar (January 28), a Jewish madman met a gentile girl in the city of Neuss and murdered her on the street in broad daylight, for he was insane. The inhabitants of the city arose, killed him together with the rest of the Jews, and reached out their hands for booty. They dragged the Jews out of their homes and strapped their bodies on the rack in order to abuse the people of the Living God. On the Sabbath, the eleventh of that month (February 1st), they also captured the mother and brother of the insane murderer, burned her while she was yet alive because she had refused to change her faith, and fastened the brother on the rack. Another Jewess, together with her three daughters, were forcefully converted from the Lord, the God of Israel, and the Bishop punished the others with a fine of one hundred fifty Guilders. And those Jews who lived in the surrounding territory were equally burnished[138] by the Bishop and the Duke, and large sums of money were extorted from them. After a short time, the Jews succeeded, through bribery, in having their brothers taken off the rack, whereupon they carried them off, via ships, to a place below the city and buried them near the Pious,[139] who had been buried there in 4856 (1096). But, the Jewess whom they had forcefully converted returned, before Purim, to her faith and to God; and He saved her. These are the names of those who forfeited their lives in this plague: Rabbi Isaac ben Hasan ben Gedalia, Rabbi Samuel ben Nathan, and his son Nathan, Rabbi Isaac ben Shimshon, Rabbi Samuel ben Natronai, and Baruch ben Joseph. All of them are mentioned in the book of Rabbi Ephraim ben Jacob, which we wrote at that

---

[137] Concentrate, i.e. he did not bother them.
[138] Burnished, i.e. their possessions were put to the torch.
[139] The Pious, i.e. the Jewish martyrs.

time, in these words: "Praised be the Lord, the God of Israel, who has saved me from this plight, for I, Ephraim, was among the inhabitants of Neuss, (near Cologne), but went three days before this calamity to Cologne and thus saved, at least, my life; but they broke into my house, robbed me of my possessions, and took all which they desired. May God offer me restitution."

In 4962 (1202) many Christians volunteered to go to Jerusalem in that very same year (4. Crusade). The Jews emptied the cup of suffering in those days, and the author of Even Bochan[140] says about them,[141] "For two long years misfortune was in the land, the evil ones flourished and rose to our destruction, they cast the lot over the Holy Scion, and in their ire they killed our young and old, lads and maidens, sucklings and old men, and a great multitude of Israel died on that day on which these miserable Shepherds prepared perils for all of us. All this was so ordained by our Lord, because we had forsaken His Torah, and He had refused to forgive us. Tremulation was in all loins as we heard about those who had been expedited to their death or had escaped the slaughter. To sanctify the Holy One of Israel and to proclaim His glory, they were killed as if they were sheep designated for the butchery, on the day of the Great Manslaughter; and they did not worry or tremble when, on that cloudy, stormy day, not enjoyed among the other days of the year,[142] this great bloodbath took place. On that day, a part of my People changed their religion and chose new gods, since it would have been unbearable for them to see their sons led to death. Their hearts were hypocritical as they entered a new covenant, which, though entered at first through force, was later accepted out of their own free will. Add to this, one misfortune after another, for the Ruler listened to calumnies with which the Congregation of Israel was accused. For, when our enemies multiplied, they slandered the Jews and said to him, "We have found poisoned water enough to empty the Land; all this has happened through the ignominy of the Israelites who have counselled to kill us all." As they talked to him from one day to the next, and the talk became increasingly vehement, the people began to believe it, and a royal command went out to search for the alleged truth, for more could not be done. The people of the land wanted almost to swallow us up alive, while the King[143] and his throne remained free from guilt. Who was there to harken to the need of Israel? And considering the pressure with which the oppressors tortured them to extort confessions,

---

[140] Here again Kalonymus refers to the persecution of the Shepherds; c.f. note 104.
[141] The original manuscript of Kalonymus' Even Bohan is non-extant.
[142] Job 3:6
[143] Referred to here is Emperor Otto IV (1198-1218). If an Austrian ruler, then Leopold VI (1198-1230).

which would never have come to mind, who would not have desired to commit suicide? Who has handed Jacob over to plunder and to such heavy pain and torment as they have never experienced on all the Earth or among all the nations? God has found Israel guilty; therefore did He pour out His wrath. And the fire of the Lord consumed them. The Holy Ones of the Most High entered this conflagration, each one with his family. Like a groom who withdraws himself from his chamber, they walked out of their incarceration to sanctify the Name of their Father in Heaven. Appear, Oh God of vengeance. Vindicate the blood of Your servants, which was shed, although they had done no evil . . .

These two persecutions took place in the course of one year. Hardly before twelve months had passed, when the second followed quickly upon the first. A third kind of suffering also took place through which the one, perfect and sanctified teaching of God's Torah was now destroyed. Discounting, for a moment, the pressures of exile, the hatred of the nations weighted heavy upon us. I am already too tired to suffer their grudge, and their envy of me depresses me all too much. Strangers break into my gate and tear away the belongings in my own abode. Ten men, talking with strange tongues which I cannot understand, grab the garment of a Jew to deprive him of his coat; and, if he shows the courage to defend this infamy with the sword, one of the Gentiles will hurry to the scene and grab his neck. Thus, God protects him not. And so, Holy One of Israel, behold this on High; see our suffering; on Your account we are murdered every day and put on a par with cattle. Lord, champion our battle, for the sake of Thy great and fearful Name. Why shall the nations say, "Where is their God?"[144] Let us praise Thy great Name, Selah.[145]

In those days, God made Rabbi Moses Maimonides appear. He went to Egypt and there became the personal physician to the Egyptian Sultan[146] who honored him very much. He was more erudite than all of his contemporaries and composed books about the Law; and he also swung his sickle over[147] the profane sciences. His fame spread all over the world. The translation of Maimonides' opus, Moreh Nebuchim,[148] was instigated by Rabbi Samuel Ibn Tibbon and finished in the year 4965 (1205). When Maimonides

[144] Psalm 79:10
[145] Selah is a pause sign which most likely demanded a change of voice by the recitator of the Psalm. In the Book of Psalms we encounter this word no less than seventy-four times (see also Habb. 3:3,9,13). Selah is usually placed at the end of some remarkable passage designed to excite and quicken the attention of the reader or listener.
[146] The author refers to Saladin.
[147] I.e., he was at home in the other sciences also.
[148] A translation from the Arabic Dalalat al Hairin or Guide for the Perplexed.

saw it during his stay in Egypt, he rejoiced in his heart, wrote to Rabbi Samuel in the most flattering terms, lauded him in his letter and also informed him in detail about his living-conditions, among them that he was the physician of the Sultan.

In the year 5000 (1240), a terrible war took place in the Kingdom of Naples and the King[149] was forced to collect all of his own money as well as that in the possession of his servants, for they occupied the highest positions in the State. Also, all the Jews who lived in the towns of his realm assisted him with an open heart and with great enthusiasm. Through this, the King acquired great strength and power, and chased the enemy from the land. For this, the King honored the Jews and elevated them. But when they became haughty, misfortune befell them: for the King died. But before he died, he gave his son the following order: "Compensate the Jews for their money and show them your courtesy in the same manner as they have behaved toward me to this day." Soon the new King spoke to his counsellors and dukes: "What kind of honor and award can I bestow upon the Jews for all the good which they have shown my father?" And they answered, "All the gold of Ophir[150] cannot repay their kindness. But you can save their souls from perdition if you can move them to change their religion so that they become like us, and we be one nation." The King liked that. He called to him the heads of the Congregation and announced the favor which he had agreed to proffer to them. This saddened the Jews very much; terror and panic gripped them and they said: "We don't expect from you any other favor than to talk to us about this matter; neither evil nor good, Oh our King and Master."

And the King replied, "I am disposed to repay the faithfulness with which you have honored my father in this important matter, and I can not deviate from it any more." As the Jews realized what he meant by that, they said, "Give us time and we shall see how we can respond to you, Master and King." And he said to them, "Prepare yourselves now to accept this favor from me, for then I shall grant you all you may wish to demand from me." But they countered slyly, "We wish to oblige you, if all the nobles of the realm will become related to us by marriage," for they thought in their

---

[149] The King referred to here is Frederic, the son of the Holy Roman Emperor Henry VI, and who later on became Emperor himself (in 1220) ruling as Frederic II. He died in 1250 and was succeeded by his illegitimate son, Manfred, who ruled as regent to his legitimate half-brother Conrad (Emperor Conrad IV) and upon the latter's death in 1254 for his son, Conradin, until 1266 when he was defeated in battle by Charles of Anjou, brother of Louis IX of France, at which times Naples became a Papal fief under Charles.

[150] Ophir: King Salomon is supposed to have imported his precious stones from this fabled land. Old Testament scholars have suggested India, North Africa, the East coast of Arabia and even an island in the Red Sea.

hearts that the King would reject this, and then they would be free from guilt. Yet the King replied, "Be it so, as you have spoken." But when the Jews gave themselves away by uttering another thought, he became angry, and this grieved them much. This order of the King was then publicized in all the towns of his land: that the Jews within a given time, namely, from the proclamation of the royal edict to the burning of the cap,[151] had to change their religion or be killed. Many of them were seduced during this fateful time, and after the decree of the King had been made public, they intermarried with the nobles of the realm. And their Synagogue was converted into the Church of St. Catherine. Those, however, who refused to turn away from the Lord, the God of our forefathers, were slain with the sword. Behold and study it, if such has ever occurred before.

In 5001 (1251), the number of Jews had grown in England, and in London alone lived two thousand men with their families besides those who lived in other cities of the Kingdom. There, a priest from among the monks fell in love with a Jewish girl, and tried to persuade her for a long time without her giving any attention to his voice. He even hid himself under a Jewish costume to be able to talk to her daily. The girl was poor and had no father, but when the mother saw that the priest was rich and brave, she gave him her daughter for a wife on the condition that they should settle down in a foreign country, for otherwise she would fear for her life. However, after this matter became public knowledge, the monk became a laughing stock and the object of talk; they were despised and had to suffer their disgrace. They talked it over with another priest who was close to the King[152] and who gave the Jews a bad reputation in his eyes. Moreover, the common people talked continuously to the detriment of the Jews and hated them much. They also accused them, saying, "The Jews circumcise (debase) the royal coinage[153] and eat up our treasures at the same time." They even presented all kinds of coins which they had cut down at home with the words, "The Jews have committed these evil deeds." Many others came with them who joined their clamour and defamed the Jews. Upon the King's orders, the judges pronounced their judgement: the Jews were to be expelled and were not to be allowed to take

---

[151] The "burning of the cap" is a very obscure reference. No commentary or medieval work on folklore has this custom listed. This translator suggests this hypothesis: the burning of the cap may be a pars pro toto coinciding with the custom of publicly burning a scare-crow, topped by a hat, that dangled in the wind during harvest time. In this context then, the Jews would have had to move on during the time from the issuance of the edict until the burning of the scare-crow, i.e. harvest-time.

[152] The king referred to here is Henry III (1216-7?).

[153] Circumcise the royal coinage: unethical people often filed metal off gold and silver coins, and then sold it on the market in ingot or bullion form. This practice often included even the Kings themselves.

even the most insignificant of their belongings with them. Thus, they had to leave behind all their possessions as a ransom for their lives.

Thereupon, the monks rose and said, "Behold, the Jews have converted a cleric in our land, and such a crime can only be atoned, if they change their religion or die by the sword." And the King said, "As you have spoken, so shall it happen today." They immediately tore the Jewish children out of the arms of their parents and sent them to the northern territories on the border of the Island where they were re-educated and turned away from the Lord, the God of Israel, and where they remained under the power of the people in the land, so that they no longer remembered the Jewish way of life nor their parents. Many of their parents, and especially their mothers, died of broken hearts; and the Remnant was expelled from the land. Even today one can find Synagogues there which were converted into churches, and many inhabitants of the land still bear Jewish names to this very day.

However, after this King had died and a new King[154] ascended the throne in England, he recalled all the Jews who had been expelled from the land, whereupon they gathered in all those places where they had lived. And they declared: they would not return at any price or resettle there unless they could see their children again. The Christians thought to make them return to their Faith through persuasion. And thereafter, each Jew left his domicile and went wherever the inhabitants of the land received them with kindness and deference. They were most happy.

After a short time, pestilence broke out in England, and several people died daily. This was followed by a famine in the land so that every staff or bread was broken.[155] The war was weighing heavily upon the inhabitants – the Scots waged war against them[156] – because they had risen against the People of the Lord of Hosts, the God of Israel. After the King had gathered his nobles and asked, "Why and through what are the Scots sitting on our necks," they replied, "This happened through the evil deeds of the Jews." "But what is to be done to turn the wrath of God from us?" the King asked. And it was replied, "Nothing else, but that they should change their religion

---

[154] The new King is Edward I (1272-1307)

[155] The Jews could not make a living and consequently starved; c.f. Psalm 105:16.

[156] I.e., the war of independence of the Scots against Edward I of England and the English invasions of Scotland in 1302-04. Our author like so many other medieval writers, believed that wars were ordained by God. Particularly when rulers of a given country mal-treated the Jews, His people. Thus, God appears often as the Defender and Judge of Nations. The same philosophy is applied when a given ruler, who was hostile to the Jews, died either prematurely or due to a severe illness, or perhaps in battle. The Scottish-English conflict, or the Turkish invasions of Germany-Austria, the personal tragedies of Ferdinand and Isabella and other historical events are pictured by our Jewish author as God-ordained.

and become like us; and if they refuse, force ought to be applied." And the King's order was announced that no Jew was allowed to leave England, and if anyone tried to emigrate illegally, he should be killed. Thereafter, he called them all together and said, "Choose another God so that you become like us, and then we will give you everything that your hearts desire." But when they rejected this, they were baptized by force.

But when, later on, the suffering and agony of the English doubled, as pest, hunger, and war took their toll in the land, the King gathered again his counsellors. Many held that this calamity was the direct result of the repression of the Jews and that the King should permit them to return to their former faith, so that only those who wished to remain with the Christians might do so, since a voluntary convert has a greater value, after all, than one who has been forcibly converted. This opinion seemed to find the concensus of all, when a man, hostile toward the Jews, made his appearance, saying, "Don't you believe that once the Jews are allowed to return to their teachings, they will never wish to become Christians like us, since their Law sits as tight in their hearts as nails; and you have proof of that, in that they offer resistance, as much as they possibly can, before they change their religion and become like us, leaving their God altogether. But if they now return to their teachings, the sin will also come back which has brought us to much suffering. Because of the decree in their favor, our suffering has doubled, as we have become involved in all these evil incidents which has befallen our necks." "But what is there to do?" the King asked. "Nothing else but to abrogate the decree in the land. Then our guilt will cease," was the answer. This talk found favor in the eyes of the King, and he did the following: on his order two tents were erected at the shore of the sea. Into one, they put the Torah of Moses; and in the other, the Cross. A high place was also erected there for the King to take his seat upon. Those, who had seemingly turned from Judaism, were ordered to gather, and the King said to them with friendliness and benevolence, "Of course, you know that I have turned you away from your God by force to avert suffering. But now I see that it has doubled, and that we are up to our necks in deep trouble because of the decree against you. Therefore, I order you to be free as heretofore, and to choose what you want to do. Know that in one tent by the seashore, the Law Code of Moses rests, while in the other the New Testament is. Each among you Jews may choose now what is right and proper in his eyes, and in that faith may he walk for all times." All of them ran toward the Law of Moses; they, together with the women and children. But the Christians had dealt with them treacherously, for they were only allowed into the tent one at a time. And each of them who entered that tent was murdered and thrown into the sea so that one did not know about the other. Thus, very many of our People fell, serving the fish of the sea and the birds in the sky as a welcome meal.

In Flanders also miserable people gathered who betrayed the Jews, saying, "They have stolen a Host; and, as they perforated it, blood came out." And they thought that this blood called for vengeance against the Jews, whereupon they rose against them like bears and wolves of the night and killed many of them with the sword in this terrible time. They also turned away many hearts, saying, "Choose yourselves another god and become like us, for then you shall live," and thereupon many of them were traduced and converted. This land is filled to this day with many of the descendents of Israel, namely, those who accepted the new teaching.

In the year 5023 (1263), there were, in the city of Schweinfurt, Germany, two city leaders who hated another one very much. The son of one of them was murdered by one of his father's enemies. It did not become public knowledge who had killed him, and since hatred was great amongst them, the relatives of the murdered boy kidnapped, through the accomodation of an old woman, one of the daughters of the other party who was then seven years old, killed and buried her outside the city. But when the relatives sought her without success, they accused the Jews, as was customary since they walked in darkness, and rose to make an end of them. However the Mayor went out to them and quieted their emotions; and their hatred subsided, whereupon they desisted from the nefarious plan which they had dreamed up amongst the Jews. But this matter became known later on through the old woman herself. Nevertheless, the citizens of that city did not take off the cover of blindness from their faces.[157]

In a book composed by a German in Latin[158] it is written: It was reported to the Pope[159] in 1272 that a Jew had fallen into the grime of an outhouse on the Sabbath day and, although he had implored help, the Jews refused to pull him out before the end of the Sabbath. The Pope's heart was repulsed by this, for he believed these people, and he ordered that in all the cities of his realm whosoever acted contrariwise (i.e. continued to observe the Sabbath and also the Sunday according to his orders and decrees) should be killed. The Jews got very weary of living.[160]

[157] I.e., they still hated the Jews.
[158] Cosmographia Universa by Sebastian Muenster, a profesor of theology and Hebrew at the University of Heidelberg, Germany.
[159] Pope Gregory X (1271-76)
[160] In reality, Jewish Law commands that in the face of danger to individual life, Sabbath Laws can be set aside. This also goes for times of war, from Massadah to the Warsaw Ghetto.

In the book of Sebastian Muenster, we find the following account: In 5047 (1287) the Jews living in Bern, Germany, were accused of having murdered a child. Many were tied to the rack, others were expelled from the country, and when because of this, the Jews made presentations before the Emperor Rudolph,[161] he marched fully armed with thirty thousand men against Bern, and attempted to subdue them twice. But he was unable to do anything and every one of his soldiers returned to his home.

In the same book, on page 828 we find: The Emperor withdrew, by his power, the authority of the Bishop over the city of Nordlingen and permitted the Jews to settle there. But when they became very prosperous, the citizens became envious and refused to have friendly relations with them. In 5050 (1290) they suddenly fell upon them, killed many with the sword and spared neither man nor woman. Rudolph, the Emperor, took vengeance on them, and Counts and Nobles demanded the return of clothes and utensils which they had captured and pawned off to the Jews. Nordlingen declined thereafter.

On page 644 we find this: After King Adolph[162] had conquered Ruffach[163] in 5058 (1298), he burned it down. After a year had elapsed, the inhabitants of the city arose against the Jews in January, burned them on a pyre outside the city, and no savior arose for them on that day of God's wrath. Twenty-nine years later they killed the Remnant which was left. Behold this, Oh Lord, and champion their cause.

And for nine years after that the soil did not yield any harvest, trees in the fields did not bear any fruit, and the country-side languished in hunger. They entered this into the history books as a memorial so that future generations could talk about it.

In 5066 (1306) the King of France, Philip IV,[164] son of Philip III, grandson of Louis IX, great-grandson of Louis VIII, and great-great-grandson of Philip Augustus, made this proclamation to all the cities of his realm: every Jew had to leave without taking the least of his belongings with him, unless he adopted another religion and became one with the people of France. When the Jews learned this, they became terrified. They did not respect their property or possessions and emigrated from France, saving only their very lives. This took place in the month of Ab, that is, the fifth month. Only very few, whose hearts were not permeated with the love of God, remained in

---

[161] Referred to here is Rudolph I of the House of Hapsburg

[162] The king referred to here is actually the Holy Roman Emperor, 1273-91 Adolph of Nassau (1292-98).

[163] In Alsace-Lorraine.

[164] Philip IV, the Fair, was a very unscrupulous King (1285-1314). He brought the Papacy to France in 1305, the so called Babylonian Captivity of the Popes at Avignon.

France as did those who lived in Toulouse, and only a fraction moved away; namely those who had God before their eyes and who followed Him faithfully. Thus many of Jewish descent remained among the Christians, and therefore, many can be found there today who believe other religious doctrines.

After almost nine years had passed, Philip, who had gone on a hunting trip, galloped after an elk on a rock ledge and plunged, together with his mount, from the crest of a hill into the sea, so that both died. His son, Louis X, reigned in his stead (1314-1316). He invited the Jews to return to him, and they dwelt there for seven years. After that, he chased them out again,[165] for he had to yield to the wishes of his people which were bad and nefarious. At least they were permitted to emigrate with their belongings and treasure. After Louis' death, his son, John, ascended the throne, but he was a mere child and died after a reign of only twenty days; Charles IV ruled in his place (1322-1328).[166] Again the Jews were allowed to return to France, and they remained there unmolested as long as they lived. But after their deaths, when Charles of Valois had become King,[167] many rose up against the Jews, killed a great number with the sword, confiscated their belongings, and chased out the rest against the wishes of the King: and the Jews have not returned to France to this day.

In Spain there lived a seventeen year old boy in the year 5080 (1320) who stated the following: "At even-tide a dove flew toward me, sat on my shoulder and on my head. The Holy Spirit came over me and prompted me to catch her. I envisioned a virgin, beautiful to behold, who spoke to me, 'Lo, I have chosen you to be my shepherd in the land. Fight against the Moors, and the vision, which you have seen with your own eyes, may it serve you as a sign.'" And he countinued, saying, "I also found this happenstance written down upon my arm as it had taken place." Thereafter another boy arose and spoke, "I have found the sign of the cross upon my shoulder." But in reality, he had only dreamed this. When the nobles of the land heard this, they directed their attention to the boy and honored him much. And the lowliest scum joined him in large numbers, saying, "Let us march in battle against Granada." But when a Jew scoffed at the boy, they hated him and planned to kill him. The number of those who gathered about the boy was almost

---

[165] Louis X died in 1316. Our author here refers to the oppression under Philip V.

[166] John was born five and one half months after the death of Louis X and lived only five days (not twenty) during all of which time Philip V, the Tall, was regent, After John's death, Philip V ruled until 1322. Charles IV followed him until the year 1328 and was, in turn, succeeded by Philip VI, the son of Charles of Valois, his cousin (1328-50).

[167] The king referred to as Charles of Valois is Charles V (1364-80) who was the third French king from the House of Valois.

thirty thousand; and they suddenly fell upon the Jews of Tudela, in Navarre, killed them with the sword, and no one came to their assistance.[168]

Many separated themselves from the Shepherds[169] and marched toward Martel to destroy the Jews. When the Count, the commander of the army in Toulouse, heard this, he rushed and sent troops there, who captured many of the Shepherds, put them in chains and brought them along on ten wagons. When the monks learned this, they rose at night, liberated them, and as they went on their way – now that they had been saved from the power of the soldiers – they said, "A finger of God has shown itself in this matter." And all the people joined in, "Behold, this is a wonder which God has done." Thereupon, they spilled out their harted against the Jews, and in a short time, killed two hundred persons. The commander of Toulouse, who had come to their aid, almost stumbled and his feet slipped.[170] Thereafter, many Jews gathered before the ire of the enemy in the Citadel of Narbonne and stayed there. After they had heard that the Shepherds had been chained and taken away on carts, they came down to the city. The commander sent one of his relatives with them in order to bring them quickly to safety in Carcassonne, a walled-in city. But this enemy of Israel handed them over to the citizenry of the open cities, who fell upon them like wolves of the night, and killed men and women mercilessly, and without sparing the old men. Their corpses are like the dung in the open field, and they served as fodder for the beasts of the fields and the birds of the heavens. May God see this and judge.

As the news spread into the province of Bordeaux and to the other locales under English sovereignty,[171] the castles of Sarrazin and Agenois, they contemplated to kill all the Jews who were living there and in the cities of Toulouse, Bigorre, Marsan, and Condom. Thus, through the Shepherds, one hundred ten more Communities were destroyed, just as had happened in the open towns. Many of them, who had hidden in the Castle of Sarrazin, preferred to kill each other before the enemies could fall upon them. They cast

---

[168] Tudela was the home of the famous world traveler and writer, Benjamin of Tudela in the 12th Century (see also Hitti, *The Arabs*, p. 357)

[169] King Louis IX of France (The Pious 814-40) asked for help to make a fresh attempt to conquer The Holy City. He waited like a "Royal Beggar" in the ports of Syria. Some of the common folk in Northern France made an abortive attempt to save their King. They called themselves The Crusades of the Shepherds. (see Henry Treece in his *Crusades*, p. 248, Random House, N.Y. 1963: "But this unprepared rabble, already excommunicated because of their openly stated denial of the Pope, was met and destroyed by their own French army at Ville-neuve-sur-Cher". The rest of the bloody account is rendered by Hacohen.

[170] Psalm 73:2

[171] Meant here are the Dukedoms in Gascogne and Guyenne which came under British control through the marriage between Eleanor of Aquitaine and Henry II of England. They belonged to England for almost three hundred years.

lots amongst them to see who would kill his own brother. Thus, all of them died, and the two, who remained, leaped from the watch-tower and killed themselves.

In Toulouse, many perished through the sword, the others converted from the Lord, the God of Israel, and only one escaped: a nobleman of the city, friendly to him, saved him. In Gascogne, of all the remaining Jews, only twenty were saved; the rest were slain. In Lerida, seventy Jews handed their fortunes over to the commander of the city so as to give themselves safe conduct to the Kingdom of Aragon; but, when they had come out into the open, they, too, wereslain. Avenge his meanness, Oh Righteous God. The Jews of Aragon were greatly scared, and had not God, whose mercy never ceases, permitted them to find grace in the eyes of the Archbishop, all of them would have lost their lives. After that, the nefarious Shepherds divided themselves into four groups: some marched to Valencia, some to Barcelona, some to Jaca, and the rest to Montserrat. When the man, wearing the cross on his shoulder, came to Jaca, they slew four-hundred-ten Jews on the seventeenth of the month of Tamus, and only ten, who had fled to the Castle, saved their lives.

Hereafter, about fifteen hundred Shepherds marched from this place, terror and panic gripped the Jews of Barbastro and the other towns. They lifted up their eyes toward Heaven, and God sent them mercy in the eyes of the city's noblemen who had pity on them; and the evil odor of these nefarious Shepherds ascended into the sky.[172] The King of Aragon[173] then sent his son to their destruction and about two thousand men were killed by the sword; the others took to flight. The King of France[174] also drove them out of his country and made it known in his name that anyone, who found the Jews in France and killed them, would not be found guilty of murder. The Pope[175] also forbade his Bishops to spare the lives of the Shepherds living in their countries.

When the enemies marched to Navarre, the Jews of Pampelona feared and trembled very much and they marched out of the city to go to Monreal, three miles away from Pampelona. As they were on their way, the people, who accompanied them, handed them over to the Shepherds, who killed many of them and pursued those who escaped. After they had come near to the city, God inspired the Jews with fortitude: They fought against them and slaughtered one hundred seventy of the Shepherds. But the man who had

---

[172] They came into ill repute.
[173] The King of Aragon here is Alphonso IV (1327-36) and his son is Pedro IV (1336-87).
[174] The French King is Philip V.
[175] The Pope is John XXII (1316-34)

borne the cross was killed with an arrow by one of the servants of the city's commandant who had come along. When the Shepherds now saw that their leader was dead, they turned around and fled. Even after the power of the Shepherds had been broken, three hundred of them marched to Tudela, but when they saw that the place of residence of the Jews was strongly fortified, they too, turned around and walked away. The Jews now realized, in the possession of their wealth, that God had saved them, they praised Him and gave to the poor amongst them for three long years as much as they needed for their sustenance. Thus the name of the Shepherds was blotted out from under God's heaven.[176]

In 5081 (1321) Sancha,[177] the Pope's sister, thought to destroy the Jews, and since she could not bring it about, she demanded that her brother at least expel them from his territory. After he had lent her his ear, a period of suffering came to Israel. But God granted them mercy in the eyes of Robert, King of Naples,[178] who stood up with determination against all who rose against them. And after the Jews had given this shrew (Sancha), twenty thousand Guilders, her voice became quiet and her plan came to naught.

It happened in the same year, during the reign of Philip V, King of France, as the number of sick people in the land increased and many of them died, that several physicians declared that a pestilence had broken out. Other stipulated that the deaths had come through poisoning, for God had confused their tongues.[179] They accused the Jews and lepers as follows: "You have thrown poison into our wells"; and all the people of the land believed it. When Philip arrived in the province of Narbonne, the lepers had just been burned to death, and he let it be known that the Jews in Narbonne ought to be proceded against in the same manner. And he made it known throughout France that like was to be done to all the Jewish residents and lepers, whereupon all Jews were arrested and thrown in jail. But when the Jews engaged the services of physicians in that area to visit the sick and to investigate the matter truly, so that after their judgment the plague could be dealt with, they came, started an exact investigation, gave dogs water to drink from that which was supposed to be poisoned, and declared, "Here is no deadly poison; but this plague is the finger of God which afflicts you because of your sins." The investigation lasted for nine months, during which time the Jews remained in custody where they became fed up with life. After the course of nine months, five thousand persons were sentenced to death, and it was said

[176] Exodus 17:14
[177] Or read Sanchia
[178] Robert of Naples ruled from 1309 to 1343. He was a great defender of the Papacy.
[179] Genesis 11:9: they had different views

to them, "Only then can your guilt be atoned, when you secede from the Lord." And when all the Jews refused to listen to their voices, they were burned to death while calling out: Hear, oh Israel, the Lord is our God, the Lord is One. This much I found in the book of the Portugese writer, Samuel Usque.[180]

In Sebastian Muenster's book, Cosmography. we find the following account: "forty Jews were arrested in Vitry and thrown in jail. When they saw what fate was ordained for them, they chose two men out of their midst who were appointed to slaughter their brethern so that the Christians could not torture them. And so it happened. When these two men finally remained, the older man said to the younger, 'Draw your sword and kill me,' whereupon the younger man rose and killed him. And he was the sole survivor. Thereafter, he took all the gold which the people had with them, cut up their garments, and tried to descend from the tower with a rope he had made. But, as he tried, the rope tore and he fell to the ground and broke his leg. He was then apprehended and executed."

In the year 5082 (1322) Charles IV (1322-1328) began to reign in France, and the Jews again returned there and lived in safety. After Charles had died, leaving his wife widowed, all the princes cast their eyes in her direction, for she was pregnant. They began to quarrel amongst each other for they all wished to become regents until the unborn child had grown up. In these days, the people of the land rose up against the Jews, killed many of them with the sword, and reached their hands out for booty. The rest of them were chased out of the land and have never again settled down in France. When the King of France, who ruled over Navarre, died in 5088 (1328) the entire population of this land rose up suddenly against the Jews on the twenty-third day of Adar (March 6th). In Estella and the other towns, some six thousand persons were killed and there was not one who escaped their power. They also felled Rabbi Menachem, son of the holy Rabbi Aaron ben Serach, in this unmerciful time. When he had sunk unconscious to the ground and slept under the dead from near evening to the middle of the night, he was saved: a friend of his father had pity on him, pulled him secretly out from among the corpses, had him restored to health, and showed him much good. He then moved to Castile, but his father, mother and four younger brothers has sanctified the Name of God and the Name of the Holy One of Israel was glorified through them. Rabbi Menachem reported this himself in his

---

[180] Samuel Usque is of Marrano origin. In 1553 he published Consolacem as Tribula-coens de Israel (Consolation for the Sorrows of Israel) composed to strengthen the "steadfastness of the Marranos." He later lived in Safed-Israel. His poems were written in Portugese and were well known by his contemporaries.

book.[181] He descended from the exiles of France who were driven out in 5066 (1306). When, hereafter, a new King came to power in Navarre,[182] the remaining Jews presented their complaints to him, but he did not listen to their voices.

In the year 5108 (1348), a terrible pestilence raged from sunrise to sundown,[183] and there was not one city which remained untouched. This is recorded in the book Emek Rephaim,[184] written in those times by Rabbi Hayim Galipapa. A pitiful out-cry arose from one end of the earth to the other, unequalled until now: for a town evacuating one thousand sick people had only one hundred persons left, and a town of one hundred had a mere ten survive.[185] On the other hand, if one single Jew took ill and died, then one hundred people of the land took ill and died, and the Gentiles were filled with envy and would not talk to the Jews in a friendly manner.

In these days, no King ruled in Aragon,[186] and had not God stood by our side, not one Jew from Aragon or Catalonia could have escaped or run away, for out of meanness, accusations were circulated which proclaimed: "All this happens through the guilt of the Jews; they have brought this deadly poison into the world; they have caused it, and only through them is this horrible plague come upon us." As they voiced this terror causing rumor, the Jews panicked much, castigated their bodies through fasting, and cried to God; and this year was a time of need for Israel, of grimness, and of punishment. On a Sabbath eve, the Gentiles rose against God's people in Barcelona, killed twenty persons, reached out for loot, and no one said, "Restore it."[187] While they were still fighting, God let it thunder, and a rain poured down and lightening lit up. It scared those who had risen against them, and God confused their tongues. Hereafter, the Jews went out to the nobles and dignitaries of the city to save the rest from the hand of the attackers, but even before the thunder and rain had come, they were powerless to save them because too many had risen against them saying, "Let us destroy them, so that they won't be a people any longer, and the name of Israel will no longer be remembered." May God award the good, but those who fawn upon their crooked paths, may the Lord carry them off together with the evildoers,[188] Amen, Amen.

---

[181] Seder Laderech.
[182] Presumably Philip VI of France and Navarre (1328-51).
[183] From the Orient to the Occident. Ref. to Black Death (plague) of 1348
[184] Valley of the Giants
[185] Amos 5:3
[186] The King of Aragon is Pedro IV
[187] Isaiah 42:22
[188] Psalm 125:5

After a while, they rose against the Jews in the city of Cervera, killed eighteen people, and stretched out their hand to rob them. The others saved themselves through flight, castigated their lives by fasting, and many put themselves in sackcloth and ashes. After another three days, on the thirteenth of Ab (July 26th), when the Jews had a Fast day,[189] the inhabitants of Tarrega also rose, slaughtered more than three hundred Jewish persons, threw them into an empty pit and reached out their hands in plunder. The remaining Jews saved themselves by fleeing into the houses of their acquaintances, where they kept themselves hidden with the aid of secret presents, until the storm had subsided. On that terrible day they were completely denuded of all their possessions, but they were not ashmed.[190]

The Spoilers came also upon the inhabitants of Salsona and Tarragona due to the multitude of their sins. Those of imposing stature were hewn down, and the lofty were brought low;[191] about three hundred people in these two cities were slain with the sword. Behold this, Oh Lord, witness it and champion their cause. In the Provence also, the Jews emptied the cup of frenzy in these bad days. When this sad news reached the city of Monzon, the Jews became frightened, believing that punishment was now to be meted out to Israel. They initiated a day of fasting, girded themselves with sacks, implored God, and fortified their streets, courts, and hamlets. They kept a vigil in the night and interrupted their businesses during the day. They did not leave the Jews-Street until the people, who made attempts on their lives, were dead. They remained at their posts for a long time. Also in Lerida, Huesca and in all these locales where Jews had strong, reinforced walls, they gathered, defended their lives, and posted armed guards until He, who is enthroned in Heaven, looked down upon them and saved them.

In Germany, too, the Jews were accused with the words, "They have cast poison into our wells; chastise them with rods and thorns;" and after that, they burned them. These are the words of Rabbi Hayim Galipapa to this point.

The Portugese, Samuel Usque, wrote as follows: "The Jews in Germany multiplied much in the province of Thuringia in 5108 (1348), and since the inhabitants of the land were filled with envy against them, they thought of ways to kill them. Now, as many of them took ill, they said, 'The Jews have thrown poison into the wells to kill us.' They suddenly rose up and killed

---

[189] Jews commemorate the 9th of Ab, on which day the two Temples in Jerusalem were destroyed and other misfortunes befell the People, as a Fast Day. If the 9th of Ab falls on a Sabbath the Fast is observed later: the Sabbath, a day of rest and of a joy, is never disturbed by an act of mourning.

[190] Genesis 2:25

[191] Isaiah 10:33

many with the sword; others were flagellated with whips and then burned. Behold this, Oh Lord; witness it, and champion their cause!"

Sebastian Muenster adds this account in his book: "Many Jews gathered in their homes, locked the doors behind them, and set fire to them when they saw that this misfortune had befallen them. Thus, the fire consumed their families and relatives. In Mainz, the bell of the big church[192] melted because of the heat of the inferno. Behold! Such happened: in the Imperial cities, they tore down the houses of the Jews and used these stones, along with tombstones from the cemeteries, to build walls and watch-towers. They also traduced many of the Jews to fall away from their faith." Here ends the report of Sebastian Muenster regarding the Jews.

In the year 5108 (1348), the Jews were expelled from the Kingdom of Hungary; and they also were chased from their domiciles in other countries in that year. After the course of one year, most of the Jews of Germany had also to drink from the bent cup of frenzy. They were like a frightened deer or an urn with which one is displeased. Only those, who lived in Vienna and the towns of the Duke of Austria, (Albert II, d. 1358), did not hear the voices of the oppressor, for God had mercy on them and did not permit the Duke to entertain the thought of doing them any harm. Many Jews fled there and remained until the storm was over, and God had saved them.

And the Jews who had inquired about their permission to return to England were expelled from this bewitched land in 5118 (1358); and they never returned.

After Alfonso IX, King of Castile, had died and his son, Don Pedro ascended the royal throne, his brother Enrique, led a war against him.[193] There was no town that was superior to him, and he mocked at every fortification. He besieged Toledo in the month of Siv (Iyar)[194] in the year 5128 (1368), and he held a tight grip around the city. After the course of a year, King Pedro mustered an army and moved out of Seville to free Toledo forcibly from his hands. Don Enrique marched against him; when he had reached Montiel, they clashed, and King Pedro was overwhelmed and died in battle. The government fell to the hands of Don Enrique who now occupied the royal throne.[195] In those bad days, the inhabitants of the land rose up against the Jews in all the towns of Castile where they lived scattered, killed many with the sword, and reached out for booty.

[192] A reference to the Church of Saint Quentin

[193] Hacohen is here mistaken in his chronology: Alphonso IX was King of Leone from 1188 until 1230, and of Castile from 1214 until 1230. The king referred to here is Alphonso XI (1312-50), and his son is Peter the Cruel (1350-69).

[194] Siv and Iyar seem to be identical here.

[195] Enrique ruled from 1369 until 1379.

It was then a time of suffering for the Israelites as never before. Though the Jews cried out to God, He wrapped Himself in a cloud and no prayer broke through to Him. Also, in Toledo, the Jews were forced to drink from the rounded cup of frenzy and, because of the total absence of all necessities, they consumed even the flesh of their children. Behold this, Oh Lord, and see how I was degraded.

Because of want, some eight thousand persons died in these sad days. Only a small number of them remained alive, and even after the war clouds had been dispersed, they found no rest, for the nefarious Don Enrique kept them under a heavy yoke; and the People of the Lord marched down to the gates.[196] Rabbi Menachem ben Aaron ben Serach was also affected by all this: he was denuded of all his possessions and remained without clothing as he reports in his book, Tseda Laderech.[197]

A new Regent[198] appeared on the scene in Austria who was still a child, and consequently, the whole of the populace was ruled by the decrees of the counsellors and dukes. In 5131 (1371), the counsellors of the young Regent had the Jews in all the towns of his realm arrested and thrown in jail, where they remained for so long a time that they became disgusted with life, although they were at least not tortured or abused.

Although I don't know why, an expulsion from France took place in 5143 (1383).

On Sunday, the twenty-second of Nissan of the year 5149 (April 18, 1389), the people of Prague, in Bohemia, surrounded the Vinyard of the Lord of Hosts, the Israelite families. All of these people crawled out from the ends of the earth, each with an axe in his hand, as if he were a wood-chopper, reached out, and slew many of them, so that the mountains trembled. The corpses of the Jews were lying in the streets together with the sweepings. They blasphemed the Torah of the Lord and reviled the words of the Holy One of Israel. Doing all this, still their wrath did not subside, and they stretched forth their hands, burned many, pulled those who slumbered in the dust from their graves, and smashed their tombstones to pieces; there was no one who saved them from their power. When many of the Jews saw that the hour of fate had arrived, they sacrificed themselves.

---

[196] Judges 5:11; i.e., their fortunes declined.

[197] Ibn Zerach was a Spanish codifier. His Tsedah la-Derech was a concise Handbook of essential Jewish religious laws for the use of busy Jews in attendance at the royal Court." (c.f. Roth's Standard Jewish Encyclopaedia, p. 950)

[198] After Rudolph IV's death (1365) "a dark period followed" (see Enclop. Britannica Vol 2., p. 757, 1956. His succession was divided between his brother Albert II (1365-95) and Leopold (1365-86). This division of authority led to a long and devastating dispute between the two lines. The Jews must have been caught right in the middle.

King Vencislav[199] was not in Prague then, for he had travelled to Eger, and because of that, misfortune befell the Jews. They then killed each other, some his brother or his friend, some his dear wife or his sons and daughters, all, so that the Christians could not torture them. And their entreaties went up to Heaven. Behold this, Oh Lord; see it and champion their cause. It was Avigdor Kara who mourned over them in a Selicha (poem of forgiveness).[200]

After Pope Urban (VI) had died, a Spaniard named Peter of Luna was elected Benedict XIII in 5154 (1394), and because a struggle among the Cardinals had broken out, they elected Boniface IX in Rome, who then occupied the papal throne.[201] Many persecutions took place in Spain in those days because the monk, Fra Vicenza of Valencia,[202] who belonged to the Dominican Order, mounted the pulpit and said hostile things against the Jews. When he had incited the populace of the land against them, they arose to annihilate the Jews: many were slain with the sword, and many forcibly converted from the Lord, the God Israel. In these most hopeless days Israel was degraded much. The Torah Scrolls of our Lord were burned and trampled upon like street-dirt. My own grandparents, Cohanim, moved away from the city of Cuenca, from the furor of the oppressors, entered Huete, and stayed there in these terrible days. Of the remainder, a part was murdered, another part killed their sons and daughters, so that they would not have to change their faith, and a third group was forcibly turned away from the Lord, the God of Israel. The number killed in this bloodbath amounted to one hundred fifty thousand, and those who were converted to about fifteen thousand.

At this time, many fled into the land of the Moors and many saved their lives by going to Portugal, and they stayed there. This miserable monk also had the intention of going there to set the teeth of the Jews on edge,[203] but when he inquired about that before King Edward, then reigning in Portugal,[204] he was told, "You will enter Portugal with jubilation but emerge in

[199] Venceslav (or Wenceslaus) was king of Bohemia from 1378 until 1419 and Holy Roman Emperor from 1378 until 1400.

[200] Rabbi A. Kara died on Saturday, April 25, 1439. He is buried at the Old Cemetery in Prague.

[201] Actually, Hacohen is a little misleading here: this takes place during the Great Schism. Urban was elected in 1378 and died in 1389. At the same time, the anti-Pope Clement was elected in 1378 and died in 1394. Urban was succeeded in Rome by Boniface IX who was Pope until 1404. Clement VII was succeeded in Avignon by Benedict XIII, 1394-1423).

[202] Fra Vicenza is St. Vicente Ferrer (1350-1419). He was an advisor to King John of Aragon.

[203] Jeremiah 31:30

[204] Hacohen is mistaken here: while Edward was alive during the lifetime of Vicente,

flames bearing an iron crown upon your head!" And thus, he withdrew in ignominy. However, the King of Aragon[205] listened to his voice: there were many converts in Catalonia, Aragon, and Seville at that time, and the number of apostates from Judaism was numerous in the whole of Spain. But later on, after the storm had subsided, many did return to their God. Yet inquisitions were imposed upon them, a practice which is conducted to this day. The Jews lived then in Fort Huete and Fort Soria, as also in other citadels, where they had sought refuge, until they emigrated from this land which God had cursed.

This infamous tyrant also stretched the plummet of confusion[206] against the Jews of Savoy. I, Joseph Hacohen, saw a book, the exterior of which was in bad condition, that belonged to those who kept Jews hidden in wells for a long time in these evil days. Yet, this Fra Vicenza was regarded as a holy man in the eyes of the Christians because Calixtus[207] had put his name amongst the Saints, and they celebrated his name in a memorial on the fifth of April. Oh Lord, avenge his deeds and help us for Thy Name's sake.

Joseph Hacohen is speaking again: Although I wrote in the Book of Chronicles[208] that this had taken place in the days of Pope Eugenius IV,[209] the story is more accurate in this account, for I have found it recorded in the Hebrew language and also in non-Jewish language and literature. In addition to these, I have found the following Hebrew account, though the handwriting was German: In those terrible days, a thick darkness reigned all over Spain because of the decision to annihilate the Jews, and erudite people declared that this was the finger of God. Because of this, the Christians' ire against the Jews acquiesced, for God had mercy on Israel, and they dwelt in this land where they were fertile and multiplied.

After the Jews had appealed for permission to live once more in France, they were again chased away in the year 5155 (1395). And in these days, a terrible false accusation was brought up against the Jews living in Germany near the water-rich region at Bodensee (in Zurich and Schaffhausen and environ) to corrupt and destroy them, and then to rob them of all their possessions. They were ordered thrown in jail, though they had committed no

he was not crowned until 1433, some forteen years after Vicente died. Their meeting, while Edward was king, would have been impossible.

[205] John I was king from 1387 until 1395

[206] Isaiah 34:11

[207] Calixtus III (Alfonzo Borgia) was Pope from 1455 until 1458.

[208] The Book of Chronicles is commonly known as the "History of the Kings of France and the House of Ottoman." It is a kind of world history depicting the struggle between Moslems and Christians during the Crusades.

[209] Eugenius IV (1431-47)

crime, punished in the usual manner, and then more than one hundred men, women and children were murdered in this terrible time. In them, the Name of the Holy One of Israel was glorified. Moreover, other false accusations were brought against a Jew in Germany, his life was embittered in the customary way, and he was put in chains and sentenced to death. When they took him outside, he said, "In a few days, much blood will be spilled in this city, and nobody will be able to stop it: up to their thighs will they wade in it." Those who heard this were much astonished and remembered it. And after a short while the Swiss people rebelled against their masters, the Dukes of Austria; they carried on a war with them in which many sank, lifeless, to the ground. Two Austrian Dukes were killed in this battle.[210] Thereafter, the Swiss went out a second time, spilled blood, as if it were water in this waterrich region which they call Bodensee as also in Zurich, just as this man, whom they had slain, although he had committed no crime, had predicted. Hereafter, the Swiss threw off the yoke of the Dukes of Austria and elected Judges and Prefects from the elders of their Confederacy as they still do today.

In 5166 (1406), a fire broke out on the Sabbath eve in the Synagogue located in the Jews Street, and it consumed all the homes of the Jewish neighborhood. This caused the whole city to shudder on account of them: Jewish homes were rendered to plunder, and the enemies let their hands glean like grape gatherers over the branches;[211] and there was no one to save them from the power of Christian hands. One Jew took heart and tried to save his clothing, but only endangered himself: they wounded him mortally, so that he died. To the other Jews came no harm, only their dwellings were destroyed speedily, and no gleaning was left for them.[212] They praised God for His mercy and for His wonderous deeds to His sons of man because He saved their lives from perdition in this fateful night.

After three years, King Sigmund of Hungary[213] was defeated by the Turks, Kuerishdshi Tshelebbi,[214] and had to flee. His soldiers were slain with the sword in the neighborhood of Shalumviv on the seventeenth day of the fifth month. In 5120 (1410), the remaining Jews, who had wished to

---

[210] This probably refers to the defeat and death of Duke Leopold III of Austria at Sempach in 1386, and to the defeat of his brother, Duke Albert III at Naefels in 1388.

[211] Jeremiah 6:9

[212] I.e., none of their dwellings was spared.

[213] Sigmund or Sigismund was King of Hungary from 1387 until 1437, King of Bohemia from 1419 until 1437, and Holy Roman Emperor from 1411 until 1437.

[214] "The Ringer." This futile Crusade is linked to the name of Nicopolis who was defeated by Sultan Bajazid in 1396 (see also R. S. Atya, *Crusade of Nicopolis*, London, 1934.

return to France and live there, were expelled. The dispersed went here and there, one part to Savoy and Piedmont, and another to Germany, that is to Alsace-Lorraine, i.e. to Lorena (Italian), and to other German provinces,[215] and there they settled and remain to this very day.

In 5179 (1419), the adherents of a new religion rose up in Bohemia,[216] killed all the city fathers of Prague, destroyed the monks' cloisters, put the torch to them, and smashed their pictures into pieces, so that Prague became desolated. King Vencislav died in that year, and Sigmund ruled in his stead. The inhabitants of Bohemia rebelled against him with all their leaders and Dukes, and many people were slain then. After the course of a year the Christian Kings decided to war against the adherents of this new religion, called the Hussites, and to exterminate them from the earth so that their name would never be remembered. But when King Sigmund marched against them, together with the Dukes of the Empire, they were decisively defeated by the Hussites, despite the fact that they had mustered an army of one hundred thousand soldiers. The majority of these were slaughtered, and the King was forced to flee on foot, and barely escaped with his life. The others fled from there and were forced to beg for bread to save their lives at the doors of generous people in all the places to which they had dispersed. They also engaged the Hussites in naval battles (Moldau River), and they conquered the whole of Bohemia which then had to pay them tribute. Many of those who had gone to war intended to deal arbitrarily with the Jews once they had returned safely to their homes. Therefore, the Jews were very much afraid for their lives. Among them was the pious Maharil (Rabbi Jacob Moeln Levi). They decided on a fast of three days, day and night, in the month of Bul and said those prayers normally reserved only for the Day of Atonement; and God saved them.

In 5181 (1421), the following happened: in the cities of Austria, Jews had been rounded up on the tenth day of Sivan (May 24, 1420), and thrown in jail. Eight hundred persons, children and women, were chased away and were forced to flee insecure and unsteady, naked and bare, together with their infants. Many found their death. About one thousand people were kept in the jail. Women and children were separated and kept apart in the homes of the inhabitants of the land, where they given all sorts of forbidden food to eat, extraordinarily tortured, and turned away from their faith.[217] After a

---

[215] Here again Lorraine is typed as a German province. It is historically true, however, that Lorraine, up to the 15th Century, was mostly a fief of the German Empire.

[216] The new Religion is Hussitism, named after John Hus who was declared a heretic by the Council of Constance (which was convoced by Sigmund) and burned alive in 1415. His teaching resembled those of Wyclif.

[217] This technique of separating men from women was used to persuade the latter to

year had passed, on the ninth of Nissan (March 12, 1421), four hundred of them were slain, and the Name of the Holy One of Israel was sanctified through them. Now, Oh Lord, Spirit of all Flesh, keep pure their souls in Your treasure-chambers, and may their reward be of help to us; Amen, Amen.

In the year 5190 (1430), the Jews of Germany were accused falsely in the cities of Ravenburg, Ueberlingen, and Lindau. They were thrown in jail, tortured, and an entry was made into the Protocol-Book as to what they did neither confess nor ever had planned doing.[218] Thereupon, they were sentenced and burned, and their pure souls ascended to God. Look down, Oh Lord; witness this and help us for Thy Name's sake. Then they plundered the considerable riches, and it was this which was the cause of this nefarious deed and which had prompted all the accusations.

In these days, the Dauphin[219] fought with his mighty army in the cities of Switzerland. All of the locales, through which he passed, were pillaged and the Jews, too, were handed over for plunder. He had an army of about thirty thousand men. All the inhabitants of the land gathered, and nobody stayed behind; and then, suddenly, they fell upon the enemy and caused them to flee and hide in the mountains. But the Swiss followed them on the same routes in order to annihilate them completely. The Dauphin had divided his troops into three contingents, and those of the Swiss, who were laying in wait, directed their fellows' attention to the second contingent, for they believed that the Dauphin was in their midst. Thus, the first group, with which he actually rode, was allowed to pass by. However, the other two were beaten and a respectable amount of booty was made.

On the thirtieth day of Shevat 5190 (January 24, 1430), the people of Aix rose up out of the blue sky against the Jews of the Provence and killed nine of them. They reached out their hands in plunder, and there was no one who came to the aid of the Israelites. Seventy-four persons converted, for a fear of the people had befallen them. Thus, they were turned away from the Lord,

---

accept Christianity. Many did under duress. However, after their escape, most of them returned to their ancient Faith.

[218] This sentence is vague. We must assume that Germans plundered from the Jews, but that the crime was attributed to the Jews who in turn were forced to admit their crimes.

[219] The Dauphin, the eldest son of the King of France, afterwards Louis XI (1461-83), was seven years old in 1430. However, it was quite common for a Dauphin to assume his duties as a commander with the help of a deputy or viceregent. King Charles VII sent his son, the Dauphin to Switzerland in 1444. This means that the Dauphin was about twenty-one years old and not a mere child. It is interesting to note that this invasion of about thirty-thousand soldiers was by invitation of Emperor Frederic III in Zurich. In other words, we are talking here about a Swiss Civil War.

the God of Israel. May this fatal day remain forever a single incident, for the Congregation was unexpectedly robbed and its homes suddenly destroyed. Look down, Oh Lord; see this, and help us for Thy Name's sake. This calamity is alluded to in the Psalm,[220] "for the water reached up to my neck (life)," means this: the Hebrew word "Kí" (for) corresponds in value to the numbers of days in the month, the word "Bá-u" (came) to the number killed, and the term "Mayim" (waters) linking the word to the name of the city (Aquae-Aix); the date after our abbreviated computation of time, the term "Ad" (to) the number of those who were converted, and the word "Nephesh" (soul-life) to the date of the abbreviated Christian computation of time.[221]

In 5200 (1440), the Duke of Bavaria, Germany, died. This was a decent and just man, god-fearing, avoiding evil, who was mourned, "Ah Lord!"[222] And he was honored. The Jews who lived under his dominion became numerous, and also the deer and other wild beasts in the fields multiplied, for he had not permitted to do them any harm. But when his son took his place, he did not walk in his father's path,[223] and he began to devour the Jews in the land, the deer and the other wild beasts in the fields. He had the Jews thrown in prisons, though they had committed no crime, confiscated all their belongings, and then expelled them from the country. He also dealt cruelly with the deer and wild beasts, so that they became fewer and fewer from one day to the next. After a short while he took sick, leprosy spread over his face, the people were repulsed by the sight of him, and he died.

When Philip Maria Visconti, Duke of Milan, died,[224] the Venetians started a war against Milan. In the year 5207 (1447), Francesco Sforza, the son-in-law of the Duke of Milan, became the leader of his people. This man rose in power, built castles for himself, and practiced law and justice. The Jews also multiplied in his land. After he had reigned for twenty-five years, he died, and one of his five sons, Galeazzo, followed him to power.

In 5215 (1456), a young lad walked out of his house in Salamanca, Spain; it was a Christian holiday. He was adorned with golden trinkets, and he wore festive clothing. Two evil men came up to him, tore off his golden chain, and when the boy cried out and wished to return to town, they attacked him a

---

[220] Psalm 69:2

[221] "Ki" equals thirty, "ba-u" equals nine, "mayim" equals ninety, "ad" equals 74. An abbreviated chronology omits the hundreds and/or thousands.

[222] Jermiah 22:18

[223] Duke Adolph of Munich (Bavaria) died in 1440. His son was Albert the Pious (1440-1460). He reformed the monasteries. Hence, his hostility and religious fanaticism toward the Jews. He died in 1460, not a "short while later," as Hacohen has it.

[224] He ruled from 1412-1447, and was the last of his line. Sforza is his son-in-law who fought for three years to enter Milan in 1450. And he was succeeded by his son Galeazzo (died in 1476).

second time, murdered him and covered him with soil. Nobody saw it. Thereafter, people looked for him, and it was publicly announced that the finder of the boy would get a reward. After some shepherds' dogs had found him and torn off one of his arms, the shepherds brought the arm to the city. Then several burghers, together with the father, went out to see the body. After he had identified him, the father wept very much for his son. But when the judges asked, "What kind of man would dare to commit such a crime?" the opinion was expressed that the crime was certainly committed either by a captive Moslem or a Jew. Many were convinced that the Jews had done this, to bring their God a sacrifice. Whereupon all, roaring like bears, stormed into the city, saying, "The Jews have torn out his heart, baked it, and they all consumed it." Then the relatives of the slain gathered, preparing before them the implements of war with which to annihilate the Jews instantly, and had not God in His mercy bestirred the King[225] to investigate the matter thoroughly they would, most likely, have lost their lives. Through the investigation the matter was cleared up by a goldsmith to whom the murderers had sold the golden trinkets which had belonged to the lad. The ire of the people against the Jews then subsided.

In this year, it was during the days of King Juan II, who was then still a child, and his mother, Catherine of Lancaster, that the nobles of Castile became envious of the Jews of Segovia, because they had a great influence at the court of the King. And they conspired evil things against them. They sought out a certain monk, whom they agitated, saying, "The Jews have thrown a Host in a pot of boiling water which turned to blood." Their words were believed, and many were cast in jail. They then assassinated Don Meir Alguadez,[226] the physician of King Enrique III and, after their fashion, two of the most prominent members of the Jewish Congregation. They dragged Jews through the dust, quartered them, and converted their Synagogues into churches; and if this matter had not been seen in the light of day, all of the members of the Congregation would have lost their lives then.[227] It, further-

---

[225] The King is Alfonso V, the Magnanimous, of Aragon (1416-58).

[226] Rabbi Meier Alguades or Alvarez, the translator of Aristotle's Ethics, died in 1410 (he was murdered). Wiener suggests that Hacohen perhaps mistook Alvarez for Alvaro de Luna, who was greatly favored by Juan II and then assassinated in Valladolid in 1453.

[227] There seems to be a problem of historical accuracy in this paragraph, as is suggested in the previous note. Reluctant to challenge Wiener, there is perhaps a better, or at least a simpler, answer to the question here. The paragraph begins, "In this year. . ." which leads one to believe Hacohen means 1456, the date given at the beginning of the preceeding paragraph. It seems however, that he means the phrase "In this year. . ." to refer to a date during the reign of Juan II which he leaves unspecified. First of all, the year 1456 was not one during which Juan II reigned. He was born in 1405 and crowned King of Castile on the death of his father, Henry (Enrique) III, in 1406. He died in 1454. Thus, it seems that

more, happened in these days that a quarrel between one of the magistrates of the city and the Bishop broke out. This man hated the Bishop much, thought to kill him, and even persuaded one of his servants to poison him. He promised to do so, and when the poison was found on him, they tortured him, as is their custom, in order to find out who had ordered him to do such a thing. But when he refused to confess, his master prompted him to testify that the Jews had commanded him to kill the Bishop. His words were believed, and he was spared. But then many of the Jews were slain and the rest were forced to flee. You, Oh Lord, have witnessed my injury; please grant me justice.[228]

In Savoy, many Jews lived in safety after they had emigrated from France and became very powerful there. Later on, in the year 5221 (1461), they were burned, whereupon they settled in the Romagna where they live to this day.

The moon wrapped itself in darkness in the night before the fifteenth of Nissan in 5235 (March 23, 1475). During the time of Pessach, the evil-doer, Enzo, in Trent, murdered a two year old child, Simon by name, tossed it secretly into a pond by the house of a Jew, Samuel, and nobody saw it. As is customary, the Jews were accused, and their homes were entered into on the orders of the Bishop; but those who did it returned soon without having found the child. Later on, when the searchers found him, they went to the Bishop's command to the scene to identify him. The Bishop had all Jews apprehended, and embittered their lives and tortured them,[229] until they

one cannot interpret "In this year..." to mean 1456, if we also wish to maintain that this year was during the reign of Juan as the rest of the paragraph so clearly maintains. Secondly, his mother was Catherine of Lancaster, daughter of John of Gaunt, whom Juan I had married to his son Henry III as part of a treaty settlement between himself (Juan I) and Gaunt who had been at war. But, presumably Catherine would have died before 1454 and thus the whole sentence "... it was during the days of King Juan II ... and his mother, Catherine of Lancaster ..." would have little meaning. This would not be the case, if the "day" referred to were the first few years of Juan's reign. Thirdly, it seems likely (to say the least) that the Castilian nobles could have had influence over Juan II and used this influence to direct an anti-Semitic policy during the King's infancy rather than when he had grown older. Thus Alguadez's death (which took place in 1410, when Juan was merely five years old) would have been more or less at the time described in the paragraph. Fourthly, as the murder of Henry III's physician is supposed to have taken place when his son (Juan II) was a child, it hardly seems likely that Hacohen would confuse Alguadez with de Luna who died in 1453, i.e., when Juan was 48. Fifthly, it certainly would not be out of place for Alguadez the philosopher (or translator) also to have been a physician (compare the fact that Maimonides was also physician to Saladin). Thus, it seems more likely that Hacohen was merely in error in his remembrance of dates by a factor of something like fifty years, if, indeed, it be insisted that "In this year..." be interpreted to mean 1456.

[228] Lamentations 3:59

[229] Incidently, March 24th is celebrated in Trent with great pomp as the Feast of St. Simonin even to this day.

confessed all that came to their minds. Only one old man, very aged indeed, by the name of Moses, did not confess to this evil untruth, and he died while being beated up. Award him, Oh Lord, for his decency.

Two erudite Christians, who were well versed in the law, came from Padua to find out the circumstances of this matter, but when the wrath of the people became aroused against them, they were threatened with death. The Bishop then sentenced the Jews, embittered their lives, had them pinched with the points of tongs, and then burned them. Their pure souls went up to Heaven. The Bishop then confiscated all their belongings, as planned, and filled his home with the booty.[230] After that, it was said that the child was holy and caused miracles. The Bishop had this made public in the towns. The people came close to see the body and did not come with empty hands. All over the hatred against the Jews was rampant among the populace in which they lived, and nobody wanted to say a decent word to them. After that, the Bishop challenged the Pope to declare the child a Saint, since it had proven itself holy. The Pope sent one of his Cardinals, with the title Legate, to investigate the matter scrupulously.

When he arrived, he investigated the matter and found, that it was all an empty delusion and foolishness. He also examined the corpse of the child and found that they had embalmed it with the spices and perfumes used for embalming. Thereafter, he made fun of them, and when he proclaimed in the presence of the entire populace the whole matter as a hoax, the ire of the people grew so that he was forced to flee and to retreat to one of the towns nearby Trent. He then had the entire dossier, containing the confessions of the Jews and the decree over them, brought before him. One of the servants of the evil-doer, who had committed this crime, was arrested. He then confessed that this ignominious deed had been ordered by the Bishop who had planned to annihilate the Jews. The Cardinal brought this servent with him to Rome and reported accordingly to the Pope,[231] who, in turn, did not elevate the child to sainthood, as the Bishop requested of him day after day. The child was called Beatus Simon, but to this day he is not called Sanctus or Saint.[232] And now, Lord of Hosts, Righteous Judge, remove the veil of blindness from the eyes of those people who are of an uncircumcised heart,[233] who believe such untruths and who give them the stamp of verity, for because of

---

[230] Nahum 3:1

[231] Pius II (1405-64) was originally one of the anti-Popes, excommunicated and then "reformed." He revived the Holy Orders in 1446. After the fall of Constantinople he worked feverishly to get a new Crusade started.

[232] This child was not canonized until 1588.

[233] Uncircumcised heart means lacking in understanding or faith.

such lies we are butchered every day and led to the slaughterer's bench. Help us, for Thy Name's sake.

The Duke of Brandenburg (Albert Achilles 1470-86) died in these days, a brave and honest man. And he was much mourned: Ah Lord! After his death, the Jews were expelled from the land of the Franks and from the principality of the Bishop of Bamberg, from Wuerzburg and all the locales over which he ruled.

In 5235 (1475) Isabella became Queen of Castile.[234] She was the wife of Ferdinand, King of Aragon. On account of those who had been traduced into conversion since the days of Fra Vicenza, of cursed memory, the Inquisition was reinstated, and many were burned at the stake. It was then that the Lord fulfilled the prophecy of Jonathan ben Uziel which he verbalized to Ezekiel with these words: "From the Torah, given under fire, they have receeded. Therefore, they will be handed over to the whim of the nations which are as strong as steel, and they will be burned in a mighty holocaust."

In 5237 (1477) the Duke of Milan, Galeazzo, was assassinated in the church,[235] and his oldest son, who followed him as ruler, married the daughter of Alphonso, King of Naples. His uncle, Louis, with the nickname, il-Moro acted as his guardian and stood continuously and hamperingly in his way. This nefarious and miserable Moro[236] also dealt badly with the Jews, had them thrown into the jail, and extorted from them a condiserable amount of money, although they had done nothing wrong. He ruled with the help of his golden treasures and married the daughter of Hercules, the Marquis of Ferrara. She bore him two sons, Maximilian and Francesco, whom he loved very much.

In 5241 (1481) [237] Ferdinand and Isabella, ruling in Spain, expelled the Jews from the city of Seville, and then from the entire province of Andalusia, and they were forced to migrate to a different country. And in 5249 (1489) Louis Moro, the protector of Milan, accused the Jews wrongly, arrested and expelled them from his realm, after he had extorted a huge sum of money from them.

In those days, in one of the open cities of the territory of Tortone, a certain Jew was accused, as in the case of Trent, and the child was also

---

[234] Isabella became Queen of Castile in 1474. She died in 1504.

[235] I.e., in the Church of St. Stephen. John (Gain Galeazzo Sforza (d. 1494)) married Isabella of Naples. His father was King Alfonso II (1494-95) of Naples.

[236] A play on words: in Hebrew "mar" means bitter, and hence, Moro is "the bitter one."

[237] In this same year the Jews of Seville were sacrificed four times.

named Beatus Sonin (Simon?) and they adored him. This caused the Jews much trouble.

A little time later, after the death of John Galeazzo, his brother's son rose up and Heaven uncovered Moro's guilt. Louis XII, King of France (1498-1515), tore the whole land away from Moro (he acted in the service of Higher Powers), abducted him, and took him to France; and thus he died in a foreign country and was buried there in 1508.[238]

At that time, Rabbi Isaac from Leon was respected and highly esteemed among his contemporaries in Spain. He died before the expulsion of the Jews from Spain. But one year, before the exodus, this rabbi appeared to his wife three times during her nightly dream and said to her, "Remove the tombstone from my grave and have it plowed over, so that no one may know my place of rest." When she related her dream to the sages, they instituted a Fast and allowed her to do what her husband has asked her. Rabbenu Asher and Rabbenu Jona, and other famous men, were also buried there: over their graves the plow was also dragged, and nobody knows their grave site to this day.

After Granada had been under the rule of the Moors for two hundred years, Ferdinand and Isabella, the rulers of Spain, besieged it and conquered the whole territory of this realm by their power: the city of Granada was delivered unto them in January of 1492, and the Jews living in that province fell victim to plunder and booty.

The number of Marranos[239] had increased in Spain much since the days of Fra Vicenza. They had intermarried with the most aristocratic citizens of the country and were highly respected. The Jews also grew in number until the days of Ferdinand and Isabella. These two appointed Inquisitors over the Marranos to find out whether or not they followed the precepts of the Christian religion. They made the name Jews into a horror, a by-word and object of satire.[240] Many of them were burned then. God also did not lift His hand to spare their destruction; one stormed against the other, a lad against an old man, the despised against the venerable. And if a woman longed for the silver and gold vessels of her neighbor, or a woman who shared the same building with her and the woman refused to hand them over, she was denounced. During that time the Jews became disgusted with their

---

[238] This is incorrect: Moro died in 1510 in the Castle of Loches in Berry.

[239] Marranos, a name applied in medieval Spain to a christianized Jew. Especially to one who merely professed conversion in order to avoid persecution by the "Holy" Inquisition. Incidentally, the Oxford English Dictionary Vol., VI M p. 180 rejects the etymology of Marranos, equating the term with the word "pigs".

[240] Deuteronomy 28:37

lives. Now, as these two rulers saw that many adhered to the House of Israel, they expelled the Jews from their country so that the Marranos would not follow in their paths, as many had done to that day. All the Hosts of the Lord, the Exiles of Jerusalem in Spain, emigrated from this cursed land and in the fifth month of 5252 (1492), and from there they dispered to the four winds of the earth. On Friday, the tenth day of Ab (August 3),[241] sixteen large ships sailed from the harbor-town of Cartagena filled with Hosts of Humanity, without those (of course) who did the same thing in other parts of the kingdom; and they went where the whim of the moment drove them: to Africa, Asia, Greece, Turkey; and they remain there to this day. Stark, grave suffering and all kinds of perils met with them; the mariners of Genoa abused them daily and people languished on the way there. The Moslems killed a part of them in order to rob them of their gold some of which they swallowed in order to hide it. Others were devoured by pest or by starvation. They cast another one overboard into the waters; others were cast off naked by the ships' captains on the islands of the sea, and still others were sold as male and female slaves in proud Genoa[242] and its surrounding territory in this terrible year.

Among those who had come by ship to Italy was a Hazan (cantor) by the name of Joseph Zibhon with a son and several daughters. One of them caught the heart of the ship's captain. When the cantor's wife learned this, she preferred to commit suicide: she cast her daughters into the sea and plunged after them. When the seafarers learned this, they became full of terror and descended into the sea to bring them back on the ship, but only one fell into their hands. The name of one of the sisters was Paloma (the Dove). Her father cried over her with a lament of these words: "And they took Jona (the Dove)[243] and cast her into the sea."[244]

Many remained in Spain who had not the strength to emigrate and whose hearts were not filled with God. Thus, many of them were lured away from their faith. Behold this, Oh Lord, and witness it. To whom have You done this? Where else has man eaten up the fruit of his own loin?

Among those who were cast off on the islands of the Provence was a Jew with his old father who, smarting from hunger, begged for bread. No one gave him anything in this foreign land. The son went out and sold his own youngest son for bread so as to revive the old man, but when he returned to

---

[241] The same day Columbus set sail for the Americas.
[242] Genoa is called by its citizens, Genoa la Superba.
[243] Paloma is Spanish for dove while the same word in Hebrew is Jonà.
[244] Jonah 1:15

his father, he found him laying dead. Thereupon he rent his clothes, returned to the baker to retrieve his son; but when that man refused to hand him over, he began to cry out loudly and bitterly, and no one stood by his side. Oh God, all this happened after five thousand years had taken their course and in the month of Ab in that year. The word "Rabim" corresponds to the numerical value of that year as alluded to in Isaiah:[245] "For *numerous* are the children of the desolate." Yet we have not forgotten You and did not renege on Your Covenant. But now, Oh God, do not stay away from us; hurry back to our aid, for You, Oh Lord, are our help; champion our cause and save us for Thy Name's sake.

The King of Navarre,[246] however, did not exile the Jews from his country, and many who had come from Aragon settled there. After the course of one year, as those men whose hearts were filled with God wished to move away from this iron oven,[247] because they feared for their lives, the King of Aragon[248] permitted them to cross his land. They reached the Provence by ship and remained for a short while in Avignon.

Among the arrivals was my uncle, Don Bonafous, his mother, Preciosa, his wife, Orazetta, and my mother, Dolca, who spent her youth in the house of her mother as did the sons of Don Bonafous. Also Don Abraham Official and his wife Myrrha and many others whose names I have forgotten arrived with them. There they found my father, Rabbi Yehoshua, from the stock of Cohanim (Priests), who had moved away from Fort Huete. They gave him my mother, Dolca, for a wife on the 15th of Ab in the year 5255 (1495). But they did not remain there for long and moved to Turkey where they have lived to this day. After a short time, the King of Navarre expelled those Jews who had remained there, but when, because the road had been barred, they could not migrate, they fell away from the Lord, the God of Israel.

The Jews of the Provence were also to be expelled in those days, but they refused to leave this land of destruction and chose another faith. They have remained there to this day. In the Provence only those who lived in Avignon and in the towns belonging to the Pope remained. In the meantime, the Lord

---

[245] Isaiah 54:1; the numerical value of Rabim is 252, the event taking place in 5252 (1492).

[246] Ferdinand II's father, John II of Aragon, once owned the little Kingdom of Navarre in the Pyrenees (populated mostly by descendants of Basques, a highly unassimilable ethnic element). Since then, Navarre had passed in turn to the French noble families of Albret and Foix. Ferdinand used a pretext to invade Navarre because of their alleged pro-French attitude

[247] In the Bible, the "Oven" is Egypt which is here equated with Navarre.

[248] King Ferdinand, the husband of Isabella.

was zealous for His people and retaliated against the two rulers[249] for their handiwork: their daughter died in Portugal and Ferdinand's oldest son died of a dread disease so that no male heir, who could inherit the crown, was left to them. His wife, the infamous Isabella, was also fed up with her life because a part of her body had been eaten up by a bad and grave disease, called cancer; and she died. Verily, God is just.

Joseph Hacohen speaks: The exile from France and the above named fatal and terrible banishment have prompted me to compose this book so that later generations of Israel may know how we have been afflicted in these countries and places. For, behold! new days have arrived! About six hundred family fathers[250] migrated, in the Year of Exile, from Castile to Portugal with the consent of King Joao II,[251] who had made a pact with them in consideration of a headtax of two guilders to be paid to him. He also promised to deliver ships to those who did not wish to remain in his country. With the aid of the ships, these Jews were to be allowed to go to whatever places their hearts desired. However, the plague reigned in that year in Portugal, and it had also begun in Italy, where many died. After a short while, many expressed the desire to emigrate to the land of the Moslems[252] and to Turkey. These demanded ships from the King, but he procrastinated with much double-talk. But when they remained persistent, he gave them ships, and they began their voyage without harm and went on their way.

---

[249] I.e., Ferdinand and Isabella

Ferdinand (II) of Aragon (d. 1516)	Isabella of Castile	(d. 1504)	
Juan (d. 1497)	Maria – Manoel I of Portugal	Juanna la Losa- (Joanna the *Mad*) married Philip the Handsome (d. 1506), son of Emperor Maximilian I	Catherine of Aragon Henry VIII of England
		Charles V Emperor 1519-56 (He became King of Aragon in 1516, and Emperor in 1519)	Ferdinand I, Emperor 1556-64

[250] It was Rabbi Isaac Aboab who went with a delegation of some thirty Jews to Joao and persuaded him to accept the Jews for a period of six years. After that, Portugal was to furnish ships for those six hundred Jews to help them emigrate. Unfortunately, some twenty thousand families went to that country as a temporary domicile. Unexplained is the question why Joao tore the children of the immigrants from their parents and shipped them to the Portugese Islands.

[251] Joao II, the Perfect, ruled from 1482 until 1495; he was also regent during the absences of his father, Alfonso V.

[252] I.e., to north Africa; more precisely: Marocco.

En route, however, the mariners rose against them, tied them up with ropes, raped their wives before their eyes, and nobody came to their aid. Thereafter they brought them to Africa, and then ejected them on a barren, empty, and unfertile land which seemed uninhabited. Their children asked for bread, but no one could give them anything, and their mothers lifted up their eyes toward Heaven in this fateful time. Those who dug the graves cried out to the mountains, "Oh cover us!" for many sank feint to the ground like dead; and they wished to forfeit their lives because of the heat of hunger. But as they lifted up their eyes toward Heaven, some Arabs came upon them and stopped and waited to see if those people would face up to them. When they did, the Arabs reproached them and talked to them harshly because the Jews had come into their land without making a covenant with them beforehand.[253] Then they made them into slaves and dragged them along behind. But these poor ones, eaten up by hunger, regarded this as fortunate and they praised God. Then the Jewish inhabitants of the country brought them out of bondage and presented them with clothing, food and drink out of pity. May God remember them forever. After this became known in Portugal, the remaining Jews there became filled with fear and did not dare to emigrate. And in the second year after the Israelites had moved away from Castile, the King of Portugal inquired if more than the original six hundred family-fathers, with whom he had made his pact, had entered his country. When it was found that, in the haste, more than that number had come in, he had the excess arrested, declared them to be his slaves, and refused to accept ransom. Then was their life truly embittered.

His servants who plowed the sea with his ships discovered an island which they named St. Thomas. Not only can large fish, called lagartos, be found there, but also snakes, toads, and basilisks.[254] The King used to send common criminals there, and those who had been sentenced to death. There he sent the poor Jews, together with the criminals, and no one came to their aid. The mothers rose their voices with weeping when these barbarians tore the children from their laps, and the men tore out their beards because of their souls' grief in this time of terror. Many prostrated themselves before the King, saying, "Please, let us go into exile with them," but, like a deaf viper, he refused to listen and ignored them completely. One woman, who clutched her child to her bosom, plunged into the sea because of her grief, and thus both found their death. See and witness, if such a thing has ever occurred before! When they were

---

[253] Rabbi Jehuda Hayyat describes the suffering the Jews underwent in Marocco in the preface of his book *Ma'arehet Elohut*. (Ferrara 1557)

[254] Lagartos are lizards (the Latin term implies some large sea-fish); basilisks were serpent or dragonlike creatures whose breath or even look was supposed to be fatal.

on St. Thomas, some of them were swallowed up by the lagartos and others died of the deprivation of all necessities. Only a handful were able to save themselves, and their parents mourned them for a long time.

The oldest son of King Joao, Don Alfonso, married the daughter of the Spanish King, Ferdinand, and he loved her much. But when he rode on his fleet-footed horse on that day of his rejoicing, God punished him, and he fell to the ground and died on the following day. His father mourned him. After a short while, King Joao also passed away, for he had been poisoned. And he left no heir for his kingdom. He was followed by Manoel[255] who had been hostile toward him and had planned his perdition. After the course of five years, from the time the Israelites had emigrated from Castile, Manoel let it be known publicly in Lisbon and all the other cities of his realm that those who bore the name of Israelite, had either to leave the country or to accept a new religion; and any other Jew who was found there later on[256] was to be killed. Through this decree the Jewish Community in Lisbon was destroyed. In their great travail the Jews decided to emigrate to serve their Lord, the God of their forefathers. But when the King heard that, he ordered them to come to Lisbon, promising to provide ships for their departure. When they got there, they were cast into prison and were told, "Choose another religion and become like us, and if not, it will be done by force." But they did not listen to the King's voice, and when he saw that he had no effect on them, he ordered all the young Jewish men up to twenty-five years of age to step forward from the circle of their parents. When they were surrounded, a loud and mournful cry went up; and, in the King's name, spurious promises were made to them, and they were asked to leave the Holy One of Israel. But when they paid no attention to him nor lent an ear to his impressive entreaties, they were grabbed by the arm or the hair of their beards or the curls of their heads, and then dragged to the church where they were sprinkled with baptismal water, given different names and handed over the authority of the country's populace. Thus they became converted.

Thereafter, one of the King's servents went to the aged and said to them, "Your youngsters and sons have already accepted a new religion: do as they have done so that ye may live." However, as they refused to listen to him, the King commanded that they be given neither bread nor water, and when, after three days of fasting, they still refused to listen to him, they were dragged to a church, mercilessly beaten – not even the faces of the very aged

---

[255] Manoel (Emmanuel) the Great reigned from 1495 until 1521 and was married to two daughters of Ferdinand and Isabella, Isabella and Maria.

[256] The respite lasted eight months.

were spared – and then, forcibly baptized. Many refused even then and preferred to be killed. One man wrapped his son in a prayer-shawl and exhorted them to sanctify the Name of the Holy One of Israel, whereupon one died after the other, and he himself after them. Another man killed his dear wife, and then plunged the sword into his body so that he died. Those, who wished to bury the dead, were murdered by the Christians with pikes. Many plunged themselves into graves just to remain faithful, and many jumped through fences and out of windows, and their corpses were thrown into the sea by the Christians in the presence of all the other Israelites. This was done to intimidate their hearts so that they would no longer persist in their obstinacy. Later on they were continuously defamed, ridiculed and daily falsehoods were testified against them in order to destroy them and to usurp their possessions. And they became weary of living. The monks also conceived evil things against them and created a bad name for them in the eyes of the populace, saying, "When pestilence, war and famine come to your land, it will happen solely because of the greed of those who cling in their hearts to Judaism."

In 5266 (1506), two Dominican friars set out for Lisbon, the cross in their hands, gathering the people of the country and asking them to join in taking vengeance for their Messiah. They suddenly fell upon the forcibly-converted like the bears and wolves of the night, killed four thousand of them with the sword and reached out their hands in plunder. They raped the virgings and women, threw the pregnant women out of windows onto the waiting pikes which were held up below. One of the women killed one of the friars who wanted to defile her with the cross which he held in his hand. Meanwhile the judges rushed to the scene to halt the proceedings, for God showed mercy upon the remaining. The King also rushed from the city of Abrantes, and the bloodbath was stopped. The monk was apprehended, burned to death, and a few of those who belonged to the Spoilers were expedited from life to death by these Marranos so that they earned their ignominy. Many emigrated from Portugal and moved to the Orient (Levant) to serve the Lord their God as heretofore, and they dwell there to this day. But many of them remained there, vacillating to and fro, or they feared the Lord, while at the same time, they paid allegiance to the cross and went to church daily. From this time on there remained not one in the Kingdom of Spain who carried the name of Israelite.

After this inhuman Manoel had died, Joao II[257] ascended the throne and the Judeo-Christians multiplied, spread out in Portugal, forgot the Lord,

---

[257] Joao III was the son of Manoel and ruled from 1521 until 1557; he instituted the Inquisition in 1531.

their Creator, and bowed down before another god. After a short time, the King ordered Inquisitors to sit over them who accused them of not obeying the royal laws, embittered their lives, and cast many in jail. And in 5291 (1531), a few more were burned because of hatred and wrath.[258] Many were also caught in their nets before they emigrated, many were hauled out of boats where they had hidden, and were burned. Many also sank down to the bottom like lead as they fled hastily to the sea, and no one came to their aid.

Many fled on seven routes[259] in all directions as if before a sword. And this happened daily. After they had fled from Portugal, the iron oven (may God curse it), they met upon the road with numerous and heavy sufferings. Some were captured in Spain, some in Flanders, and they were hated in England and France. Thus, they went under with all their possessions. Those who had gone to Germany perished in the mountains, leaving behind their wives as widows and their children as orphans in a land where their language was not understood. The frail and soft-hearted women who were near to giving birth, gave forth the fruit of their wombs in the mountains and perished there of want and the effect of the bitter cold. And when they migrated to Italy, they had to face the hampering Spaniard, Juan della Fuja who, on the border of Milan, stood in the way like an adder. He ordered them apprehended and their belongings confiscated, and then he had them castigated with rods so that they would confess what they had kept hidden and who was to follow them. He also had the women beaten up and he embittered their lives so that they would hand over the silver and gold which they had carried with them. He did not spare the dignity of the aged and filled his apartments with robbed goods. Many of them became impoverished that year, and the otherwise hated had to hire themselves out for bread. Others served the fish of the sea for fodder, still others died because of the cold, and yet others died in the populated towns to which they had finally come. But most of them returned to the Lord, the God of their Fathers who had pity on them, and they served the Lord, the God of Israel. When Eraclio, the Duke of Ferrara, permitted them to live in his land, many of them became circumcised. However, many of them who lived spread around among the citizens of the country, conducted seemingly strange religious services[260] in the same manner, for they, too, had emigrated from the iron

---

[258] It was primarily the Bishop of Badaioz who tried to persuade Joao and the Queen of Spain to introduce the Inquisition in his letters of March 20 and May 13, 1528.

[259] Deuteronomy 28:25

[260] Our author, a Spaniard, is used to the so-called sephardic prayer ritual with its rather "Oriental" pronunciation and intonation. In contradistinction is the ashkenazic service used by the western Jews with which Hacohen was not familiar.

oven[261] because of the Inquisitors who had been after their lives. Many of them removed themselves completely from Europe in order to serve their Lord, our God.

The Emperor, Frederic III, lived eighty-five years. He had reigned about fifty of them.[262] He passed away in 5253 (1493) and commanded Maximilian, his son, to show himself benign toward the Jews. Maximilian I (1493-1519), after he had succeeded his father, walked in his paths. However, the imperial crown was not put on his head.

The King of Naples[263] ended his life in those days, and his son, Alphonso II, ascended the throne in his stead. Both of them dealt tolerantly with the Jews, and many Jews, exiles from Spain, went there and grew in numbers in the cities of his realm. After the year had passed, that is, two years after the expulsion from Spain, Charles VIII,[264] King of France, invaded Italy with a mighty army and advanced on his way as far as Naples. Ferdinand II, son of King Alphonso, fled before him to Fort Castelnuovo. The whole town was in turmoil, and the numerous Jews residing there, were delivered to the French as prey. Thus, Israel's fortunes declined much in this fateful time. The other details of this war are described in my book which I composed about the Kings of France and the House of Ottoman.

In 5257 (1496), I, Joseph, Son of Yehoshua from the stock of Priests (Cohanim) expelled from Spain, was born on the 20th of December (Tevet) in the Provence, to be exact, in Avignon located on the river Rhône. When I was five years old, my father led me away from there, and I have lived in the territory of proud Genoa until this very day.

A German Jew by the name of Lemlein, a false prophet, a crazy man, a mere bag of wind, arose in these days in Istria, near Venice. Jews streamed to him and said, "Yes, he is a prophet, for the Lord has sent him as a leader to His people, Israel. He will gather the dispersed of Judah from the four corners of the earth." Even some of the erudite bowed down before him,

[261] I.e., Portugal and Spain.

[262] Frederick III actually ruled fifty-three years. He was elected Emperor on February 2, 1440 and died in 1493. The last sentence in this paragraph may be an allusion to the fact that he was not crowned until 1452 by Pope Nicholas V.

[263] The author has Ferdinand I in mind; he died on January 25, 1494

Geneology of the *House of Naples*

Ferrante, King of Naples (1458-94)

Alfonso II, King of Naples (1494-95)

Ferdinand II (1495-96)	Isabella married G. Galeazzo Sforza, the Duke of Milan (d. 1494)

[264] Charles VIII crossed the Alps in the fall of 1494 to Pavia and entered Naples on February 22, 1495. He ruled from 1483-98. Ferdinand II, 1495-96, was the son of Alfonso II.

designated fast-days, put sacks around their waists, and everyone foreswore his evil ways, saying, "Our salvation is nigh, and the Lord will fulfill it hastily at His appointed time."[265]

The soldiers of the King of Spain[266] marched against Bugia, in Africa, in 5269 (1509), conquered it and led the inhabitants of the city into captivity. Also, the Jews who had lived in that country ever since they had come from Spain, together with those who had attached themselves to them, were led before the enemy. After a year had passed, they also marched against Tripoli in the Barbary, conquered it, and turned it over to plunder. Tripoli then lost its whole splendor; all the Jews – a large Community existed there – walked as captives before the enemy. They were brought to Naples, where many of them perished due to want and mental anguish.

When we were at Novi in the territory of Genoa, the son of the city's gatekeeper went out in the field during the week which the Christians call the Week of Martyrs, to collect herbs. He fell into a ditch filled with water, and no one saw it. But when his father became saddened and feared for his son's life, mean people said to him, as was customary, "The Jews have butchered him, and the sacrifice was offered in the house of the Hazan (cantor) Michael." Our hearts melted and turned to water when we heard these inflammatory orations. And when the gatekeeper told this to Monsignore Piedro Fregoso, the city's mayor, he treated him roughly, saying, "Don't tell me those thisngs any longer, for I know the customs of the Jews and their laws; it is far from them to do such a thing." The Jews also visited him and threw themselves at his feet. And he inspired them with courage, saying, "Peace be with you, don't be afraid. Verily, no dog shall sharpen his tongue against you." Thereupon, they left him in peace. After three days, the body of the boy was found, the herbs he had collected were in his breast pocket and the knife in his hand. Those who had spread lies were ashamed. But for the Jews, it became a time of Light; they celebrated Passover in gladness and praised their God.

Ottaviano Fregoso (may the names of evil ones rot) drove the Jews out of proud Genoa in 5276 (1516). My father, Rabbi Yehoshua Hacohen, together with all the other Jews residing there, left Genoa. After two years had passed, I married Paloma, the daughter of Abraham Hacohen, and we settled down in Novi. When my father passed away he was 68 years old; he died and was gathered to his forefathers on the 4th day of Tevet in the year 5280 (November 26, 1519). I buried him near Novi and the city (Genoa) in honor

---

[265] Isaiah 60:22

[266] The King of Spain at this time was Ferdinand (1506-16) of Aragon. Actually, there was no Spanish crown yet!

at a resting place. My wife conceived in the same year and gave birth to a son, whom I named Yehoshua. The lad grew up and found favor in the eyes of all who cast their eyes upon him; and I found solace after the death of my father.

When Monsignore di Lautrec resided in Milan in those days, he spilled the blood of aristocratic Christians like water, so that they hated him much. But Lautrec also treated the Jews very badly and ordered them to wear yellow high-pointed hats like the Moskovites in order to blaspheme the people of the living God. But God did not will it, and a few days later he was driven out from the soil of Milan. After that, he marched with his great military might against Naples. However, he was unsuccesful, took ill there, and died.[267] Many of his troops also died in this destruction which was not caused by man. The others retreated and returned to their country. Ottaviano Fregoso was also dislodged from Genoa by the Lord in 1522 and died in the power of his enemies in a prison. God is just. The proud city of Genoa was also given over to prey, as is recorded in my book, the Chronicle of the French Kings and the House of Ottoman.

Achmed, the Vizier of the Turkish Sultan, Suleiman,[268] revolted against his master while visiting Egypt and wished to destroy all the Jews unless they handed over all their silver and gold. At that time, the Jews of Egypt were in a great plight. They designated fast-days, girded their loins with sackcloth, and prayed to God who heard their entreaties. At one time, Achmed said to the elders of the Congregation, "When I come out of my bath, then you shall see that your fate has been sealed, and that the name of Israel will no longer be remembered." In the meantime, the Turks who had conspired against him slew him, even before he came out of his bath, and trampled on his body as on one only worthy of contempt. Thus the Lord brought upon his head that which he had wished to inflict upon His people; and, because of this, I thank You, Oh Lord among the nations, and praise Your name.[269] And in those days, the Turk Suleiman, sent many Jews away to settle in Rhodes, where they live in safety to this day. After a year had passed, the Jews took up residence again in Genoa according to an order of the Adorni, the enemies of Ottaviano, who were merciful rulers. They brought with them my brother-in-law Rabbi Joseph ben David, although this was not permitted according to the laws of the proud city; and he remained there until his dying day.

On the first day of Shavuoth, 5287 (May 6, 1527), Emperor Charles V

---

[267] Marshal Lautrec, the Governor of Milan, was unable to hold his territory and returned to France in 1522. In February 1528 he returned and invaded the territory of Naples, but soon succumbed to the Plague.

[268] This is Suleiman the Magnificent who ruled from 1520 until 1566.

[269] This event was celebrated by the Egyptian Jews at their Purim Festival (the Feast of Lots) on the 27th of Adar.

lead his troops against Rome, conquered it and allowed it to be plundered. Rome's splendor was totally lost. Also the Jews were handed over to plunder and several of them lost their lives. On February 24, 1530 (5290), Pope Clement VII[270] put the Imperial crown on the head of Charles V[271] of Austria in the city of Bologna. This made the citizens of the country very happy; however had it not been for God's mercy, which is never ending, the Jews would have been almost completely robbed, for the Emperor's people opened their mouths against them, hissed and gnashed their teeth.[272] But God saved them.

Andrea Doria, the fleet-admiral of Emperor Charles, marched against the Turkish cities in 1532. Koron was besieged in the seventh month, and the Turks surrendered it into his hands on the festival of the Great Hoshanah in 5293[273] (September 20, 1532) and entered into a pact with him. The Jews were handed over to rape and plunder and marched as captives before the enemy, and no one was there to help them. Patras was also conquered and the Jews there – or a major part of them – were forced to drink from the cup of frenzy. One part was redeemed in Xanten, others were sold as slaves in different markets and other liberated in Italy in this very same year. Among the exiles arriving by boat was a brave woman, Esther by name, the wife of Rabbi Jacob Hacohen. When the ship's captain said to her, "I would love to approach you," she followed him, wrapped herself up, and plunged from the ship into the sea, where she died before anyone knew where she had gone; and nobody was really very much concerned about her.

A Jew, David by name, had come to the Court of the King of Portugal, Joao III, from a distant land, India,[274] and said to him, "I am a Hebrew and fear the Lord, the God of Heaven. My own brother, the King of the Jews, has sent me to you, oh Sire and King, to seek your help. Therefore, be our savior, enable us to march against the Turk, Suleiman, and to rescue the Holy Land from his power." The King replied, "Be welcome, but now I shall send you to the highest cleric, and whatever he will say, I shall do." He then retired from him and resided in Lisbon for a few days. Those who had been forcibly converted put faith in his words, saying, "He is our Messiah, for God has sent him." Many gathered about him and honored him extraordinarily. This man then moved away from there and went to Spain, and in all places to which he came he was greeted by the many who streamed to

---

[270] Clement VII reigned from 1523 until 1534.

[271] Charles V (1519-56) was not crowned in 1527 as Hacohen states, but in 1520.

[272] Lamentations 2:16; i.e., they slandered and threatened them.

[273] I.e., the seventh day of Succoth (the Feast of Booths).

[274] According to Farissol, David Reubeni came from Baibar (The Arabian Desert). Others have held that he came from the Tartar country.

him: those who had been induced to convert and who lived there; but he proved to be a source of embarrassment. From there, he went to France, visited Avignon, and then traveled to Italy. There he designed a banner of artistic work and wrote holy names upon it; and many believed in him. This man also came to Bologna, Ferrara, and Mantua, and proclaimed that he had come upon the prompting of the Christian Kings and wished to lead the Jews among them to his land and domicile. He even talked this over with the Pope, and the Israelites began to fear very much. But when the people countered, "What shall we do with our women-folk in case we go to war? And what with our children to whom they have given birth?" he replied, "There are many of them in our country; don't be afraid, because, for God, there is no obstacle to help." He also invented a letter in his heart and he said, "My brother, the King, has sent me. It is written and a royal seal is affixed to it." Later on, his secret was discovered and nobody believed him anymore, for he had recorded a falsehood.

A scion from the tribe of Israel, Solomon Molcho went forth from Portugal where he had lived among the dispersed since the days of the forced conversion. He had spent his youth among the royal chroniclers. But when he saw this man David, God touched his heart, and he returned again to the Lord, the God of our forefathers, and had himself circumcised. At that time, he did not understand the least bit about the teaching of the Lord or the Holy Torah. However, after he had been circumcised, God bestowed wisdom upon Solomon, and he became, in a rather short time, more learned than the rest of men and many admired him.

Hereafter, he moved to Italy, took for himself the right to lecture the teachings of our God before Kings, and did not retreat one inch before them. In the meantime, he had traveled to Turkey and had stayed also in Rome where he held conferences with Pope Clement VII who showered him with favors against the wishes of the legal experts. The Pope also gave him a sealed permit, with his name affixed to it, to settle wherever he wished and even allowed him to call himself a Jew. He also became most knowledgeable in the Cabbalah, and his mouth brought forth graceful words[275] because God's spirit spoke through him, and his word was always in his tongue. He wrote down precious teachings which he had drawn up from the deep well of the Cabbalah[276] and sent them to his friends in Salonica where they had them printed. In Bologna, he preached in public, and in other places many

---

[275] I.e., he spoke in a pleasing manner.
[276] In the Sepher Ha-M'phoar & Havat Kanah (acc. to Wiener). Transl.: "Tradition". Actually a book of Jewish speculations on the mysteries of God and the Universe (*UJE*, Vol. 2, p. 614).

followed him to partake in his wisdom and to test him through riddles. But Solomon gave them enlightenment on all problems; nothing was hidden from him, and he told them about that which seemed hidden. As they recognized his wisdom, they said, "It is true what we have heard about you, and your erudition is far greater than your reputation which penetrated to us." Yet, many were filled with envy against him, but they could not charge him with anything evil in Italy, for he was highly respected in the eyes of the Dukes. He enjoined with David (Rëubeni), and both followed one and the same goal. He also wrote to the learned philosophers and theologians about the visions which he had, as I have recorded in the Book of Chronicles of the French Kings and the House of Ottoman. There one can read it in more detail, how and what happened to him, including what he had written about David: "I have heard people say, David the Prince has come to Italy; but the cup of slander has been poured out over him by the evil ones amongst our own Jewish brethren. It was my intention that, when I saw him, he should give me insight. But this matter turned out to be just the opposite, for he put questions to me. I therefore believe about the whole matter only that he is a very learned man, and that, when he pretends not to be knowledgeable or not to understand the Law, this is so only because he wishes to deceive people, and also to see how I behave toward him. Since this is his intention, I behave toward him like a servant in the presence of his master." So much for Solomon's words in his epistle as I have recorded them in the Book of Chronicles. Later on, Solomon intended to have a lengthy conference with the Emperor on matters of religion. He therefore undertook a journey when the Emperor was in Regensburg, where he conferred with him. But the Emperor (Charles V) remained steadfast and did not listen to him because of his broken spirit[277] and had him and his friend, David, together with his adherents, thrown in jail where they remained for a while.

When, after that, the Emperor returned to Italy, the two were brought in chains on a wagon to Mantua and locked up in a prison. Then, the Emperor conferred with his learned advisors, and when they determined that he merited the death penalty, the Emperor had him led outside to be burned. On one of the following days, they put a muzzle around the cheek-bone of Solomon[278] and led him to his place of execution. When the whole town was in turmoil because of him and the fire burned before him, one of the Emperor's dukes said, "Take the muzzle from his teeth, for I have to give

---

[277] Exodus 6:9; i.e., a shortage of time; perhaps this is also an allusion to Charles V's increased misgivings with the Reformation controversy and his growing political and international troubles (Turks etc.).

[278] To prevent him from speaking.

him a message from the Emperor." After they had done so, he said to him, "The Emperor sent me to you, Prince Solomon, to inform you that in case you should leave your path, he would forgive you. He would keep you alive, and you could even live near him. Otherwise, your fate has been ordained." Solomon neither rose nor moved, but replied like a holy man, like an angel of God, "Only during the time in which I belonged to the Christian religion was my heart saddened and contrite. But now, do as you please, and may my soul return to the house of its Father as heretofore, because it was better there than here." They were filled with anger against him, threw him on the wood pile which was burning, and sacrificed him to the Lord as a whole burnt offering which went up in smoke. And the Eternal smelled this lovely savor, and received his pure soul in His paradise where it was to join Him like a fledgling and a daily delight. His servants were released from the jail and allowed to walk away freely. Only his friend, David Rëubeni, the Prince, remained in prison. A guard was posted by his cell. When the Emperor returned to Spain, he took David with him, and kept him in custody. After he had died in jail, many of those, who had been seduced by him and by his dreams, were burned in Spain. Many in Italy believed at that time that Rabbi Solomon Molcho had been saved from the hands of those who conspired against his life through his knowledge and that the fire had no power over him. One man swore before the assembled Congregation that Solomon had been in his house eight days after the cremation and that he went from there on his way, but that he had not seen him afterwards. Only God alone, Our Lord, knows this, and I wished to be able to write down in truth and candor whether or not His words confirmed the truth.

Alfonso I, Duke of Ferrara, died in the eighth month of the year 5295 (1534) and his son, Ercole, followed him. This man permitted forced converts who had fled from the iron oven in Portugal to settle in his country and to return to the Lord, our God. Many of them were then circumcised also.

When the Emperor Charles marched against Tunisia, in the Barbary, he conquered it on July 21, 1535 (5295) and Tunisia lost its whole splendor. Many of the Jews who lived there in great numbers fled into the desert because of hunger, thirst, and want. The Arabs took everything away from them under great pressure. Many perished, and a part was slain by the sword when the Christians came into the city. The other part marched as prisoners before the enemy, and no one helped them.

Rabbi Abraham wrote from there the following description of the incidents which befell them: "The earth swallowed some here, some fell victim to the sword, others perished due to hunger and thirst; what is there to do?

God has decreed it thusly, and if He killed me also, I'd wait for Him regardless." That much for Rabbi Abraham.

Since they had been sold to the four corners of the earth as slaves, the Italian Congregations in Naples and Genoa bought their freedom. May God remember them for their good.

The Greek, Ibrahim Pasha, was all his life a Jew-baiter. And since the Turkish Sultan, Suleiman, had honored him highly, he became haughty in his heart and conspired evil against his master. But when this became known, the Sultan ordered his execution on the 15th day of Adar Sheni[279] (II) in 5296 (March 8, 1536). Light and joy shone for the Jews, and they thanked God.

The Emperor surrendered Montferrat to the Duke of Mantua because his wife, Margarite, had inheritance claims on it, and the Duke had prepared to march there. But before he arrived, William Viandro marched outside and brought the French secretly in the middle of the night to Casale on September 22, 1536. There they created a great amount of noise so that the whole town became agitated against them. The Jews became victims of plunder, and their homes were destroyed in a very short time. On the following day, the imperial troops arrived at the city in great strength. It was plundered a second time, and the same befell the Jews in these horrible days.

In 5298 (1538), I, Joseph Hacohen, went down to settle in proud Genoa, while the Emperor dwelt in Regensburg, Germany; he ordered, in 5300 (1540), the Jews expelled from the Kingdom of Naples. And they emigrated here and there like a herd without a shepherd. Some migrated to Turkey, others drowned in the sea, others were captured by a ship's captain from Ragusa who brought them to Marseille where they nearly perished. But Francis,[280] the King of France, had pity on them, drew them away from the power of the tyrant and sent them on his own ships to the Levant; for God had mercy on them. May he be blessed for this. Also those people who had been seduced into conversion aided them. May God remember them forever.

The Duke of Mantua died in June 1540 and his son, Francesco, was elected in his stead. But since he was still too young, the people obeyed the statutes of the Cardinal, his uncle,[281] until he had reached maturity. He liked the Jews and communicated with them in a friendly manner.

In the same month, darkness carried off to death my first born son.

[279] Adar Sheni, or V'Adar; 13th month, containing 29 days and is inserted before Nissan. Hebrew Leap Years occur seven times in every cycle of 19 years: in the 3rd, 6th, 8th, 11th, 14th, 17th, & 19th year of the cycle. One day is added to the month of Adar, and the 13th month is known then as Adar Sheni.

[280] This is Francis I (1515-47)

[281] And also his mother Margarita

Yehoshua of blessed memory, as he had wanted to take a bath in the river Reno by Pieve on the ninth day of the third month, Tammuz. His hands had not been bound,[282] and his feet not tied together in iron fetters, but he sank down like lead into the fleeting waters, and no one could save him. Therefore, I say: May dew not descend upon Pieve, nor rain into the land of Ferrara, nor fields bear the first fruit,[283] for there fell the delight of youth. If only I had died in your stead, oh my son, my son. Woe unto me, oh mother, who hast born me; cursed be the day on which I was born, to experience hardship and grief so that my days dwindle away in sorrow. Why did I not die in my mother's womb so that she would have been my grave and her womb my eternal vault?[284] Woe, for I have sinned, my wound is as large as the ocean. Who will restore me? Fourteen days later, after this mournful message had reached me, his brother also died, a suckling, still at his mother's breast. Yet, may the righteous Judge be praised. Whether I turn to the left or the right, I shall praise the Lord, my God, until the end. I will obey His commandments even if it affects my life. Thus I shall tarry until my redemption comes. Thus my solace is my distress: Though He afflicts with wounds, He also binds them. He shall bind their souls in the bond of life!

In 5302 (1542), many cities in Germany were consumed by fire and their smoke ascended unto the Heavens. Yet, the arsonist could not be found. The Jews and the Shepherds were accused with the words, "They have committed this nefarious deed"; and when they were tortured, they confessed that which had never entered their minds, whereupon they were led to the stake. Behold this, Oh Lord, see it and champion their cause.

At that time the Jews were also expelled from Prague;[285] and they moved away on wagons in the month of Adar, arrived in Poland and settled there. Many of them died on the way, and others were killed with the sword. Yet the Lord blotted out their ignominy: after their departure, the city of Linz burned down. It was a large city, the perfection of beauty. Not twenty buildings remained standing, and for a long time it was a constant heap of rubbish.

In 5303 (1543), (al) Mansour conspired against his master, the King of

---

[282] Samuel II, 3:34; i.e., he did not die on the battle-field.

[283] Samuel II, 1:21

[284] Jeremiah 20:17

[285] In 1541 Ferdinaad expelled the Jews due to the people's excitement caused by a conflagration. At first only ten Jews returned, but when the real cause of the fire was established, he called them all back and treated them in a friendly manner. Actually, Ferdinand, the brother of Charles V, was not Emperor yet in 1541. However, he did govern Charles' interests in Austria and Bohemia as his deputy. Was Emperor from 1556-64.

Tlemcen, in the Barbary (near Oran-Algeria), and called in the Spaniards who were in Oran and who invaded the city with a huge army and then plundered. The Jews also, living there in great number, fell into the captivity of the enemy, and they were sold as slaves in the month of Adar. In the meantime, a part of them was redeemed in Oran and another in Fez. But a third part of the Captured was taken to Spain and there led astray from the Lord, the God of Israel.

May this month be desolate, for on the 18th of Adar, 5303, (February 22, 1543) three shameless persons broke into the house of my brother-in-law, Rabbi Moshe Hacohen, in Pieve in the territoty of Ferrara, while he was away. They barricaded the door, killed his wife, Hannah, his daughter, Judith, and his sons, Samuel and Shemtov, with the sword; and no one came to their aid. His servant, the Frenchman Samuel, was also killed near the others; they reached out their hands in prey like a grape gatherer over his branches[286] and then went away. Moshe becried the destruction which God had caused, together with his whole father's family, and he wept loudly and bitterly.

As they carried out their funeral garments[287] to bury them in Bologna, the whole Congregation became highly moved, rose its voice and cried. A few days later, one of the culprits was apprehended, publicly whipped with rods in Ferrara, and then expedited from life to death. Oh Lord, may all Your enemies find their end thusly.

When the pestilence raged in God's Community of Salonica during the month of Sivan in 5305 (1545), the whole population moved about unsure and in flight as they were fearful of the Lord; and many died. One day, fire broke out in the house of the spice dealer, Abraham Catalano, Monday night the 4th of Ab, which is the 5th month (July 14), consuming eight thousand dwellings and one hundred human lives in a very short time; and the prayer of the others went up to Heaven on that fateful day. Woe unto the eyes which had to witness how eighteen synagogues and their Torah Scrolls, together with so many fellow Jews, fell victim to the flames which made saving them impossible. Young and old, lads and virgins, were lying on the

---

[286] Jeremiah 6:9

[287] Jews do not believe in resplendent funerals. The mummification of bodies or their incineration are forbidden. Even a public display of a dressed up and beautified body is frowned upon. All of these practices are associated with Paganism. It is customary, after a body has been properly washed and cleaned by the Hevrah Kadishah (ten men, lit: Holy Fellowship, composed of elders and men of integrity in the community) to wrap the dead into the so-called tahrihim (long, white linnen shirts). The only other items accompanying the dead are the prayer-shawl (tallith), the T'phillin (phylacteries) and a small sack of earth from the Holy Land. The latter is put under the head of the deceased.

ground and in the streets naked, suppressing their feelings of shame. Afterwards, a pest broke out among the populace so that the grave diggers tired
and a paucity of mourners prevailed; and Israel declined much. The Turks
then cast the spice dealer into prison where he took ill and committed suicide.

In those days news came to my ear which made my inside tremble, and
rumors which made my lips quiver.[288] There was a poor Jew in Greece who
came daily to different Jewish homes to work in order to earn his livelihood.
Vulgar and mean Greeks thought out ways to conspire against the Jews:
they sent this man away under a crafty pretext, and nobody knew anything
about it. The Jews were accused of killing him, as was customary, before the
Turkish authority, the city judge. This man then ordered them to be thrown
in jail where they were tortured, and after they confessed to what they had
never thought of doing, they were hanged. The physician, Rabbi Joseph
Abiob, was also burned in that fateful time. After several days, a Jew met up
with the poor man in one of the Greek towns and said to him, "Are you so
and so?" whereupon he answered, "Yes, certainly." Upon further inquiry as
to who had brought him there, he told the whole story and what had happened to him. The Jew persuaded him and brought him back to the city with
friendly words, presented him before the city judge and wailed loudly
before him. The Judge was very shocked, put his hands to his loins,[289] and
had these miserable Greeks put in jail. When this matter became known to
Sultan Suleiman, ire rose in his nose, and he had these evil doers expedited
from life to death. Thus, they paid for their infamy. After that, the physician,
Rabbi Moshe Hamon, appeared before the Sultan, implored him with tears
and said, "If it is right in the eyes of the Sultan, may this be recorded in the
law books of the Empire so that in the future similar happenings could only
be tried before the Sublime Porte, and that one would have to appear there
for judgment." This was granted in his favor. The Jews of the city Tokat fell
victim to a similar accusation, but came to light, for the Lord had mercy on
them; and they praised God.

In Asolo, a little town among the cities of Treviso, lived four German Jews
and their families, and because they did not flatter the inhabitants of that
place, they were much hated. In the month of Tevet, in the year 5308 (1547),
about fifty miserable creatures gathered, suddenly invaded the Jewish homes
as they were eating, killed twelve persons with the sword, and reached out
their hands in plunder. The others fled and saved, at least, their lives. There
was one woman with a seven year old daughter; and, as they were about to
break into their house, the threw ovensoot into their faces, blinding them, so

---

[288] Habakkuk 3:16
[289] Jeremiah 30:6; i.e., a sign of terror.

that they could not harm the woman. They merely slapped the girl's face. She recovered and the Lord saved her. When the city overseer learned about it, he was shocked and sent out his officials, but the murderers had already defiantly escaped.[290] Later, four of them were captured alive and sent to Treviso where they were dismembered as one cuts up a little goat; and they found their death because of their blood guilt. Seven of them who had fled to Trent were sent by the Cardinal to Genoa to serve on the Emperor's fleet, thus paying for their crime.

Henry II, King of France,[291] permitted the Jewish merchants in Mantua to travel to the cities of his Empire and to do business in the Land. He also exempted them from paying taxes, and when they paid homage before him for this, he showed himself most friendly.[292]

On the mountains I shall break out in tears and lament because I, Joseph Hacohen, hoped for good news. But evil tidings came and my zither became a lamentation. I hoped for peace, but there was none, for the loveliest of young men was torn away from me, the joy of everyone's eyes. Therefore, I cry and mourn, for my shadow left me when the fruit of my loin was taken from me, the son of my vows. Yet, God is just. Why did the womb conceive me so that I had to experience twice in the course of nine years such distress and agony? May the day on which my mother bore me be unblessed. I cry out loud because this terrible time, so displeasing me, added days to my years; for in what could I find pleasure after such a painful experience? The arrows of suffering which hit me were directed at the Gate;[293] they wounded and hurt me, the arrows of the quiver were brought to my kidneys, they smashed me and did not even leave me swallow my spittle; and I spent my days in sorrow. My sad and agitated heart rages like the sea, my eye weeps and does not rest; in the evening weeping alights, and in the morning I ache and moan like an ostrich. If only my head were like waters and my eyes a fount of tears, for this was not good tidings! My son, Yehuda, was like a lion of whom I hoped that we could live in his shadow, but because of our sins he cowered, stretched himself out, and was gone. God took him unto Himself on Sunday night, the 29th of Shevat, 5309 (1549). He went to sleep, but he left us behind in mourning. Praised be the righteous Judge. May that night be lonely, for in it my house was suddenly devastated and my dwelling destroyed in one instant. My eyes vanished in tears, my zither became a song

---

[290] Exodus 14:8

[201] Henry II (1547-49) was the second son of Francis I.

[292] Henry allowed several Spanish and Portugese Jewish refugees to settle around Bordeaux and Bayonne in 1550.

[293] I.e., they were aimed at me, at my heart.

of mourning, my flute sounded of wretchedness; for my sun became dark, the crown of our head is fallen and the stars in the skies have retreated. Who can believe my narrative? My grief is immeasurable; the event has hit me hard. There is no solace. Tall like a cedar, a father of wisdom, planted with the finger of God, he was felled only seventeen years old. Woe to the eyes that had to behold this. Yet I assayed my sad and agitated heart in the knowledge that our Creator has prepared for us the fountain of eternal life, through which we could find solace, and eternal salvation in the House of the King; Lord of Hosts is His name. My hope rests in the Lord of Spirit of all flesh. He will firmly bind up his pure soul in the bond of life so that he may slumber in honor. But I and my wife, Paloma, who are left behind with a troubled, aroused, and saddened heart, may He have mercy and pity on us and may He permit us, for His great Name's sake, an end that is happier than our former times, for our souls trust in Him. Therefore, we abide in Him.[294]

When Francis, Duke of Mantua, had married the daughter of Ferdinand I, the Roman King (The Emperor), and they were marching with drums and dancing into the city in 5310 (1550), his mother, Marguarite, confiscated the Jewish cemetery and donated it to the monks for the enlargement of their estate. And although the Jews cried out for help, nobody came to their aid; and those who slumbered in the earth were pulled out of their graves. A few days after that, her oldest son, Francis, died, and his brother, William the Hunchback, who had his eyes solely on profit and oppressed his people heavily, followed him.

When I, Joseph Hacohen, was in Genoa, a Jew by the name of Hayim arrived to settle down with us. The craftsmen became very jealous of him. One day, four Jews came to his house in the company of a Christian girl and ate a meal with him. They dined like drunkards and created a bad reputation in the eyes of the inhabitants of the city. After a year had passed, my sister's son, Zecharia Halevi, a physician, also moved there with the intention of settling down. But the physicians were so filled with envy of him that they conferred with the nobles and the Dominican monk, Bonifacio of Casale, may his name be cursed, who was preaching then. On the second day of Passover 5310 (1550), he sermonized as customary before an audience of physicians and nobles who afterwards went to the Palace and talked there with the rest of the nobility.[295] There were also two physicians in that inner council. As they were all talking together, the Doge was unable to persuade or reconcile them. The effect was that they released against us the Decree of

---

[294] This elegy is like a mosaic of verses and quotes from the Old Testament.

[295] I.e., the Palazzo della Signorie. The inner council of the Doge was comprised of one hundred prominent Genoese nobles, twenty-two years of age and older.

Banishment on the second of April, a law which was promulgated in Genoa by the sound of trumpets as they had done in the days of my father, Rabbi Yehoshua Hacohen. On the third of June, we left Genoa, and I settled down in Voltaggio where I practiced medicine until 5328 (1568).

After a year had gone by, several large towns in Bohemia were consumed by fire whereupon, as was customary, the Jews were accused of having committed this deed. But when the matter had been investigated, it was found out that the Jews were innocent of the crime, and God saved them.

In the year 5312 (1552), the ships of the monks of Rhodes[296] set out for Malta to take booty and met a ship coming from Salonica which had about seventy Jews abroad. They captured it and proceeded to Malta. These poor Jews had to send all over to obtain ransom money which they then had to turn over to the miserable monks, and only after that were they permitted to move on.

In 5313 (1553), some mean persons entered the Portuguese synagogue in Pesaro by night, took a Torah Scroll from the Holy Shrine, had fun with it, and then took another outside and threw it into the Garden of the Castle. The phylacteries (T'phillin) they strung up on oak trees. Five days later, they forced their way into the synagogue of the city's Congregation, took thirteen Torah Scrolls, wrapped a pig into their covers and put it into the Holy Ark. Oh Lord, do not erase their sin and deal rightly with them in the time of Your anger.[297]

At one time, before Pope Julius III[298] had become the Father of all Christendom, he had seen a poor and needy young man and taken him to his house. After the Cardinals had elected Julius, the youth became an outstanding man and was made a Cardinal which irked the other ones very much. One day, the youth saw a Jewish girl who was beautiful to look at. He sent for her and tried to persuade her to give in to his wishes, but she rejected them decisively. When her parents cried out, she was returned to them. They hid her, and no one knew for a long time where she was. After a while, the young Cardinal again asked for the maiden and, when she could not be found, he ordered the heads of the Congregation to come before him and demanded that they procure her for him. But when answered that they did not know her present abode, he became quite irate against them and had

---

[296] The Maltese Monks were the Knights of St. John of Jerusalem, also known as the Hospitalers, a famous crusading order. When driven from Palestine by the Saracens, they went to the Isle of Rhodes; they were driven from there by the Turks and given Malta by Charles V.

[297] Jeremiah 18:22

[298] Julius ruled from 1550 until 1555 and was succeeded by Marcellus I who ruled during a few months of the year 1555.

them thrown in jail. Meanwhile, the other Jews had taken flight because they feared him. But when he saw that all his actions thus far were to no avail, he ordered all the women and infants to be apprehended. And so they were also forced to flee with their children. In Rome a great outcry was heard then. When the father of the girl and the heads of the Community saw that all was bad for them, they handed the girl over to him. She was sent to a convent where, under constant pressure, she turned away from her God. They also laid hands on some part of the Jews, saying that these were now Christian children because their mothers had sinned against them; and no one assisted them.

In these days, undignified people from our own Congregation secretly committed illegal acts against the Torah of God, our Lord. They became stiffnecked and abandoned God and scorned the Covenant into which God had entered with our forefathers. They followed the other nations with whom to deal God had forbidden, made Him angry with their prattle, and heaped sins upon sins. They also voiced a disadvantageous judgment about the Talmud before Pope Julius III, saying, "The Talmud which is taught among the Jews entails laws different from those of other nations; it preaches desertion from your Messiah and it doesn't profit the Pope one whit to keep it in existence."[299] Thereupon, the intolerant Julius became quite irate, anger flamed up in him, and he ordered it to be removed and burnt. The order had hardly escaped his mouth, when his officials went out quickly and nimbly, broke into Jewish homes, brought all of their books to the city square, and burned them on the Sabbath, the beginning of the month of our Festival (Rosh Hashanah) in 5314 (September 9, 1553). The Israelites decried this conflagration, instituted by the enemies of our God. These are the names of those slanderous human beings: Hananel de Foligno, Joseph Moro, and Samuel Romano. Oh Lord, may their transgressions never be extinguished; judge in the hour of Your anger.

After that, curriers rushed swiftly to the tall and smooth people[300] in the entire Romagna. In Bologna and Ravenna an innumerable number of books were burned, and the Israelites ached and cried out, but they lacked the power to help. Books were also burned in Ferrara and Mantua on the order of the Pope, and nobody helped the Jews then. The Pope had also strung the plumb over Venice, and he did not withdraw his hand from the destruction. There it was also an enemy and adversary, the Physician Elazar ben Raphael, who had also left behind him the teachings of the Lord, who gnashed his

---

[299] Esther 3:8
[300] Isaiah 18:2

teeth against the Talmud,[301] and uncountable many books were burned in the month of Bul (Marcheshvan), which is the 8th month. They even wanted to stretch forth hands against the Torah Scrolls standing the Holy Ark; but the heads of the Community made protests, and through their intervention, they were saved. And in all other locations which were reached by the order of the Pope, a great mourning arose from the Jews: fasting, and crying, and moaning. And the Israelites appealed to God, prostrated themselves and said, "God is just." After they had done so, God's ire vanished and they were not destroyed completely. But in the Dukedoms of Milan and Montferrat no houses were searched because the Pope's order was defied by the viceregent, Don Ferdinand Gonzaga, for the Congregation's heads found favor in his eyes through God; and the Pope's voice was not obeyed.

The Corrector is speaking: This happened because of their meritorious conduct for the Academy which existed then in the faithful city of Cremona; for God had willed for them[302] a patron in the person of Gaon Rabbi Joseph Ottling[303] who spread the Torah in Israel; and God's ire did not afflict them because they enjoyed His Torah and were not deterred from studying it day or night. Thus God saved them until 5319 (1559) when the Academies ceased to exist and the cup of frenzy came over them from the side of the Princes. There was no peace for those who busied themselves with disputations about the Law. Also his brother, the Cardinal of Mantua, conferred at least twice with the Jews before he undertook anything either weighty or insignificant,[304] so that they should know what to do. May God remember them for the good. After that, the heads of the Congregation went to the Pope who then concerned himself with the work of the Poskim (The Masters of Halachic Decisions), and he permitted the writings to remain in the country. But in regard to the Talmudic writings he refused to lend a willing ear. Oh Lord, witness this and see how little strength we have before those who rise against us. We raise up our eyes to You.

The Germans, the servants of the Emperor, were then in Asti, and a young Christian lad of eighteen was found dead in an abandoned house situated outside the walls of the city-limits. Nobody knew who had committed this ugly crime. A German got up, a miserable creature who had valued this young man's affection,[305] and declared, "The Jews have committed this crime, as they always do." The whole town became agitated by this man's

---

[301] I.e., he told lies against it.
[302] I.e., the people of Cremona.
[303] Ottling was a German Rabbi who came to Cremona. He died in 1570.
[304] I.e., before he interfered mercifully or decisively.
[305] Homosexuality seems to be implied here.

testimony, and as it is recorded in the judges' chamber, they had all the Jews arrested on the 9th of Tishri, 5314 (September 17, 1553), and they sat captive for many days. When they were in the prison's courtyard, they fasted, vowed donations for holy purposes, and sought God with all their heart and soul. And as they longed for Him, He let them find Him, gave them tranquility, let right come to light, and they were freed. Therefore, I praise Thee, Oh Lord among the nations, and laud Thy name. But the judges refused to lay their hands on the German and released him, because they would not get to the cause and root of the matter. But now, Lord God, witness how we are like the blameless lambs, and yet they conspire against us day by day with ig- nominious thoughts saying: We want to devour them from the Land of Life. Help us, for Thy Name's sake.

Ye mountains, break out in jubilation because Pope Julius de Monte, who wanted to convert us and who had burned the Books of our Fame, died on March 21, 1555 (5315). Oh Lord, God of all spirit in all flesh: may his worm not die, his fire not be quenched, and may he be an abhorrance to all flesh.[306]

When Don Ferdinand Gonzaga, the Emperor's Deputy, had also died, he sent Cardinal Christophulus Madruzzi[307] to Milan to guide his affairs there. At that time, the war between the Emperor and the King of France was being fought at the border of Toscana (Tuscany) and the territory of Pied- mont. The French marched in the middle of the darkest night into Casali- Montferreto, occupied it and plundered the Jews. The Lombards, hearing of the arrival of the French, began to panic because the French excelled in cruel deeds. But since there was no money available in the entire country, the senators in Milan sent for the Jews to negotiate with them a loan and for equipment for the army. After they had handed over ten thousand ducats, they were given permission, in the name of the Emperor, to remain in the country over a period of another twelve years. It was initialed with the im- perial insignia. The Cardinal and the senators acted as mediators between the Emperor and the Jews. On April 8th[308] the Cardinals chose Marcellus II, but the days of his life did not last long, for his end was near though he did not know it.

In those days, a Spaniard took ill in Rome, set his house in order and entrusted his son and his entire lot of possessions to the care of his friend. He died and was buried, but his friend had a Spanish whore for a lover, and they conspired evil against the lad, fell upon him, throttled him, and nailed

---

[306] Isaiah 66:24

[307] The Cardinal of Tridentinum (Trent) (1512-78); he was used by Charles V and Philip II as a troubleshooter.

[308] April 9th, 1555.

him to a post so that he could not weave to and fro. They carried him secretly during the night to the hill site of Campo Santo and, when he was found there, the whole town became uproarious. Mean persons preached persecution against the Jews and brought their disadvantageous talk before the Pope. Marcellus became quite shocked and, without God's never ending mercy, the Jews' feet could have become weary. When the Jews heard of this, their hearts were touched: they called a Fast Day, donated money for holy works, and prayed to the God of their fathers who allowed them to be answered. He put words into the mouth of Alessandro Cardinal Farnese[309] with which he quieted the people and before their ears addressed himself to soothing tones, whereupon the Pope's ire subsided. He also spoke to the heads of the Congregation thus, "Do not be afraid; be calm and mark the help of my Master which he will extend to you today." Then a clever statement was issued: on order of the Pope and his Cardinals everyone was to come quickly to see the lad, for he was to become sainted. The people, from young to old, hurried to the scene to view the boy while the judges and officials remained there all day to see who would recognize the lad. A physician also happened to be there who recognized him and said, "This is the son of the Spaniard. You'll find a scar on his head, for I have treated him and his father as a doctor." Thereupon, the people left the scene and he led them to the boy's home. The judges walked ahead and, as they found the man and his mistress there in hiding, arrested them and had them thrown in jail. When Hananel Foligno (see page 102), the enemy of his own people, heard this, he was angered and he preached even greater persecution against the Jews. Thereupon, the elders of the Congregation said, "Let him be brought here, so that we can conduct a disputation before your eyes and see what will become of his fantasies." The judges ordered him to appear, but he was unable to stand his ground: Heaven revealed his guilt, and the earth rose ud against him. After the man and his woman had been whipped, they admitted their crime and did not deny anything that they had done in the least. When asked, "Why did you nail him to the cross?" the woman answered, "Because we thought it would later be said that the Jews had committed this deed, and the guilt would not be attributed to us." The Pope was already old, and he took ill and died on April 21,[310] while the Spaniard and this woman were still in jail. Afterwards, Alessandro Farnese had them brought to the Tower where they were incarcerated. A few days later, their lives were embittered

---

[309] Allessandro (1520-89) was a member of the famous Italian family of the 16th Century, a literary patron, who completed the Farnese Palace in Rome.

[310] He really died on the twenty-second day of his Pontificate, according to Ranke, *Ibid.*, p. 278 (April 30) See *Encyd. Britan.* Vol. 14 p. 864.

and they were tortured with tongs before the eyes of the public. After that, the calumnies against the Jews stopped. I therefore praise Thee, Oh Lord among nations, and praise Thy name.

On May 22, the Cardinals elected the Theatine monk, Cardinal Caraffa,[311] a Neapolitan, and called him Pope Paul IV[312] to his dying day. This Paul was, because of the plenty of our sins, a mad and irate human being who repeatedly brought new suffering upon the Jews, aggravated their lives through heavy labor, and made them feel the yoke quite heavily. But he also dealt miserably with the Christians. Because of his avarice, a mighty war broke out amongst them in Italy and France and about one hundred thousand people died. This does not include the cities which were consumed by fire during the hostility as described in the history books in great detail. To the Jews he was a snare; he made them all, including women and children, wear badges at their homes and in the streets.[313] He also sent deserters from our Faith to the homes of the Jews as Inquisitors to see if there were still Talmudic volumes in their hands. And Israel declined much. He also permitted the Jews in Rome to worship in two places only, and in Bologna at one. Punish him, Oh Lord, for his baseness. Many people fled Rome but, when they were on the road, mean people met them and harangued them. Witness this, Oh Lord; see it and champion their cause. Upon his decree, they were forced to sell their homes for whatever price they could get, had to live alone at the edge of the city, and no Christian has been allowed to live in their midst until this day. He also stretched the rope of confusion[314] over the forcibly converted ones in Ancona[315] in order to destroy them quickly.

One day, an evil spirit of the Lord came over him and he spoke to his brother's son in the middle of the night, "Go down and burn down all the Jewish homes. But do not reveal one single thing to anybody which I ask you to do." The latter felt quite sorry about it, but when the Pope became insistent, he left. On the way he met Cardinal Farnese and told him, "My

[311] His full name was John Petrus Caraffa, formerly the Bishop of Theata, founder of the Order Clericorum Regularium.

[312] Paul IV reigned from 1555 until 1559.

[313] Papal bull of July 3, 1555; it consisted of eighteen chapters, restricting the Jews to Ghettos, special clothing and trade in old clothes. Caught with other items, they were forced to sell them within nine days. They were also forced to sell their homes and farms and lost about four-fifths of their wealth.

[314] Isaiah 34:11

[315] Ibn Yahya reports that Paul IV, the Theatine, ignored all those who refused to be converted a second time (forced converts were always suspected by the Inquisition as potential backsliders), suffered terrible punishments: some twenty-three men were burned alive and thirty-eight were sentenced to serve on galleys.

uncle is determined to destroy the Jews, and now he has sent me out to set fire to their houses." The Cardinal replied, "Be careful not to commit such a fiendish crime. Let's see tomorrow what the significance of his dreams is." He went home, but Paul's servants brought news to him hurriedly for a second time. And when he had arrived at his uncle's residence, he asked the Pope, "What does the Master want from his servant?" This one asked him at once, "Have you accomplished what I ordered you to do?" And when the other answered in the negative, the raging Paul said, "Do nothing else now. I'll send urgent letters to Ancona via curriers so that the Marranos can be jailed and we can learn what will happen to them." When Paul's letter arrived there, they were jailed, their property confiscated, and they had to languish for many days in the gaol. But Thou, Lord God of Hosts, lead their strife and remember at all times the derision of Your evildoers so that it be known that God reigns over Jacob; and I shall be jubilant each morning because of Your mercy as You judge each man according to his deeds. All the thoughts of this evil Theatine Paul in relation to the Jews had only one intent, namely, to harm them, and never to do anything good for them. Thus he behaved always. When the elders of the Congregation went to him one day, he talked to them roughly, identified them with the dirt in the streets and did not even turn his face toward them. He also strung the plump over the Marranos[316] who had come from Turkey to Ancona, had them jailed and reached out after their possessions.

In Constantinople lived a very respected lady by the name of Beatrice,[317] who also stemmed from the forcibly baptized. She visited Sultan Suleiman who, upon her pleas, made a presentation to this miserable Paul to free these people. This evil Theatine, although he gave her an audience, took out his wrath upon the secretly believing Jews in Ancona: he burned twenty-four men and an old woman who, before they gave up their last breath, exclaimed the "Hear, Oh Israel." Their pure souls rose in a column of fire to the Heavens. The others he turned away from the Lord and took their whole property. At no other time has such an evil deed been committed in Italy. Daughters of Israel, weep over them, do not clothe yourselves in silken garments, do not cover yourselves with purple because the Glory of Israel is gone. My inside, my whole inside, raged because of the assassinated; and because of those who were seduced to convert, my soul rejects all solace. Witness this, Oh Lord; see it, and champion their cause.

This ugly person sent thirty-eight Jews laden down with chains to Malta (to serve) in galleys. However, they managed to escape on the way, for God

---

[316] Also on page 115, line 15 "strung the plumb", i.e., he tripped them up.
[317] Possibly the famous Donna Gracia

saved them, and they worshipped God as heretofore because He had assisted them. Upon the order of the anti-Jewish Theatine, a proclamation was issued in Rome to the effect that every Jew, who would not contribute to the common good, had to forfeit his life if he was found living there after a certain date. The hands of the Israelites became limp and they became fearful, but when they inquired as to what he really meant, he replied, "You'll find out in due time; and, when the respite is over, I shall know what to do with you." As it was felt that he was only seeking a pretext to harm them, a few more Jews were sought out for possible conversion. Israel was then like a frightened deer, and many of the weaklings among the Faithful were alienated from the Lord, the God of Israel, in those days. May God punish this evil-doer according to his worthlessness. At that time, the walls of Rome were reinforced and the Jews were conscripted for work on these walls and heavily beaten while so doing. Those who were forced to sell their homes were daily accused with the words. "You have not sold them for good, and the writers (of the bills of sale) have written matters in an ambiguous language." Those who lived in the towns under the jurisdiction of the evil, anti-Jewish Theatine were cast into jail and accused arbitrarily; and they devoured Israel with a wide open mouth.[318]

In 5316 (1556), a pestilence raged in Venice and about twenty-eight thousand people died during this epidemic. But there was light in the homes of Israel and none of them came up missing, for the Lord passed over them and did not allow the Destroyer to enter their houses.[319] For this, I thank Thee amongst the nations, Oh Lord, and praise Thy name.

Guido Ubaldo, the Duke of Urbino, expelled the forcibly baptized Jews living in Pesaro at the order of the Theatine of cursed memory in March of 1558 (5318). A ship left Pesaro on April 1st (13th of Nissan) with about seventy people who were bound for the East. When they arrived at Ragusa, fifteen of them disembarked while the rest continued the journey. On the way, men without honor came aboard the ship and captured them, because the ship's captain, who was hostile to them, had betrayed them, whereupon they were sold as slaves in Apulia and nobody came to their aid. Later on (on April 27) another ship left filled with people. But as soon as this became known in Ancona, they were pursued. When the Jews found this out, they begged the captain to take them to Istria which belonged to the Venetians. Thus God saved them.

All thoughts of the miserable Philip, who, as a Jew, was known by the

---

[318] Isaiah 9:12
[319] Exodus 12:23

name of Joseph Moro[320] focused at all times on doing evil to his former fellow Jews. In that year, he visited all the towns of the Romagna in which the Jews lived and entered synagogues on the orders of the Theatine. He held the cross arrogantly in his hand, put it on the pulpit, and preached about it before their eyes. In 5319 (1559), he went in his extra-ordinary meanness to the synagogue in Recanate on the Day of Atonement and put the cross in the Holy Ark. When the entire congregation showed its excitement and ordered his exit, this evil man made so much noise that the people of the town surrounded the building. Without the never ending mercy of God, their feet could have faltered on this horrible occasion. Upon the orders of the mayor, two members of the Congregation were caught, tied, and flailed with whips in the open street as if they were robbers in the night; they were beaten up, and no one came to their aid. Oh Lord, see how low our honor has sunk among the nations. They detest us like a quaranteened woman,[321] How long shall Your adorment remain in captivity and Your treasure in the hands of the enemy? Arouse Your strength and zealousness against Your opponents and may all Your antagonists perish. Amen, Amen.

In that year also, the monks were like thorns in the sides of the Jews of Cremona and brought them in ill repute with the people. During Martyr's Week, two monks preached before Milan's viceregent against the Talmudic literature, and, the Poskim were burned at their instant command, even before the heads of the Congregation could protest against it. All of this was caused by the feuding of two German Jews, Joseph Ottling and Yehoshua ben Het. May God avenge this according to their just desert. After a few days, Yehoshua ben Het was murdered, and it was not known who had assassinated him. He was buried in Cremona at some remote spot near the wall.

Since Ottling was disposed against me, because I had written down the above, I wrote to him the following letter the next day: "May the Counselor and wise Expert of Art, the Pride of our Age and its Ornament, find the Mercy of the Lord. When I learned that you, Sire, were annoyed for the things I wrote down in my book, I wondered for a while. Yet, my kidneys exhorted and aroused me, like a man who has been awakened from his slumber, saying: What makes you sleep; why do you behave like a disinterested person? Open your mouth, so that your words will become clear. And I replied to him as follows: Look backwards and inquire from the former times. Has it not been recorded that Cain slew Abel, that Lot slept with his daughters, that Jacob betrayed his brother, that Rachel stole the

---

[320] Also Solomon Romano after another version.
[321] I.e., segregated from her husband's couch due to her monthly period.

images, that Reuben did defile the bed of his father, that his brothers sold Joseph, that Moses destroyed not only the Egyptian, but also the calf Aaron had made, that Abimelech murdered his brothers, the sons of Jerubaal, seventy people in all, that Saul purged the priests of the Lord, that David lusted after a woman, Bathsheba, and made her come to him with the help of messengers, and then issued the written order to put Urias in the front-line of the battle field so that he be killed, and that Solomon loved heathenish women who, in his old age, turned his heart toward alien Gods? Behold, have the authors felt offended as they wrote down everything these men and kings have done, or has their wrath been aroused against those who have publicized their offenses? If this is so, dear Sire, after it became known by all, and there are many more whom I do not wish to single out by name, why does this upset you so, and why does your ire burn against me because I wrote that your quarrels have caused all this? To this, one should add that I know that, what I wrote down, has come to me from the mouths of truthful reporters who have told me all of it two and three times, so that it is not the figment of my imagination. Besides, God forbid, I have not done this, Sire, to make light of you, but in the fulness of my agony and pain when I saw that Torah Scrolls containing the Law of our God became the victims of flames, and no one said, Restore them.[322] I am astounded because of you, Adornment of our Age, that you did not take the verse to heart: Do not become disheartened because of bad companions.[323] Evil comes only from evil-doers like him (ben Het), and from the root of an adder came forth a serpent. Especially since you have heard what he caused in Germany and that the name, Jew, can be applied to him only metaphorically, just as one can call a picture on a wall, a man. Therefore, I had to write, as I intended it, for your quarrels have been the cause; but not to degrade you in the least, for who could dare to say anything against a man of your like and get away unpunished? Be it as it may, since I did not fail against you purposely, so please forgive my guilt, in your great goodness, and also my aberration. See and behold: I have written also about the Kings and counselors of the land, what has happened to them as it happens to take place on earth, be it good or bad. Be consoled with the rest of the mighty rulers whom I have discussed here and against whom we do not take a hindseat. In this way, your name will be immortalized for all time in this book, which is quite something to state. Saying all this, if my words however still do not put you at ease, you may, Sire, also write all these things down in a book with an

---

[322] Isaiah 42:22
[323] Proverbs 24:19

iron pen and a point of diamond,[324] you Ornament of our Age. Especially
since you know and must have heard that my antagonisms and labors may
have been the cause of many bad or even worthwhile things. I do not
pay attention to idle things; and one who is not very truthful himself ought
not to be so particular toward him. But since you are very wise, like an
Angel of God, so I shall not add anything more to this but only pay homage
to your radiance and eminence and shout Peace in your direction. Again I
beg of you, since love covers all sins of omission,[325] please forgive my
transgression and my guilt for the sake of your goodness; and, farewell.
Anticipating all your best wishes, I remain, your obedient servant: Joseph
Hacohen."

As the Jews in the towns around Milan feared that the trouble might
spread into their towns also, they petitioned the viceregent, the Duke of
Sessa, and the senators who accompanied him to Milan. He promised to
report favorably to the Pope about the Jews and to change his (the Pope's)
mind so that he would permit them to reprint the books of the Talmud.
Destroy, Oh Lord, the council of those who rise against us, for Thy name's
sake, and help us in Your great mercy.

This evil Theatine put his hands also on the books of the Christians then,
and where his influence could be brought to bear in Italy many works were
burned in the month of May and in many locales. This made his decrees
hated even by the Christians. The scientific writings which German Lutherans had composed and printed he devoured from the earth, and even an
Italian translation dealing with the book of Deuteronomy, the Prophets,
and Hagiographa, which had been undertaken.

A certain monk, investigating metters under orders from the Theatine,
tightened the plumb of desolation over the Jews in Alessandria in the month
of August and deprived them forcibly of their books. When they turned to
the senators of Milan for help, these men wrote to the monk to deter him
from his evil plan; he refused them, and demanded, instead, a huge sum of
ransom money from the Jews. They turned again to Milan and appealed to
the viceregent, the Duke of Sessa, crying Oh and Woe, and he bestowed on
them his forbearance. Indeed, he wrote a second time to the monk with the
effect that the monk, to his anger and fury, had to turn over all of the books
to the mayor of the city on the eve of the 29th of Elul, and in doing so
atoned for his ignominy.

In 5319 (1559), the Emperor, Ferdinand I, expelled the Jews from the
Kingdom of Bohemia. Yet, he permitted a remnant to stay in Prague where

---

[324] I.e., though the press and other publications; c.f., Jeremiah 17:1.
[325] He taunts him with his new Christian faith.

about two hundred families remained. The others were forced to emigrate. A fire broke out in Jews-Street on June 22nd, (17th of Tammus), and in a short time, some sixty houses burned down so that the flames rose up to the Heavens. The whole town was in an uproar and the populace stormed against the Jews like the bears and wolves of the night, and took all their possessions; the Jews fled, fearing for their lives. During that fateful event, several women were also thrown into the fire and their cries went up to Heaven. When Duke Ferdinand, the son of the Emperor, heard this,[326] he hurried to the scene, acted as mediator, and turned the plunderers to flight, whereupon the plague ceased. Later on, the Jews were permitted to remain in Prague for a limited time.

The inhabitants of Worms expelled the Jews from their city also, and they resettled wherever they could find a domicile and have remained there to this day.

In these years, a certain German, a miserable human being of cursed memory, a former Israelite by the name of Yehuda of Modena, preached persecution against the Jews. Thereupon, all the holy scriptures of the Jews of Prague were confiscated, and even their prayerbooks were investigated; and there was not enough left over for a gleaning. They were put on wagons and driven to the imperial palace of Vienna, since it had not been determined what was to be done with them. The Jews panicked about that, their hearts became like the heart of a woman during her labor pains, and they cried out to God. And God sent mercy in the eyes of the Emperor; he returned the books to them. They praised God and were glad.

When God saw that the wickedness of the Theatine was indeed great upon this earth, and that the evil imaginations of his heart[327] were directed toward us, He punished him so that he died on August 18th. God is just. All the inhabitants of the country were glad, for when an evil person perishes, jubilation reigns.[328] His statue was dragged through the streets of Rome, was thrown into the water, and he was mocked and became the object of ridicule and barbs in the midst of the nations. It was heralded to all the people to destroy his armorial ensigns (escutcheons) so that they would be extirpated under the Heavens. They even smashed to pieces the stones with all the ensigns on them. His followers were like a chased deer or a vessel

---

[326] Duke Ferdinand is called Ferdinand I (d. 1595), son of Emperor Ferdinand I (d. 1164); but he does not seem to have been the Emperor. (*Encyclopedia Britannica* (1960) Vol. XI. 60, article on "Hapsburg Genealogy".

[327] Genesis 6:5

[328] His statue was destroyed and the headquarters of the Inquisition plundered and put to the torch. His head (i.e., on the statue) with the triple crown was dragged through the streets.

with which one has displeasure: They were slain, killed, and they fled before the sword, for then the stones in the walls cried out after them. Such an atmosphere had never been seen in Rome before. At that time, the Roman citizens and nobles gathered, decided no longer to permit dominion to the monks as they had had heretofore, and put troops into the city (to keep order). Later, in the night of December 25, 1560, the Consistory elected a cardinal from Milan, bowed before him, and named him Pius IV. He occupied the papal throne like his previous colleagues before him, and the nations obeyed him. The leaders of the Jews also visited him to pay their respects and complained on that occasion about all the bad things the Theatine had committed against them. He consoled them, spoke to them in friendly terms, and they took leave greatly relieved. What I report to you, was written to me from Rome.

In March of the same year, two monks dulled the teeth[329] of the Jews in Pavia, created a bad reputation for them in the eyes of the city's inhabitants, and conspired to drive them out of the land. The Jews despaired of their lives, for it seemed that each stone in the wall cried after them: they were beaten up in the streets of the city, and the citizens refused to speak to them decently. The heads of the Congregation leaped into the breech for them and complained to the senators of Milan about their plight, whereupon it was publicly announced in Pavia that whosoever gnashed his teeth against the Jews, would be punished. And peace returned to the land. Two German Jews of bad character, who had played a great role in Pavia, had caused all of this. This I have recorded according to the testimony of one witness from Pavia, and it has not originated in my own heart.

Emanuel Philibert, Duke of Savoy, also intended to expel the Jews from the whole of the land of Piedmont in that year. They were perturbed about this, prostrated themselves before his feet and the feet of his wife Margarete, the sister of King Henry IV, and presented her with a present. Hereafter she received them kindly, inspired courage in them, and prolonged their stay by four months. But Negron de Negri from Genoa, a miserable person, was a thorn in her side and agitated the Duke against them so that he said, "Leave my domain; clear out in six days." The Jews, in their horror, cried out to the Lord who offered them a certain physician, a juror of the Dukal Court. He spoke well of the Jews to the Duke, and thereupon the Duke entered into a covenant with them. They now live there – to this very day.

Carl Cardinal Caraffa and his brother, The Duke of Paliano, both nephews of the Theatine, did always what was displeasurable before the Lord, and

---

[329] I.e., they prepared unpleasantries for them.

their mouldering scent[330] went up to Heaven. In 1561, God turned around their hearts and they conspired against Marco Antonio Colonna to kill him. Also, Count Alife, the husband of their sister, and Leonardo di Cardine joined their plot. But on orders of the Pope they were put in jail and sentenced to death.[331] In the middle of the night, on March 3rd, officials visited the Cardinal, awoke him from his sleep, and announced the verdict to him. When he begged them for permission to put on his priestly robes, they ignored him, and threw a rope around his neck in order to throttle him. But as they were about to tighten it, the rope broke. The impetuous Cardinal became very mad and cried out loudly. But he died like one of the miserables after they had thrown a rope around his neck a second time. God is just. The three others were decapitated, and their corpses were thrown into the street and exhibited at the bridge in broad daylight. Thus they paid for their crime. This happened to the Caraffa family for their pride, for when they became too powerful, their power was directed against the people of the Lord of Hosts. The hearts of the Jews were gladdened, and they thanked God.

The daughter of the Emperor Ferdinand, the wife of William the Hunchback, Duke of Mantua, gave birth to a son in the 7th month of the year 1562 (5323). On the occasion of this great joy which the people in the land experienced, they decided to rob all of the homes of the Jews. This terrified them much, and their hearts could be compared to the labor pains of a woman. But when they prostrated themselves before the Duke, he sent soldiers of his guard with four cannons to the scene. On the Festival of the Torah (September 22),[332] many people of the land gathered in the evening and stormed against the Jews like the bears and wolves of the night. Their noise was heard all over. But the Jews, together with the Duke's men filled their hands (with cannon balls), and many sank to the ground, for the bullets fell from gardens, houses and courtyards. But not one of the Israelites came up missing. The battle against them lasted from the evening till the end of the middle watch of the night.[333] And only four shops were plundered. Then they dispersed and everybody went home. The people had also smashed the prisons, let the prisoners go free, and even devastated the Court in which the ducal secretaries and judges held their sessions. Nothing remained intact. After the morning had dawned, the Duke went out to the market of the city,

---

[330] Isaiah 34:3; i.e., their bad reputation.

[331] Pius IV (1559-65), Carlo Cardinal Caraffa and the Duke of Paliano were Nephews of Pope Paul IV (1555-59), hence hated by the rival faction that captured the Papacy after him, headed by Pius IV.

[332] I.e., on Simchath Torah.

[333] In the Hebrew time table, there are three watches per night, each four hours long and beginning at six P.M.

and many were thrown in jail. After that, the Jews thanked their God, for He had saved them from the power of their enemies; and then they donated a share of their silver and gold to the Duke.

Amongst those who had come from the iron oven of Portugal to Ferrara was Don Joseph Nassi who, after he had dwelt there for a short while, went on to Turkey, where he found favor in the eyes of Sultan Suleiman, who loved him very much: the Sultan gave him the ruins of Tiberias as a present, plus seven open towns situated in the vicinity, and named him Master and Duke over them. Thereafter, Don Joseph sent his servent, Joseph ben Adret, to rebuild the walls of the city. He also found grace in the eyes of the Sultan's son who gave him a daily stipend of sixty Asperus.[334] The Prince also sent eight of his own servants along with a decree, with the grand-ducal seal attached to it, recommending him to the Pashas of Damascus and Safed[335] and an order to do all that this man required of them. In the Sultan's name a law was then promulgated stating that all masons and load-carriers living in these towns should move there in order to help in the rebuilding of Tiberias. Plenty of stones were there because Tiberias had been an extra-ordinarily large city before it was destroyed; and there were thirteen syna-gogues standing during the times of Rabbi Ami and Rabbi Assi.[336] The inhabitants of those seven towns were also ordered to prepare sufficient clay to be able to execute their work. In addition to that, there was sand in great quantity because Lake Tiberias was quite near. The Arabs became envious, and an aged Sherif persuaded the inhabitants of the land not to permit the rebuilding of the city because later on they would only experience damages, for – so he said – he had found in an old source book that, if Tiberias were rebuilt, the religion would then go under, and they, too, would become sinners.

They obeyed him and refused to move there to help rebuild the ancient walls, whereupon, the work on them was slowed down. Much perturbed about that, Rabbi Joseph ben Adret went to visit the Pasha of Damascus and appealed to him for help because of the refusal of the citizens of those open communities to obey the order of the Sultan. The Pasha, in turn, was also enraged, sent soldiers there, had two of the main trouble makers arrested and brought from life to a quick death so that the rest should see and fear it and be deterred to act treacherously. The others returned to work, and as they

---

[334] Approximately four dollars.

[335] Safed, mountain-town in the Holy Land, six miles north of Lake Tiberias. Later on, the main-seat of Kabbalism.

[336] The two Rabbis were contemporaries during the Talmudic period, i.e., during the tird and fourth centuries A.D.

dug in to erect the city wall, they found a big stone, and almost simultaneously, beneath a ladder leading deep into the earth, a church full of marble statues and altars as are used in Christian churches. Four of those servants of Don Joseph, who were given to him by the young Prince as a present and who had been captured in the war against Dshelebbi, destroyed it and filled it with soil. Also, three church bells were found, which the Christians had buried there when their Despoilers marched against them in the days of Guido,[337] the last of the Christian Kings to rule the land. They made cannons from them. Tiberias, which they rebuilt, had a circumference of fifteen hundred yards. The building was completed in the month of Kislev in 5325 (1565) to the great joy of Don Joseph, who praised God for it. At the order of Don Joseph, a large number of mulberry bushes were planted to serve as food for silk worms. He also brought wool from Spain to make clothing from it, like that made in Venice. Don Joseph enjoyed a great reputation and his fame spread throughout the land.

In October 1566 (5326), Philibert, Duke of Savoy, again dulled the teeth of the Jews, for he was avaricious. He suddenly released an order stating: "Either you produce four thousand gold Guilders, or you leave my country within a fortnight." They all hastened to leave the country, one from this place, one from that. However, after a few days, they handed two thoudans gold Guilders over to him, whereupon he concluded another covenant with them, namely, that they had to produce fifteen hundred golden Guilders annually. After that, everyone returned to his domicile.

King Philip II[338] wrote to his viceregent in Milan in those days that he wished to send the Jews away from the entire territory of Milan. When the Jews heard this, they became very frightened. But all of this was caused by the meanness of a really bad German from among those who played a great role in Pavia. His name was Yehuda ben Jacob Morelo. This man tried to expel the other Jews living in Pavia, and thus misfortune came about. All

---

[337] Guido, i.e., Guy de Lusignan, the King of Jerusalem, who lost the battle of Hattin on July 4, 1187, following which Tiberias was lost to Saladin, and soon Jerusalem itself.

[338] Some information on King Philip II will be useful to the reader. Philip's father was the Holy Roman Emperor Charles V who also ruled Spain (1516-56) as Charles I. Charles was the grandson of the Holy Roman Emperor Maximilian I and the Duchy of Milan, and also of the Spanish monarch, Ferdinand and Isabella. Charles died in 1558 having been the first Spanish King from the House of Hapsburg. He had given up actual rule in 1556 and had retired to a monastery in 1557. On his abdication in 1556, the Imperial Crown was formally passed to his brother Ferdinand (1556). Philip became King of Naples in 1554, King of the Netherlands in 1555, and King of Spain and the West Indies in 1556. He invaded Portugal and became its King in 1580. He died in 1598. It should also be noted that the House of Hapsburg was more or less in control of Italy during the 16th, 17th and 18th centuries, and that Philip was no exception to this rule.

of this I have written down, not according to my judgment, but as it was testified to me by Hayim Cohen ben Samuel from Alessandria. However, the heads of the Jewish Community made presentations to the viceregent and the senators of Milan, and they were not expelled.

Pope Pius V[339] was a crazy, irate man, originating from a very lowly family in Bosco, who walked in the ways of the Theatine and who hurt the Jews much. This "impious"[340] man sent out the same decrees which had been issued against the Jews during the time of the Theatine into all of the provinces of Italy. However, his orders were hated by the Dukes of Florence, Ferrara, and Mantua, and they did not obey him. But those Jews, who lived in the Papal State, he hurt so much that they despaired of living. Huge sums of money were demanded of them. Many fell away because of faintheartedness and Israel declined much in those days. Oh Lord of Hosts, righteous Judge, let me witness Your anger with him, for I have revealed to You my cause.

In Cremona and Lodi, all Hebrew books were confiscated on the 10th of Av, and the Israelites mourned. But when the senators of Milan were approached, the books were handed back to them.

In September 1566, King Philip of Spain ordered the Jews in the territory of Milan to wear yellow hats and forbade them to loan money for interest. The women, too, were asked to wear insignia, whereupon, the Israelites became very upset and put their hands to their loins.[341]

On June 15th, the citizens of proud Genoa wrote to the Dukes in their cities to expel the Jews living there within a period of three months. A similar order was issued all over then. A copy was sent me from the viceregent of the city of Voltaggio in which I, Joseph Hacohen, lived. However, after all the citizens of the city had gathered and people had been sent there to arbitrate, he respected me and replied to them, "Now, may Joseph Hacohen remain in your midst as long as he so pleases." But I did not wish to live among them any longer, and I settled down in Costelleto in the province of Monserrat on October 27, 1567 (5428), where I was received by all in great joy.

Pope Pius V continued to harm the Jews in the Romagna and in Bologna. Many of them were thrown in jail, their lives were embittered, and when they cried to God, He veiled Himself in a cloud which prayer could not penetrate. They were accused of many things, and a large sum of money was extorted from them. On that day of God's ire, Pius burned the last remainder of the Hebrew books which had been left from the days of the Theatine. Oh Lord

---

[339] Pius V reigned from 1566 until 1572.
[340] A play on the name of the Pope.
[341] Jeremiah 30:6; a sign of agony, as a woman in labor.

of Hosts, Righteous Judge, permit me to see You take revenge on him, for I have bared my cause before You.

When many Jews emigrated from Italy in that year in order to go to the Levant, the Maltese (Knights) went out and heaped mountainous walls against them.[342] Many went under like lead before the raging masses, and many of them were kept in jails in this fateful time. But now, Oh God, our Strength, rush to our aid and punish the enemies of Your people and protect the heritage of Your handiwork.

After a year had passed, this impious, evil man of cursed memory, whose thoughts were solely schemes to design disaster, expelled the Jews of the Papal State in the month of May, which is Sivan, the third month. Although the heads of the Congregations prostrated themselves before him to deter him from his cruel plan they did not achieve anything, for, like a deaf adder, he did not want to listen, and they went away angry. He only permitted a few of them to be left in Rome and Ancona where they remain to this day. But the inhabitants of the other cities settled down wherever they found any opportunity, each going his own way, emigrating or moving away altogether. The inhabitants of the towns in the Provence were also forced to leave their domiciles and go to different places. Many went on ships of the sea to the Levant and went their way; whilst others traveled away to settle down in the cities of Savoy, near where they had been. And, because God had pity on them, they made a new covenant with the Christians. But now, Oh Lord of Hosts, let me see Your wrath on this anti-Jewish tyrant who has destroyed us and who is our spoiler, for I have bared my cause before You for Your Name's sake.

On November 16th and 17th, 1570 (5331), a great earthquake occurred in Ferrara. Many homes collapsed on that fatal day and caused the destruction of twelve churches, and the cloisters of monks and nuns. Two hundred dead persons were found about under the destroyed homes. But due to God's forbearance, not one Jew was missing. Not one of the Synagogues collapsed because of this quake. Therefore, I praise Thee, Oh God amongst the nations, and praise Thy Name.

In the month of March, the harvest month, upon the orders of the hostile tyrant, Pius V, the Duke of Urbino expelled all those Jews who had formerly been chased away from the Papal State. The people tried to go to Turkey by sea. Coming close to Ragusa, the Admiral of a Venetian naval squadron pounced on them like a bear deprived of its cubs. He allowed the aged and the children to disembark, while the young ones had to come onto his galleys to serve there in heavy labor as if they were slaves.

[342] I.e., they acted with hostility.

And nobody came to their aid. But when the heads of the Jewish Community protested to the Doge of Venice that this illegal abuse had been committed, he replied, "You ought to be glad that the aged, the women and children went free and that only the young ones have to serve until the threat of war has passed us by. Afterwards, we shall allow them to go home free." God, Oh Lord of Hosts, You are a righteous Judge; permit me to witness Your revenge on these anti-Jewish tyrants who destroyed us and had their share in our ruin, for I have bared to You my cause; help us for Thy Name's sake.

All the thoughts of this evil, impious man (Pius V) were directed toward harming the Jews. Thus, he wrote to his monks: "When the Jews refuse to return the pawned items without interest to those who march against the Turks, do not talk to them." And he ordered the merchants, who had lent them money, not to make any demands and not to touch anything that belonged to them, until they returned home or had perished in the war. But this decree was hateful in the eyes of the people. God punished him and he died on May 1st, 1572. Oh God, Lord of Spirit in all flesh, do not allow his worm to die or his fire to extinguish, and may he be an abomination to all living flesh.

The Cardinals then elected a man from Bologna and called him Gregory XIII,[343] and he became their Pope. In 5333 (1573), when Gregory gathered Venetian troops to send them into war against the fleet of Selim II, the Turk, they came to Rome and remained there for several days. On the second day of Passover, their day (the Christians') of mourning,[344] many soldiers invaded the Jewish ghetto, talked roughly to the Jews, and gnashed their teeth as they thought in their hearts of ways to destroy us. They raised their voices at the gates of Jews-Street as if it were a holiday. The whole town was excited and as the soldiers stepped forward to smash the door of the ghetto the Jews trembled much, and their hearts were like the heart of a woman during labor pains. Thereupon, each Jew grabbed his weapon, hurried to the gate, fought against the soldiers, and stepped into the breach. Thus God saved them. When Cardinal Sibilo heard this, he hurried to report it to the Pope. After a conference with the magistrates of the city, they all went, one to this side and the next to the other side, withdrew all troops, whereupon tranquility was restored to the city. And since God had mercy on them, not a single Jew was missing. Then, upon orders of the Pope,

---

[343] Pope Gregory XIII reigned from 1572 until 1585. This is the Gregory who changed the calendar, still in use today (Gregory, 1572-85).

[344] I.e., the Christian Good Friday. In 1573, it was celebrated on March 20 and coincided with the second day of Pessach.

it was publicly announced that not one single person should sharpen his tongue against an Israelite, and that whosoever did so with an evil intent, should be killed. For this, Oh God, I shall praise You amongst the nations and laud Your name.

The masters of Venice with their Council decreed in those days that the Jews should leave the city immediately, already during the fifth month. And many left Venice. At the same time, the Masters of Venice thought: how long shall we be at a disadvantage in our war with the Turks? Thereupon, they sent one of the senators of the city to the Sultan to obtain a peace treaty. The physician, Rabbi Solomon ben Nathan,[345] who was then at the court of the Sultan, acted as the intermediary between them. Selim II agreed, made a peace treaty with them in which Cyprus fell to him; and it belongs to him to this day. Solomon thought: now is the time for God to act; and he asked the Senator to do him a favor, namely, to write a line to his masters to rescind the harsh decree against the Jews which aimed at their expulsion. He did this although the Senator was against him. Thus, the man wrote; and his masters held a second conference, calling before them the heads of the Community and entered into a peace treaty with them[346] so that the Jews live amongst them to this day; and it was declared: "I thank Thee, Oh Lord, although You were angry at us, yet Your ire has turned away and Thou has sent us consolation"[347] A few days thereafter, the physician, Rabbi Solomon, went to Venice upon the orders of his master, Selim, and negotiated there with the Senators about the treaty which had been made with them and which they confirmed by bestowing a great honor upon him. The Jews also hastened to do him honor, gave him a reception, and congratulated him for all his help. After Solomon had discussed all the essentials with the Senators of the city, he bid them farewell, bowed, and withdrew in peace to return to his master.

Joseph ben Yehoshua speaks: I praise the Lord who has inspired me to compose this little opus which contains most of the suffering and incidents which befell our people from the Destruction of the Temple until this very day as far as I could ascertain then, and inasmuch as I was able to write a brief account of it. My work was concluded on the 21st of Tammus, 5335 (June 29, 1575). May the good Lord, in His mercy, always be at my side and

---

[345] This Rabbi Solomon came from a German family, lived in Udine and arrived in Venice on July 6, 1574 as an emissary of the Sultan Selim II. He was a firstrate diplomatic negotiator and mediated the peace with Spain in 1578. His wife acted after his death as the Sultan Mohammed III's pharmacist. Her son also served the Sultan as an emissary to Venice in 1605 (c.f., the later account of the Corrector).

[346] The historian Callicioli reports that the vote was 171 to 104 in favor of the Jews.

[347] Isaiah 12:1

dignify me to write about the advent of the Messiah so that the words of the verse may be fulfilled on us (Isaiah 66:1): Rejoice with her (Jerusalem) in joy, all ye who mourn over her. Amen, Amen.

Now the *Corrector* speaks: In the first chapter of the Tract on the Sabbath (Talmud 13 b). it is written: The Rabbis asked: who has composed the book, *Megillat Ta'anith*? The answer: Rabbi Hananiah and his pupils to whom the description of suffering had a certain attraction. Rabbi Shimon ben Gamliel commented on this: "For us the description of suffering has also a certain allurement. But what shall we do? If we were to record them all, we should never come to an end." For this stated reason, I have decided to record what has happened in those days after this Josephus[348] had concluded his Chronicles until now, in order to fulfill the commandment in Exodus 10:2: that you may tell in the hearing of hour son and your son's son.

After the Emperor Charles V had grown old, he longed for peace and intended to transfer his regimen to his son, Philip, so that he could rule over all the cities of his Empire and at the same time cloak his residence with the dignity of his office. But when his vassals, the German Princes, did not agree with his plan, he became saddened in his heart and appointed Philip King over Spain, all the cities of Italy, Flanders, and all the other states of the New and Old world. He ordered his vassals to vow loyalty to him, and to serve him in truth and faithfulness. After they had done so and sworn allegiance, Emperor Charles went away to serve God in the companionship of monks[349] where he remained to his dying day. But he invested the imperial crown on his brother Ferdinand, and the German Princes recognized him as their Emperor in 5318 (1558).

Emperor Ferdinand II now wished to expel all the Jews living in Bohemia, Prague, and all the other cities in his empire; and he had already sworn to do so, when the Jews appeared before him and presented a petition. The Jews of Prague prostrated themselves before him and asked that he not do them any harm since they had already lived there even before the destruction of the (second) Temple. He turned at them furiously and refused to listen to them. He added that he had already sworn to expel them. Thereupon, the

---

[348] A flattering comparison of Hacohen to Flavius Josephus. In a note in the German translation Wiener says, "The corrector calls R'Joseph Hacohen in an "honoring vein" a second Josephus because he has his name in common with the well-known Flavius Josephus." Flavius Josephus is the famous Jewish author and historian of the Jewish War, The Jewish Antiquities and others. In order to save his life, he turned "Quisling" by selling his services to the Romans. He wrote from the point of view of a Roman citizen; at the same time he tried to be objective regarding his former fellow-Jews. Josephus lived from 37-95 (?) A.D. He was a friend of Vespasian, the Emperor.

[349] In the Cloister Juste of the Hieronymites in Estremadura.

Jews sent a message to Pope Pius IV asking him to find the motive behind the Emperor's decision and to absolve him from this oath and solemn promise. This he did, but despite all this, the Emperor's ire was not quieted, and he still held up his hand.[350]

His sons, however, were benevolent rulers, helped the Jews, and said to them, "Do not fear; remain in the land, pursue your business, if you become useful men, then you may surely stay." When Emperor Ferdinand had grown old and lay on his sick bed, his son Maximilian directed the affairs of his House and spoke always justice over the citizens of the land; and at his word, they went out and came in.[351] When Ferdinand inquired about the Jews, he answered, saying, "The Jews have already received the imperial order and left the country. Not a single Jew has remained." Ferdinand thanked God, died and was gathered to his ancestors.

His son, Maximilian II,[352] reigned in his stead, and the German Princes elected him as their Emperor. There was light for the Jews and their Torah, [353] because he and his Empress were tolerant rulers who spun the thread of mercy[354] around the Jews. They served him with true loyalty, for they did not have to fight against any antagonism nor any prejudice.

In those days, the Pope and his Cardinals agreed to hold a united conference in regard to matters of their faith, namely, the Council of Trent, because it was centrally located between Germany and Italy. There was Ercole Cardinal Gonzaga of Mantua, the President and deputy of the Pope and, together with him, men from all the ends of the world were gathered. Discussions were also held about Hebrew writings; they wished to leave them to us under the condition that nothing was to be printed in them against their religion. This Council even permitted us to keep the Babylonian Talmud, provided its name was changed. It was therefore printed in Basel under the name, Shitta Sidrei (The Six Portions).

Pope Pius IV died 5326 (1565), and the Cardinals elected Pius V, the former Cardinal of Alessandria. In his youth he had been a watchman for swine, then became a monk. Since he was hostile toward the Jews, he soon advanced to fulfill the meaning of the scriptural verse: "Their antagonists are on top."[355] As soon as he began to reign, he promulgated hostile decrees

---

[350] I.e., in an oath – he refused to change his mind.

[351] Numbers 27:21; i.e., they obeyed him.

[352] Reigned 1564-76.

[353] They did not have to suffer for following their Torah.

[354] Our author refers to unrest in Moravia in the wake of which many Jews were burnt. When Maximilian heard this, he came to their immediate aid and prevented further bloodshed.

[355] Lamentations 1:55

against the Jews, such as the wearing of yellow hats on their heads and the fastening of yellow woolen patches on the women's shoulders. Furthermore, he ordered, besides all those other numerous, fatal decrees against them, that they had to give up all real estate such as acreages, grounds, vineyards, and houses. This hurt the Jews, indeed. This anti-Semite also wrote to all of the Italian Dukes, and the Senators and Judges of Milan. At that time, Archbishop Borromeo, who was regarded as a holy man in the eyes of the people, also lived in Milan.[356] He made his appearance as an enemy of the Jews in the territory of Milan in that he enforced the decrees and bulls which the Pope had issued against the Jews most expeditiously. In Milan itself, a law was publicly announced that all adult men and women had to wear the already mentioned signs, excepting only those children who were under fourteen years of age.

As soon as the first bull became public, a second one followed forbidding the talking of interest on loans. This caused great confusion among the Jews: they hurried quickly to the Senators and to the Rector (of the University) asking most timidly, "Why do you act this way toward your subjects? We have already the Emperor's consent and Permit of Settlement in our hands; he has bestowed it on us, and it can not be abrogated." But they did not succeed, for the decree was already announced; they (the Jews) had no guardian angel or expert-defender because the Academy in the holy Congregation of Cremona had ceased to exist, and Jacob's voice was no longer heard in the House of Learning as heretofore.[357] And because of that, all of our suffering resulted.

This tyrant also wrote to the Dukes of Ferrara and Mantua, but he did not accomplish anything, for they were compassionate Princes who did not agree with his schemes. He also designed evil plans against the holy Congregation of Bologna and envied their gold with his avaricious eye, because they were rich people. He assigned experienced Inquisitors to investigate whether or not the Jews had been guilty of any transgressions; and, if so, they were to lose their possessions to the State. Thus, many were apprehended, tortured, and burdened with monetary penalties. He also ordered them under no circumstances to ever venture outside the gates of Bologna; otherwise, their bodies and riches were to fall to the State. Now, when the nobles and charitable Jews realized that they were in a miserable situation, they took council together; they gathered, gave the gate-keeper a bribe; fled during

---

[356] The people regarded this agitator as holy because he escaped miraculously an attempt on his life. Carlo Borromeo (1538-84), saint and cardinal, Archbishop of Milan, prominent in the Council of Trent and author of many church reforms.

[357] I.e., the study of the Law had ceased; see Talmud in Genesis Rabba 65:8.

the night with their wives and children and, after they had escaped like a bird from the net, they moved to the territory of Ferrara for resettlement. Others settled in Mantua, and they live there to this day. Now, when the tyrant saw that this plan had come to naught, he convened another conference in which he persuaded the Cardinals to chase all the Jews from the Romagna; and, when they objected to the unfairness of such a deed, in that it would prove detrimental to the country, he countered saying, "I am the ruler, and there is no one who may resist my power." Upon his orders, it was announced in all the cities of his realm, that in the course of three months all, who were called Jews, had to emigrate from all the cities of his land, except those who lived in Rome: they did not have to go into exile. Even Ancona was stricken by this calamity. But when the people and the nobles of Ancona went to him declaring that it was to his own advantage and profit to leave the Jews there, because they controlled the commerce, and that he reaped a great revenue from them due to their business and trade connections with other countries, including Turkey, and that because of it, the Jews had acquired an excellent reputation, he yielded to their request.

Hereafter, the Hosts of the Lord moved out of the entire Romagna and dispersed all over Ferrara, Mantua, Pesaro, Urbino, and all the cities of Tuscany, as well as into the territory of Milan. They left their houses; their fields and vineyards fell to strangers, and they offered their tents as they were, for less than half of their value. And Israel degenerated very much. The Maltese Knights also had evil designs against the Jews and mistreated the Turks. They navigated around in the Italian Sea[358] to make prey, to rob; and on their journeys, they plundered all who were traveling by sea. They sold people as slaves if they were unable to make ransom for themselves. They also migrated to all the open cities of the Orient to make booty there and, wherever they went, they committed evil. After the complaints of the Turks came before the Sultan, he mustered the infantry and cavalry in order to lay siege to Malta. He put them on galleys in 5325 (1565) to make the trip by sea. Dragut[359] was their commander. After he had besieged Malta, he conquered a castle by force and bravery, and the Turks slew all the soldiers and cavalry in it with the sword, and did not leave one single soul alive. After that, they approached the city of Malta, fought against it without a let up, and erected bulwarks against it. But the inhabi-

---

[358] The Italian Sea implies here the Adriatic, Tyrrhenian and Mediterranean Seas.

[359] Dragut's name was really Torghud. After he came to Malta, he besieged the Castle St. Elmo. One hundred thirty knights died in the onslaught, but he had his head smashed in. After that, the Viceroy of Sicily landed to lift the siege, whereupon Mustapha Pasha and Kapudan Pasha Piale gave up their venture.

tants had also fortified the city and repaired the damages day after day. But during the battle, the commander Dragut was wounded so that he died. Now, when the Turks saw that their leader had fallen, their hearts melted and turned to water. God's hand was also against them, for they were plagued by cramps in their underbellies. Also, their commander had accepted bribes and had marched away from the city. Thus, the Turks returned to their country, to the Orient. The Maltese monks again fortified their city afterwards, repaired the damages, erected towers and built them stronger than they were before. To the Jews they are, to this day, a net and a snare, for they roam about the sea daily and travel by sea all the way to Cyprus, which belongs to the Venetians. There was peace between them and the Maltese monks, and the city of Famagosta served the monks as a place of refuge, though it belonged to the Venetians. Whenever they saw a ship going either west or to Alexandria, they moved against it, plundered it, and filled their dwelling with booty. Such is their behavior all the time.

After this, Selim II, Sultan of the Turks, sent a delegation to the Council Fathers of Venice. He inquired in the most peaceful and friendly manner as to why they gave tacit support to these evil-doers who robbed all the merchants who wished to travel to his country via a sea-route. However, they paid no attention to them, gave them instead an unfriendly reply, and sent the delegation back to their master in disgrace and infamy. This made the Sultan very angry and he said, "Indeed, I shall gratify myself on my adversaries and take revenge on my enemies." At that time Aloisio Mocenigo was the Doge of Venice.

Selim had enlarged Antioch and built a harbor by the shores of the sea for the time when his ships were to make use of it. In the seventh month of the year 1570 (5380), a fire broke out in the arsenal of Venice, and, when the powder storages exploded, the whole city shook to its foundation. A terrible panic followed; the noise was audible in the far distance, and nobody knew through whom this conflagration had started. Thereupon, Selim equipped his infantry and cavalry, plus all the chariots of Egypt and their officers,[360] shipped them to the Isle of Cyprus where they besieged Nicosia, conquering it in no time, although it had been heavily fortified. After it had fallen to them as booty, they also conquered all the other walled-in towns[361] on that island, and the Turks settled down there. All their generals started from here and began the siege of Famagosta, which lies at the sea. It remained as the sole city belonging to the Masters of Venice, because it was extraordinarily fortified. The Turks attacked by land and sea, but the inhabitants of the city,

---

[360] Exodus 14:7
[361] C.f., Hammer III, p. 581. (*History of the Ottoman Empire*)

who defended the walls day in and day out, forced the Turks to retreat and did not allow them to approach the city. Now, as the Masters of Venice realized that this catastrophe engulfed them from all sides, they laid hands on all merchants from the Orient, captured them, Turks and Jews alike, robbed and plundered them of all their possessions. And although they protested against this before the City Councelors and Senators, who occupied the highest positions in the State, no hearing was granted to them, and no one listened to their protest.

The nobles of Venice then decided to drive the Jewish population from the land because they believed that the Jews were co-operating with the Turks; they decided unalterably that the expulsion from their country should take place as soon as the Concession allowing the residence had run out. This decree, which they promulgated for themselves and their descendants, they made even stronger in that none of them should dare publicly to favor a Concession of Residence for the Jews, even if he so desired; and whosoever dared to do so, neither he nor his descendants were to be permitted to serve in the Senate. This was a time of great pain for the Jews: a Fast Day was designated, donations for Holy works were made, and God was approached through fasting, weeping, and crying by young and old. And Fast Days were also organized in all the other cities of Italy.

Famagosta was encircled from all sides and nobody could get in or out. When the Masters of Venice saw this, they made a pact with the Pope, the King of Spain, the Duke of Florence, and got together an army which they put on ships bound for the Isle of Corfu, where they met up with the Spanish, Papal and Florentine fleet. The Maltese ships joined them and served the sons of Lot[362] as an army. Don Johann of Austria, son of the Emperor Charles,[363] was their commander. They all joined with the ships of Venice at Corfu, and thus a fleet emerged in the depth of the sea. After that, they proceeded slowly on their route to Cyprus, going east. However, the Turkish fleet remained anchored at its post and waited until they had approached to give them battle. But the Christian commanders dared not attack them and remained quietly until they saw what would happen in the city. However, there raged a tremendously great famine in Famagosta. When Bragadino, the commander of the Venetian city, saw that the other Venetian generals did not consider it wise to relieve them and to help them out of the power of

---

[362] Psalm 83:8; the Moabites and Ammonites are the traditional Biblical enemies of the Jews.

[363] John of Austria (1545-78) is better known by the name Don John of Austria. He was an illegitimate son. Later governed the Netherlands for Philip II of Spain, his half-brother.

the enemy, and that all the inhabitants of the city cried out for bread (and there was no one there to break it for them), he surrendered the city to the besieging Turks (in 1571), who then occupied it with a guard. From that moment on the whole of Cyprus belonged to the Sultan Selim, and still does.

After this battle, however, the Turks were very proud, gathered all their hosts of war and put them on ships to fight against the Christians. They started their expedition while a mighty east wind was blowing, and sailed all through the night of October 7th. After they had taken their position facing each other, the war began and Turks fought like a people dedicated to death, saying, "Verily, this is the day we have hoped for." But as they were saying this, God sent a very strong westwind against the power of the Turkish fleet and the already faltering Christians mustered renewed courage, approached the mighty Admiral's Ship and the huge galleys, threw stones into the ships with their cannons, wreaked terrible havoc, and destroyed them completely. General Carcosa witnessed this battle and saved himself with forty galleys, but the remaining Turks were captured alive and only a handful survived. Naturally, the nobles of Venice were very happy, ordered torches burned in all the towns of their land, and accepted this day as a holiday and feast-day on which the people gave presents to each other. And the victory was announced in all the cities of Christendom.[364]

After that, Don Johann of Austria addressed the generals: "Let us march against one of the fortified cities situated by the sea and pry it open by force." And they answered, "Where thou goest, we shall go. Your people are like our people, and our ships like yours,[365] do it, be successful, and may God help you." After that, they focused their sight on a castle called St. Maura. When they arrived there, the generals ordered the troops to disembark and to bring up the cannons to break down the walls of the castle which was fortified. As they were taking huge preparations to shoot during the darkness and to break the walls, they raised their eyes and saw the armies coming down from the heights of mountains. They said to each other, "Don't you see these people coming down from the heights of the mountain tops?" But the watchman countered, saying, "You regard the shadows of the hills as humans." And as they were still debating, they heard the noise of the horses' shoes coming ever closer in a mighty trot. The Christians, fearing for their lives, fled quickly to their ships, left their cannons and their tents as they were, and only sought to save their lives. After this debacle, all the generals said, "Let us draw lots and divide up the loot of the enemy." And this is what happened. But a feud broke out among the dukes, and the discord

[364] The Victory of Lepanto was observed on October 7, 1571.
[365] Ruth 1:16

among them was so serious that, as a consequence of this conflict, they became separated, and each returned to his homeland although winter had already come and the sea was quite stormy. Also the galleys and all other types of ships sailed back to the locales to which they belonged. Don Johann of Austria broke camp and marched with his allies and friends to Milan and from there to Flanders, where King Philip sent him on the advice of the Spanish counsellors, to lead the Holy War against the Lutherans (Calvinists) who had made great progress in those times.

On November 14, 1570 (Marcheshvan 17, 5331), the city of Ferrara, the Crown of Beauty, experienced a terrible and mighty earthquake in the middle of the night such as had never before happened in the territory of Ferrara. The gutters under the roofs clanged at one another and the heart of him trembled who heard the noise. And the inhabitants did not know what God in Heaven had planned for them. When they woke up in the morning, they hurried outside to see, since the towers, the chimneys on the rooftops, and all that was high and fortified had collapsed. One was horrified before the other and they spoke: "Who could have done such a thing?" On the afternoon of the following day, another earthquake of lesser strength was recorded and also one at eventide. On the following Sabbath, in the first hour of the night, and at the end of the first night watch,[366] another powerful and terribly strong quake was noticed: buildings collapsed, houses and walls were split so that, whilst in the first storm the noise was stronger than the quake itself, here the tremor was greater than the noisy crash. Manifold damages and collapses took place and the place was like a divine terror. The nobles of Ferrara became most terrified, fled hastily from their hidden domiciles to the streets and to the Palace gardens. They deserted all their precious villas and all their belongings out of fear for their lives so that their houses might not become their graves as had happened to many. Because of it, many were prompted to move away fifteen to twenty miles from the city. But those who refused to move, fled at least from their homes into the gardens and from their courtyards to the fields of the city and squatted there temporarily until they could see what would happen to the city. The well-to-do and generous Jews should be remembered here for their good. They were in possession of grounds, courtyards and lockable gardens, and their homes were wide open to anybody who came near them. Nobody there refused to extend hospitality to at least one hundred persons, and they did not refuse to provide the necessities for the poor and needy so that they would not be deprived of wood or fire. If they were without clothing, it was given to them: they were nourished with bread and other food according to

[366] I.e., at seven and ten P.M.

the number of heads in a given family, and in their friendliness, the Jews did not allow any of them to suffer. And the Christians were also prepared to help their impoverished. Announce it among the nations that, because of God's help, not one single Eternal Lamp in any of the ten synagogues was extinguished, although they had suffered cracks and ruptures. The result of this fact was that, of all the people, not one single Jew lost his life or was injured, but rather, they witnessed great miracles in that God saved them. All the towns in their environ set up Fast Days and organized meetings on account of their brethren who had experienced deprivation and great sorrow. They called upon God who listened to their entreaties and recalled His Covenant. The details of this incident were recorded by Rabbi Azariah de Rossi, of blessed memory, in his book, Kol Elohim (God's Voice). This also caused Pope Pius V to write to the Duke, may his glory be magnified, that all of this happened because of the guilt of the Jews. But the Duke responded to him with these words: "Behold, and witness where the damages are more serious; in the cloisters of the monks or in the synagogues and academies of the Jews?" Praised be He who has inspired the Duke to say this. Blessed be the Guardian of Israel.

A fire broke out in 5332 (1572) at the Cathedral of St. Mark in Venice, and eleven days after this destruction by fire, a second conflagration broke out and consumed the shops at the Senso, as the marketplace in Venice is called, whereby the whole city became frightened.[367]

After Pope Pius V had died, the Cardinals elected a learned and well meaning man from Bologna, and they called him Gregory XIII. In those days, the remaining Jews lived in peace and contentment. When the Venetian nobility realized that they lacked the power to war against the Turks, that the helper stumbled, and he who had been helped fell,[368] they held a council to find ways and means to make peace with them. There also was the Gaon Rabbi, Solomon ben Nathan, from Udine, whose name was Sh'lomo,[369] who also favored a peace. He became their mediator and made peace between these two empires which became reconciled.

After this happening, the Doge, Aloisio (Luigi) Mocenigo (of Venice) arose as an enemy of the Jews, and he tried to expel them hurriedly from his land. But many of them had already moved away to find resettlement in other Italian cities where they could find rest for their feet; one went here,

---

[367] It is quite possible that this was the name of Venice' market place (in hebr: Has siussoh) during Hacohen's time. If so, then it was most likely used in the vernacular by the people in deference to the famous architect and sculptor Sansovino.

[368] Isaiah 31:3; i.e., not even outside help could aid them.

[369] A play on words: Shlomoh and Shalom (peace).

the other there, wherever the spirit drove them to go. Others had already sold all their belongings and, together with their wives and children, had gone on ships to wait for a favorable wind, so that the sails could be set to take them to other cities along the coastline. As it happened, Duke Soranzo [370] who had been away to see Bailo in Constantinople at the request of the nobles of his city, returned to Venice. When he disembarked, he heard the crying of Jewish children. When he asked those who stood around him, "What is the matter with these little sheep?," they answered him, "Sire, they are Jews; a decree has been issued to drive them quickly from the land." When Soranzo heard this, he became angry, and before he went to his own home, he visited the Doge, and ordered the reassembling of the Council of Ten (Dieci) which, in matters of state, always had the first voice. And he spoke to them: "What kind of evil deed have you performed by expelling the Jews? Don't you know that you will have to pay for it later on? Who has caused the good fortune of the Turks, and where else could he have found such expert workers in the manufacture of cannons, bows, crude shooting engines, swords, shields, and spears with whose help to fight against other peoples but in the Jews who have helped to have the masters of Spain expelled? And now your Council decided to expell the Jews who have dwelled this long in our country so that they could now side with our enemies and leave our land. You ought to know that the Jews enjoy the best reputation with the Turkish nobility who have the greatest influence in their Government. By my life, the advice you have given, is certainly not advantageous; you may rest assured that once the generals have departed, hordes of Turks will march against you. To whom will you then cry out for help? To the Pope or to the King of Spain of whom you know that their assistance is like a broken reed? Have you not experienced how ineffective their aid is?" When these wise counsellors had heard this, they accepted this new advice, for they realized that he had spoken the truth. After they had reassembled in sufficeint number for a second Consiglio dei Dieci, they repudiated what they had ordered at their first session and made a peace-treaty with the Jews. They, in turn, went back to their houses and live amongst the Venetians to this very day.

After Sigmund II Augustus,[371] the King of Poland, had died without

---

[370] It was a Rabbi Solomon Ashkenazi, a diplomat in the service of the Porte who had arranged a meeting with Jacopo Soranzo, the Venetian agent in Constantinople on behalf of the unfortunate Jews. He appeared motivated by humane considerations. However, his approach to lift the ban against the Jews was strictly utilitarian, Hacohen tells the stroy, although in a much different light, i.e., he pictures Soranzo as a friend of the Jews.

[371] Sigmund II Augustus was the last Polish King (ruled 1548-72) from the House of Jagellon. Henry, King of Poland, was the third son of Henry II of France (ruled 1547-59);

leaving a male heir, the nobles elected Henry, son of Henry II, King of France, and vowed allegiance to him. He, too, was disposed not to be friendly to the Jews and thought in his beart: if only the day would come when my reign will be firmly established, I shall then call them to account. But God's wisdom stands. In 5335 (1574), Charles IX, son of Henry II, died and left no son behind. Since this was the case, the kingdom fell to his brother who was then ruler of Poland. When he heard the news of the passing of his brother, and that he now had a claim on the throne of this huge kingdom, he mourned his brother for only a few days, and when that period of mourning had passed, he decided to run as far away as possible during the night, until he could cross over the borders of Poland. He revealed his secret to no one. Later, he made great preparations for the journey which he had contemplated and fled, in the middle of the night, with his body guard on horseback via the postal route. Only one day later the whole scheme became known. When the Poles awoke in the morning, the King was no longer there, for he had fled to Vienna. But when the Polish nobles found this out, they became very angry, for he had committed a dispicable act by fleeing secretly and betraying them. Yet, after he had fled, there was gladness and happiness among the Jews for obvious religious reasons, and because they had known his sentiments. They praised the King of Kings. May He be praised.

After that, the Polish nobles divided themselves into two parties, one which desired as king, Maximilian II, Archduke of Austria, and the other, Stephan Bathory from Transylvania. Maximilian had already moved his infantry and cavalry to the scene and was with his encampment near the main city of Cracow, Poland's capital, when the Secretary of State[372] moved against him with a great army and dislodged him from the city. They then acclaimed Stephan as their King[373] and, when he had occupied the royal throne, and the nobles of the kingdom came to offer their allegiance, the Jews also appeared, exclaiming, "Long live our Master and King!" Thereupon he made a covenant with them. But in Danzig, a large city at the seacoast, which is also considered a part of the Polish Kingdom, they scorned and refused to recognize him as the king; and they said, "In what way can

he was elected King of Poland in 1573, and succeeded to the throne of France on the death of his brother Charles IX (not the IV as is indicated in the text) in 1574. He ruled until 1589 and was the last of the House of Valois.

[372] Stephen Bathory was the Secretary of State. Maximilian II, Emperor 1564-76. His title Archduke of Austria was one of his minor titles.

[373] Stephen was Prince of Transylvania from 1571-76 and was elected King of Poland in 1575. He reigned until 1586, overcame a revolt in Danzig in 1577, and was victorious over Ivan the Terrible in the Russo-Polish wars of 1579-82.

this man help us?" After that, Stephan assembled an army, beleagured the city and subjected the populace, who were certainly not friendly toward his reign, against their will. After he had brought up another huge army, he fought against the anti-Semitic Russian Duke, Moscowa, humbled him, conquered his camp, and became far mightier than all the Polish kings before him.

The 17th of Tammuz, a fast day, 5334 (July 6, 1574) brought happiness and joy to the Jews of Venice: on that day, Rabbi Solomon ben Nathan came back to the nobles of Venice upon the request of the Turkish Sultan, Selim II. On this occasion, the Doge, Aloisio Mocenigo, and all the Senators who occupied high state offices, honored and decorated him before the eyes of the entire population. All the people were jubilant, and one man wondered before the other how such a thing was humanly possible now. When Gaon Solomon hereafter asked the Doge and the nobles to treat his fellow-Jews gently, those who were nigh or far, they presented him with presents and gave in willingly to whatever he desired. After that, Solomon went away from them in friendship and was dismissed to Constantinople with great testimonials of honor. Such an event has never been heard of before, ever since Judah was exiled from his land to this very day.

In 5335 (1575), since evil usually begets evil, pestilence (bubonic plague) spread from Trent to Verona and Mantua, and the epidemic took root from Venice and Padua all the way to Milan and Pavia. Many died of it as it became more and more intense; this was a time of deprivation for the Jews, for God's hand afflicted them also. In those days, the travellers celebrated and no wanderers were found in the streets. Preventative measures and precautions were taken, and thus, after two years, in January of 1577 (5337), the people of the city of Milan were purified and the Pestilence was stopped.

In 5337 (1577), God sat on His throne to judge the peoples, and the Hosts of Heaven stood to His right and to His left. Said He, "Who will persuade King Sebastian,[374] all his dukes and his servants, as well as the whole army of Portugal to invade a country that does not belong to them so that God's ire could manifest itself on them, for they have hurt His people and servants; on them, who accepted them at first with friendship and affection, but later treated them faithlessly by becoming their enemies? Respected men have been burned by them, the countenances of the aged have not been spared, they expelled peaceful women from their well-apportioned homes, and when they gave birth to sons or daughters, they did not remain with them, but were torn from their breasts to march as captives before the enemy. But now

---

[374] Sebastian was King of Portugal from 1557-78.

the days of revenge have come to let this sinful generation feel God's wrath."
[375]

A Christian rose then and spoke: "I will persuade him." "But how?,"
the others querried. And he answered, "I will go and reveal myself as a false
spirit through the mouth of all Sebastian's counsellors and persuade him to
war against the Sherif who rules over Fez and Marocco, because there are
still many opulent Jews settled on their lees[376] and could perhaps fill his
apartment with stolen goods and ill-begotten booty. And he could arrest the
Jews and either make male or female slaves or force them to become one
nation with him. And then, the Ruler replied, "Go and persuade him; you
can accomplish it, I am sure."[377]

In the ninth month, a comet was seen for seven weeks in Italy.[378] All of
the astrologers believed that it appeared like blood and that perhaps a king
would be killed or the residence of a great potentate would be marked for
destruction.

Thereupon, King Sebastian announced to his entire empire: "Anyone who
can use a sword expertly and so desires can join me in a war against the
empire of the Sherif: His people seem outwardly friendly and quiet, they
harm nobody; yet he has been dissociated from the rest of his brothers, the
Turks. Hence, we should pursue him as an enemy, reach him, divide the
spoil, and make a huge profit, for these people are bread for us,[379] their pro-
tection is removed, and God is with us. Therefore, fear them not." However,
King Philip II of Spain let him know, because he did not want to march and
be beaten. He did not listen because he desired to kill the Sherif and his
dukes, his entire army and his servants because of the evil deeds which they
had performed. King Sebastian then joined his navy and took his infantry
and the entire cavalry with him to sea. After they had arrived at a location
which seemed suitable, they disembarked: Sebastian's entire cavalry, his
knights and army, a numerous battle-ready contingent, all fitted out for
war and their weapons of destruction in their hands.

But the Sherif moved toward them with his army and they were locked
against one another like a pair of disorganized goat-herds. The battle began.

---

[375] It seems that an imaginary conversation between God and His Hosts is composed
here. The Christian who rises (in the next paragraph) may perhaps be compared to Jonah's
journey to Niniveh. At the end of this paragraph the "Ruler" is again God.

[376] Jeremiah 48:11; i.e, they live without troubles.

[377] King Sebastian of Portugal was raised by the Jesuits and hence a fiery defender of
the Catholic faith. The Moslems were his bitterest enemies. He fell in the battle of Alcassar
on August 4, 1578.

[378] Also reported by the astronomer Tycho Brahe.

[379] Numbers 14:9; i.e., we will devour them.

The entire Portugese encampment was ground down and King Sebastian captured by the archers. And although he fervently pleaded, saying, "I shall flee from before Israel, for the Eternal is warring for them against the Egyptians,[380] he was not permitted to live, and was slain together with his brother. The Lord had opened His magazines and brought forth the arms of His wrath because it was the Lord's battle against this evil Empire. And as the Turks dealt with others, so they dealt with them: their corpses lay like dung in the field, nobody buried them, the birds of prey summered on them, and all the beasts of the earth wintered on them.[381] This was the lot of our contemptors and the just desert of our looters. Praised be He who metes out His share on all the enemies of His people, Israel. When the bad news reached Lisbon, a great outcry was heard in the whole land of Portugal, because there was not one house where one was not dead.[382] All splendor was now gone from Portugal. Indeed, God is just.

When King Philip of Spain heard that Sebastian, his princes, counsellors, and army had fallen, and that it happened exactly as he had predicted, he rose and spoke: "Now I shall rule there, for I have a just claim on this empire." He immediately mobilized his cavalry, mustered Italian and German knights and also his own people, the Spanish army, and went out to battle. He marched toward Lisbon since this was the capital. The Portugese called a council and said, "Who would dare to fight against this powerful King, and who could resist him?" whereupon they let it be known: "To whomever this land may belong, make a treaty with us and we shall serve you. Only do not set any Spanish princes over us."[383] Philip obliged, because the Spanish had always been enemies of the Portugese. When he came to Lisbon, the entire populace went out and proclaimed, "Long live King Philip!" After they had acknowledged him as king, he put an occupational force in Lisbon and all the other cities, and then returned to his country and residence. His regimen stood firm.[384]

Philibert Emmanuel, Duke of Savoy, died on August 30, 1580 (5340). This occasion caused much suffering: his son, Charles Emmanuel, took over the government, but he was very young. Cardinal Borromeo came up from

---

[380] Exodus 14:25; the author describes the battle as if he had joined the Israelites and as if they were protected by God; he speaks in a poetic sense in that the Turks represent the forces of light, while the Portugese are pictured under the guise of the Biblical enemy of the Hebrews, the Egyptians (consider also the next sentence).

[381] Isaiah 18:6

[382] Exodus 12:30; i.e., where one was not dead.

[383] Philip was considered a Spaniard by the Portugese; but they wished to keep independent of Spain.

[384] The Spanish Kings ruled Portugal from 1580 to 1640. During this time the Iberian Peninsula was united; but the Portugese were never satisfied with this.

Milan to stand at his right side[385] and counselled him to expel the Jews. But when they prostrated themselves before him, he made a covenant with them so that they had to give up the taking of interest. To this the Jews agreed, "What you have asked of us is good, Sire, and God's law agrees with it, for it is written: 'You shall keep my ordinances,'"[386] and from that time on they lived there in safety.

In 5342 (1582), the Pope agreed with his Bishops at a council meeting to shorten the year by 10 days.[387] This ordinance became binding for all of the Christian countries, and they all accepted this new decree of Pope Gregory XIII with the exception of the Germans, who, however, accepted it also later on out of fear of derision. During this period, a manuscript with a seal affixed to it and encased in a doubly sealed container, was found in the foundation of a Temple in Aquileia. In the same year – it was August 29th (the 11th of Ellul) – a man from the stock of Levi was walking in a public street in Cremona. An unrestrained man walked up to him, beat him in the sides so that he took ill, and, as a consequence of this maltreatment, died. But his brothers, also Levites, ran after the Murderer who had fled into one of the other open cities and hugged the corner of the altar of the Church there, hoping that it might be his place of safe refuge.[388]

After they had made a presentation before the Bishop, they grabbed him and went to the Senatorial Court in Milan so that he could be sentenced to death. Indeed, he was found guilty for the Levite's death and he was sentenced to hang and then to be dragged by a horse's tail through the streets. Both of these things happened. But the Cremonese were very angry about that and held that, because of a Jew, a Christian had been unjustly punished. Moreover, he had been taken away from the altar against the Jews' own Law. They decided to demand of King Philip the expulsion of the Jews from the territory and the people of Pavia were on this point of the same opinion.

At that time, King Philip of Spain betrothed his youngest daughter, Catilina, to Charles Emanuel, Duke of Savoy. He gathered a multitude of dukes and knights to prepare for the trip to Spain. He imposed a special tribute upon the land, and the Jews were also forced to give a sum of money.

---

[385] Zachariah 3:1; i.e., like Satan. Carlo Cardinal Borromeo was quite a famous man (d. 584). He was a nephew of Pope Pius IV (d. 1566) and was noted as a great church reformer and was canonized in 1610.

[386] In Leviticus 18:5; i.e., according to the Laws. They thought the new pact allowed them to exist!

[387] Pope Gregory XIII changed the Julian calendar to out present Gregorian calendar in 1581, not 1582. The reasons, why the Germans refused to accept it was, because they were Protestants. The Russian Communist Government accepted it in 1922.

[388] This is an intentional parallelism to the biblical concept of the ir ha-miklah, the city of refuge.

Thereupon, the Duke went to Spain, where the King and the nobles bestowed great honors upon him. The King then gave him his daughter in matrimony. The Duke loved her, brought her to Piedmont and consoled himself thus after the death of his mother.

In 5345 (1585), Pope Gregory died. The cardinals elected Cardinal Montalto and named him Sixtus V.[389] He was a prudent and sensible man, who based his claims on justice. Toward the Jews he was fair, made a new covenant with them permitting them to live again in all the cities of the Romagna. After that, they resettled in Bologna also. He issued firm edicts by which they were enabled to live in the lands of their exile and decreed, that if Jews were to travel on Christian vessels plying the sea, Christians were not to steal their belongings nor to make them captives as the Maltese Knights used to do in those days. In addition, he also stipulated other beneficial orders in the interest of the Jews. When the Congregations realized that a new era of grace had arrived, the heads of the Italian Jewish Communities gathered in Padua to appeal to the Pope on the matter of the Hebrew books and the Talmud. But nothing was achieved there because the representatives from Venice did not wish to join them. The conference was dissolved. This was a step backwards and absolutely not progress.

In 5347 (1587), Duke William of Mantua died and his son, Vincent Gonzaga, followed him to power. He dealt mercifully with the Jews, inspired confidence in them with friendly pronouncements, and gave Gaon Joseph from Fano easy access to his presence. He also entered into a covenant with the Jews and reinforced it with the ducal seal. He did likewise with the Jews of Montferrrat and gave them decent laws which enabled them to exist.

In 5349 (1589), Duke Charles Emanuel gathered an army and conquered Carmagnola, a fortified town in Marchesato di Saluzzo which belonged to the King of France, but was on Italian territory. From there he went to Rivoli and took it by force, so that in all the Italian lands there remained nothing for the Kings of France. But for the Jews living there, this was a time of lamentation.

Henry III, King of France, ordered in those days the death of Duke Henry of Guise and of his brother,[390] because they had rebelled and tried to hand over the Marchesato to Charles Emanuel.

But King Henry was not, in his heart, deeply committed to his faith,[391]

---

[389] Pope Sixtus V reigned 1585-90.

[390] Cardinal Louis of Guise.

[391] Henry may not have been committed to Roman Catholicism, but it should be remembered that while he was King of Poland he was, for this reason, no less hostile toward the Jews.

and was even opposed and hostile to the monks living in his country, for
he had turned to the heretics.[392] The monk, Clement Bourbognon, conspired
against him and had him assassinated in his own palace. But when the
murderer, a monk, tried to save his own life by fleeing, a number of the
royal courtiers killed him. After all, who is allowed to lay hands on a king
and go unpunished? But as the King had no heir for his crown, he said before
he died, "Henry IV, King of Navarre, should be recognized as King."[393]

Among the people of France there was a divided opinion: many of the
people refused and did not want him for the king and the people of Paris
were opposed to him. King Philip stood by their side, saying, "Elect as King
whomever you wish: one of the Dukes of Guise, or the Duke of Lorraine,
or my son-in-law, the Duke of Savoy, or whoever it may be, if only he is true
to his faith. But the king, whose opinion you know, does not recognize him
under any circumstances, for he did not adhere to his faith."[394]

The King of Navarre was a hero from his childhood days on, and since
he had a claim on the throne as the brother-in-law of the King,[395] he said,
"By my life, I shall become your King by force." After he had mustered an
army, he beleaguered Paris for a long time and the city got into such straits
that people ate all that was otherwise regarded as vile and unclean and even
paid for an ass' head eighty francs. Hereafter, King Philip wrote to Allessandro Farnese, the Duke of Parma, his deputy in Flanders, to hurry to the
aid of the Parisians. He then marched with a huge army before this city and
saved it from the power of the enemy. The war raged mightily in France
then, one people fought against the other, for many had risen and proclaimed,
"I shall reign." The Duke of Savoy also warred against them on the border
of Marseille on the orders of his father-in-law.

Pope Sixtus V died in that year (1590) on August 24th, and the Cardinals
elected Urban IX. But when this man died after only twelve days, they
elected a Cardinal from Cremona whom they named Gregory XIV.[396] For

---

[392] Henry was assassinated on August 1, 1589 by a young Dominican monk, Jacob Clement, who was in turn killed by the Courtiers Lognac and Guesle.

[393] The text reads "Henry IV"; at the time here referred to, Henry was King of Navarre
(as Henry III) and only later became Henry IV of France. He ruled France from 1589
until 1610 and was the first of the House of Bourbon.

[394] Henry of Navarre was a Protestant (Hugenot) until 1593, hence unacceptable to
most Roman Catholics.

[395] Henry IV married Henry III's sister, Margaret of Valois in 1572, at the age of
nineteen. Henry of Navarre was also the heir to the French throne after Henry III as the
ranking male heir through fourteen generations going back about three centuries.

[396] The surfeit of Papacies about this time will be confusing to the reader; a note is
therefore added on the Papal reigns of the period; Sixtus V died in 1590, and was followed
for a few months by Urban VII (not IX as in the text); Urban was followed by Gregory

the Jews this was a time of lamentation, for the people wanted to rob and plunder them. They were forced to watch during the night and had to lock tight the doors of their shops during the day, until the storm had blown over and God had saved them.

The citizens of Cremona and Pavia had sent messengers to King Philip and asked him to expel the Jews living in the territory of Milan. Thereupon, the King wrote a letter to his Deputy, whom he had there, to travel to all the towns of Milan and to collect personally the head-tax of the Jews, so that he knew how many of them were there. Thus, a census was taken. A famine was then most depressing in the whole territory of Milan, and many died of hunger. And if the Jews had not loaned anything to the poor, the number of those who died would have been double. After this, the Pope also died, and the Cardinals elected Innocent IX who lived for only two months until he died also.

In 5352 (1592), the Cardinals elected a Florentine[397] on January 30th: Clement VIII. With him, a new ruler arose who ignored the decrees and orders of Sixtus V: the Jews were again expelled from the Romagna and Bologna. Consequently, one went here and the other there to resettle.

King Philip also wrote to his Deputy in Milan to expell all those Jews who lived in this land. When the heads of the Congregation heard this, they became very sad, set fast days and prayed to the Lord. Fast days were also set up in the other surrounding towns and a conference was convened. Upon a most imploring entreaty by the heads of the Jewish Community to the Deputy and to the Senators of Milan, they received this reply: the expulsion was the wish of the King, to whom no one could give orders. They then asked the Deputy to give them at least some time so that they could go to the King's Court in order to inquire from him whether this was really his intention. After that, they would accept his verdict, if only he would return to them the money which they had lent to him previously and on many different occasions. The Deputy agreed to this.

There was a Jew in Alessandria by the name of Samuel Hacohen. He offered to go to Spain on behalf of the Jews to plead for his fatherland. The Deputy gave him a letter of introduction in order to obtain entry to the King's Court without any difficulties. He immediately went to Genoa, got on board a ship, and after he arrived in Spain, he conferred with the Senators about the plight of the Jews. He even succeeded in getting all the way into

---

XIV (1590-91), who was in turn followed by Innocent IX (who reigned for a short period in 1591); Clement VIII reigned from 1592 until 1605 and was folllowed by Leo IX in 1605; he was folluwed by Paul V from 1605 until 1621.

[397] Hippolyt Aldrobandini.

the palace where the King and his highest ministers were. He spoke in the name of the Jews and asked him why he planned to deal in this way with his servants who had assisted him and his father in times of trial. He said that they were still ready today to help him with as much and more for the poor and indigent in case this became necessary, and that they could bring witnesses to justify them.[398] But if the King had once decided to expell them, he would then demand, in the name of the Jews, that he first repay them what they could rightfully claim; for this is what justice demanded. For after all, it was known to all, that the King's pronouncements were based on justice, and that he was certainly not ungrateful. This presentation pleased the King and he returned his favor to Samuel Hacohen. He wrote to his Deputy that nothing should be done against the Jews until he had received a second communication. But all this happened at a time when the Jewish Communities had gathered in order to obtain a second stay. At that moment, the above mentioned news arrived, and it made the Jews very happy. When the inhabitants of Pavia and Cremona heard that the King had brought their plan to naught, they met again and joined hands bringing together money as well as delegates to approach the Royal Court again in order to obtain from the King a recognition of their demand.

At that time, an anti-Semite from the people of Amalek,[399] Bartolomeo Carranza by name, lived in Milan. This man demanded a certain amount of money from the Jews and, in case they would not pay it, he promised to blackmail them before the King, holding alleged proofs in his hands. However, the Jews chose to ignore his words in the belief that many others would approach them, saying "Give, give." When he realized that he could not effect anything, he went to the senators and judges and announced to them that he held proof against the Jews in his hands to the effect that they had committed acts which were not right, and that because of these acts, a large sum of money could come into the Royal Treasury. Although the Jews then gave him all he had asked for, he nevertheless defamed them in that he said that they had taken high interest rates against the wishes of the King. He also preached against the Hebrew books, went to Pavia and from there to Lodi and demanded that the Commander search the houses of the Jews, which he did. All the books which they had in their homes were taken away and nothing remained. Even the prayer books were torn from their hands and brought on a Friday to the City Commander's house in Lodi where two brothers from the stock of Levi, who had forsaken their old faith, were living.

[398] Isaiah 43:9
[399] All the historical enemies of the Jews.

On the following day, the Sabbath, the morning had hardly dawned, they went to the house of the Commander where the city magistrates and burghers had gathered. The books were thoroughly investigated to substantiate the testimony of the informer. During this investigation, the Inquisitor made his appearance in the company of his secretary who had his protocols with him, and who had to pronounce the final judgment in those investigations. The Inquisitor said to the assembled and the presiding Judge, "What are you doing here? Why do you concern yourself about matters which do not belong before your forum?" The Censor then replied as their spokesman: "Forgive us, Sire, but we have no other intention than to prove the evil and infamy of the Jews." However, the Inquisitors served notice to him, that he should not open his mouth anymore on pain of excommunication and not to discuss this matter further. Turning to the Judge and the City Commander, he said, "I demand of you that, by threat of banishment, you forward all these books to my Inquisitorial Court, for it is my duty to judge them." He then ordered his secretary to enter into the protocol that he had warned them before witnesses. And so it was done. After that, the Inquisitor left angrily. When the Censor realized that he had not accomplished anything, he travelled from there to Cremona to discuss these matters with the magisrrates residing there. He said: "As you are aware, all these issues have been undertaken to your interest and profit, to establish the guilt of the Jews, so that they atone for their evil with their very lives, and so that the King can expel all these enemies of the state from the land." However, they replied, "Who has asked you to step on our threshold? Take your nicety and throw it upon the thorns.[400] Go away and return to the place whence you came. One used to say to the bee: I neither like your sting nor your honey." When Amalek[401] heard these words, all courage left him.

The commander of Lodi, afraid about the words of the Inquisitor, visited him after breakfast, and asked him for a respite to report back to the nobles of Milan, for he wished to do what they asked of him. The Inquisitor acquiesced and granted him a twenty-four hour delay during which he wrote to the city's senators and reported all the happenings. However, the messenger returned without a reply. The Commander, together with a friend, again visited the Inquisitor and asked for a second respite which was granted to him after a long plea. He addressed himself a second time to the senators and the Deputy, but since they were very busy with the affairs of state, the messenger returned again with empty hands. The Commander approached the Inquisitor a third time; he took many friends with him, prostrated himself,

---

[400] I.e., keep your courtesies to yourself.
[401] Amalek, i.e., the arch-enemies of the Jews in biblical literature.

and implored the Inquisitor most fervently to grant him another delay to see the result of this matter. The Inquisitor gave in to him and the Senators' requests and granted them a third reprieve. During the following night, he and his two servants started their journey to Milan and arrived there by morning. On that day, a secret session took place at the Deputy's court. When the Commander arrived at the court of the Royal Palace, the told the city's gate keeper that he had come to discuss a secret matter with the Deputy and his counsellors. After this message had reached the Deputy, he allowed them to enter. The Commander reported to them the following: "I am in bad shape since the Inquisitor wishes to excommunicate me. Give me some advice as to what I should do." They asked him to step outside, and he did so. It was then agreed that the books should be handed over to the Inquisitor, since he alone had to judge them, and that the Censor was not permitted under any circumstances to make any claims against the Jews. When they went away from this meeting after they had all concurred about this unanimously, the Chief Secretary met with one of the supervisors (Proveditori). He called on him and ordered him to send for the Censor and to inform him on behalf of the Council that he should never again dare say anything or act against the Jews, be it important or trivial. The supervisor did so and gave him order when he was still in Cremona. The countenance of this Haman[402] was covered with shame. He returned home and his head was wrapped in sadness.

Praised be He who destroys the plans of the cunning. Now, when the citizens of Pavia and Cremona saw that life had become easier for the Jews and their plan had been brought to naught by the Deputy, they sent to the Royal Court and begged for the expulsion of the Jews. They arrogated themselves to raise the money with the help of which he could pay off the Jews. In addition to that, the Father Confessor, whom the King trusted, also joined in and helped them to persuade him to expel the Jews from the land quickly. The King promised to do so. The Censor also defamed them suggesting that the Jews had nothing to receive since they had not paid the stipulated head-tax for years. He also wrote about that to the Senate of Milan telling them to institute an investigation by the court and to inquire if his testimony was not true. A long time elapsed until the Jews were totally absolved after this legal case had been brought all the way to the Royal Court in Spain. But the Judges in Lodi had to turn over all the books to the Inquisitor who gave them to our baptized brothers, the apostates. They found a

---

[402] The name Haman originally appears in the Book of Esther, read during the Purim Festival. Haman conspired against the Jews of Persia. They were saved by Queen Esther and her uncle Mordechai. Later on, Haman's name is identified with all other enemies of the Jews, such as Torquemada, Hitler etc.

few remarks which allegedly offended the Christian religion. A verdict was issued on March 17, 1597 (Adar 27, 5357) on which day they were to be burned. A fine was imposed upon the Jews and they had to pay a ransom which was as high as the Inquisitor wished for each person to impose.

A mighty war raged in those days in the region of Hungary, and a small strip of land in Flanders, and because of the many armies nobody was able to leave or enter Milanese territory in peace. Great anguish befell the Jews when they were notified of the King's decree aiming at the expulsion of the Jews. They set up fast days and prayed to God. They were also terrified in all the other neighboring towns, because they feared that other kings might learn from him, and act likewise. Therefore, this was a time of sorrow for the Jews. However, the supervisors in Milan tried to avert this catastrophe, and although many decrees of the King arrived there concerning this matter, this Deputy chose to ignore them. He was a Field Marshal of Aragonian descent, a pious regent who had always good reasons for his actions. For the Jews this matter became protracted and they remained there until 5357 (1597).[403] When the people of Cremona and Pavia realized that the Deputy ignored the decrees, though the royal seal was affixed to them, and against which there was no possible objection, they informed their delegate at the King's Court so that he could ask the King to enforce his people's and his country's request. When the King heard this, he became very angry. He issued a personal letter to the Deputy that demanded that he should drive the whole Jewish population from the land. Only two heads of families were to remain until the pronounced sentence had reached the Law Court, namely the Senators of Spain, which was either to sentence the Jews or free them to return.

This letter came to the Deputy in 5357 (1597). He then called in the most respected men of the Jewish community and told them: "As you know, I have stood at your side with all my power, so that you could remain in the land and pursue your business. But now I can no longer resist the King. Here in my hand is this fateful document, written personally in the King's own handwriting and sealed. Nothing can be done about it. However, I shall show my favor again: I shall extend the respite by another two months. During this time, send the poor and indigent from the land. Take these five thousand Guilders, so that they can buy the necessities for this journey and then depart. But this is a year of war; the whole country is filled with armies and mercenaries like wolves of the night.[404] I shall therefore issue a new

---

[403] As this persecution began in 5357 (1597), the Corrector perhaps implies that it lasted until the end of 1597.

[404] I.e., making the road unsafe for travel.

order, namely that all villages should obligate themselves to send escorts with you, and bring you from one locale to the next until they have accompanied you to the border of the country." And this then happened. Immediately after Passover the Jews made preparation to leave for Mantua, Modena, Reggio, Verona, Padua, and the surrounding territories. And those poor people, those refugees, their tears flowing, went away. Many amongst the members of the congregation of Cremona had brought their wares and household goods to the ships which were in the river Po; but robbers came during the night and stole them. When the morning broke, the whole city became excited, our people cried bitterly, and because of the theft, their clamor went up to God. A stranger from abroad came to them and said, "Give me two hundred Guilders, and all, that has been stolen from you, will be returned to you." After they had done so, all was returned to the last penny. Praised be He who sends salvation and freedom.

When the third month had approached, the few remaining Jews celebrated Shavuoth (the Feast of Weeks) and after that holiday, they, their wives, children, and all their servants left for wherever the spirit drove them. Yet they walked peacefully and composedly on their road without obstacles or accident, although the whole countryside was full with mercenaries; but these men were filled with fear of the Deputy.

It was on the 17th day of the third month that the Jews emigrated; the Hosts of the Lord from the Community of Lodi left by ship. I myself, together with my daughters and sons went through Milan to the other side of the Piedmont territory. And when I travelled through Milan the whole city was in an uproar and screamed, "Look at the Jews. They are leaving the Land." When the Deputy heard this, he was most pleased. On the 19th of this same month, the armies moved from village to village, and as they met the members of my family, they recognized them and shouted: "Those are Jews!" The emigrants became terrified until one man cried out to them, "Don't be afraid, and don't worry. If you wish to give us only a small handout, we should be willing to accompany you almost to Navarra." This they did, and the Milanese served as our guides. Praised be He, who does not deprive us of His favor and faithfulness. He led me on this path until I came to the Congregation of Vercelli which is situated at the extreme border of Piedmont. There I rested with my family for a few days and even contemplated staying there, for I believed that I could live there in tranquility. But I did not succeed: the Duke, may God magnify his splendor, had permitted the residing Jews to stay on, but none of the refugees was to dare to settle there, unless it was with the express approval of the Duke. When it became known that we had settled down in the land, he issued a new decree that all strangers who had just arrived were to move on and to settle wherever they could find a place outside his domain. Hence, I was forced to go from there to Montferrat. But even there I did not find my peace, for tragedy hit me: my wife passed away on the 19th of Adar in 5358 (1598) and I mourned her. My Rachel had died; may her soul be bound up in the bond of life eternal. Thus no Jew remained in the whole Milanese territory, except two heads of families in Cremona, two in Lodi, and two in Alessandria. The Deputy permitted all those whose wives were expectant to remain as long as they were ill, and until they were able to get up again and walk away on crutches; pregnant women could stay until one month after they had given birth. May God remember him for his good, for surely he belonged to the pious among the Gentiles who will have a share in the life beyond; to those, whom God sent to sustain us.

The Jews called another conference together and made the joint decision to send a delegate to Spain and to remain at the Royal Court until a final judgment had been issued for them. After they had been cleared, the King wrote to his Deputy to repay the Jews all the capital plus interest up to the last penny. The Jews from the Congregation of Viadana gathered and elected rabbinical leaders, charged them with the redistribution of funds among the people in this country: Gaon Rabbi Menachem Azaria from Fano, Rabbi Hanania from Gazzolo and Rabbi Yechiel Melli. These were the men to arbitrate all disputes and to negotiate all monitary transactions. Thus, such a distribution also took place in Rivvo (Reggio?) in 5361 (1601).

Alphonse, Duke of Ferrara, died in 5358 (1597). This man belonged to the pious among the gentiles and all Israel mourned his death: mourn, Oh Lord, mourn his glory. Because he had no heirs, the Duchy fell to his nearest relative, Don Caesar of Este, excepting only Ferrara proper, which went to the Pope.[405] Although Don Caesar made claims on it and even mustered an army and cavalry to strenghten himself, the Pope and his Cardinals threw excommunication at him which he had publicised in Ferrara and its total environ. He also gathered a very large army to fight him with all his power. Don Caesar realized that none of the other dukes would come to his aid and that even many of his loyal nobles and servans left him and became his adversaries, saying, "Who is he that dares to fight against God's Deputy?" For the Jews, this was a time of mourning for several of them were killed because of our sin and guilt. There was no justice and no judge, and every-

---

[405] Caesar of Este was the son of Markgrave Alphonse of Montecchio, uncle of Duke Alphonse II. Pope Clement VIII, under the pretext that Caesar had come from ignoble birth, declared his election invalid and incorporated the Duchy of Ferrara into his own Papal State.

body did what appeared right to him. When Don Caesar saw that he was powerless, he arrived at a compromise with the Pope and his Cardinals by handing over to them the city of Ferrara and all the surrounding territory, and he further declared that he would submit his claims to the judgment of the Royal Court which would solve this knotty problem. Thus Don Caesar and his family left the city and its environ.

On January 29, 1598 (5358), Cardinal Aldrobandini, the Pope's nephew, [406] approached Ferrara with his whole army in the name of the Pope and his Cardinals. All the city's Senators walked outside to greet him as regent on behalf of his uncle. Whenever he went for a walk, the people of the land hailed him: "Long live the Pope! Down with Don Caesar and the Jews!" When the Jews heard this clamor, they became afraid, took these words to heart, and prayed to God; they set a fast day and God listened to their entreaties, for He remembered His covenant and bestirred Himself in the fulness of His mercy. After the Cardinal had put an occupational force into the city, he let the Jews swear to become loyal subjects of the Pope, and designated judges and officials over them, for he was a regent who desired to base his state on justice. He then had all the books put before him in which the city's income and expenditures had been recorded. After he had listened to the recitation of their content, he noticed that most of the city's business was in the hands of well-to-do Jews. Having perceived this, he asked each and every one to come to a conference singly and conferred with them. When he discovered that these were well educated men of good character, he asked them, "What is your business?" whereupon they opened their hearts to him and asked him for permission to remain there as they wished to serve him in truth and faithfulness. They asked that he grant them a respite at least after which they could emigrate, and he promised them in a gentle manner and in the name of the Pope, that they could remain and find sustenance in the land. They left him in peace, and with a happy and joyful heart.

In those days, King Philip gave his daughter for a wife to his nephew, Archduke Albrecht, the Emperor's brother; and he gave him Flanders as a wedding present and all he owned in Burgundy.[407] To his own son, Philip III, he gave Margarete, the daughter of Archduke Charles of Austria. And after he had named him King, he died and was gathered to his forefathers (1598). A year had passed since he had driven the Jews from the region of of Milan.

The Pope intended to visit Ferrara to inspect the land, to launch useful

---

[406] He became a Cardinal at the age of twenty-three. His first name was Peter.

[407] Actually, Archduke Albrecht of Austria was the brother of Philip's fourth wife.

institutions, and to decree helpful ordinances. He arrived on March 18th, accompanied by twenty-seven Cardinals, forty Bishops, and numerous Dukes and respected citizens. The Senators of the city and the inbabitants of the land went out to greet him and proclaimed: "Long live our Master, the Pope, may he ever rise in glory. Down with the Jews!" After the Pope had made his entry and had ascended the readied throne he spoke to the Cardinals: "Who could possibly refuse the people living in this land its wish, or refuse to bestow on them honor and recognition, by expelling the Jews?" Yet, God's mercy never ends, and He always sends salvation even before he wounds: Cardinal Aldrobandini, the Pope's nephew, arose among those gathered and spoke: "I have already concluded, in the name of the Pope and his Cardinals who have sent me here in advance, a Covenant with them and permitted them to stay here for five years. They are also faithful people, enemies of unlawful profit. It would not be to the Pope's advantage to expell them from this country." And they replied, "If this is the state of affairs, it is reasonable to keep our word. For whoever speaks for somebody else must be regarded as his Deputy." Praised be He who destroys the plans of the wicked. Thus the Jews live there to this day.

On the 13th day of the ninth month, 1599 (5359), Queen Margarete arrived in Italy. She journeyed through Verona, and from there to Ferrara where King Philip's emissaries had gone to perform the wedding at the large cathedral in the presence of the Pope and his Cardinals. The archduke Albert, brother of the Emperor Rudolph, also became engaged to the daughter of King Philip, Isabella, through her emissary who was living at that time, in Ferrara. After that they travelled to Mantua, to Cremona and Milan until they came to Genoa where they boarded the ships bound for Spain, the land of Christendom.[408]

The Pope again returned to his residence, going from Ferrara to Bologna and from there to Rome. On October 24th, a mighty rain fell upon the land, and the waters of the Tiber stood for three days and nights above the river bed. Such has never been seen before, and many walls and buildings collapsed. But there was light among all the Jews, and not the slightest damage came to their houses: the water reached only up to the door of the Synagogue, but did not flow into their homes. When the Pope sent out messengers to find out if this was really so, as was reported, he found out that people had told him the truth.

[408] Genesis 32:3; i.e., the land of Edom which was always hostile towards the Jews. This Queen Margarete was probably the granddaughter of Emperor Ferdinand I (1556-64) and wife of King Philip III of Spain (1578-1621), the son of Philip II. This Archduke Albert is the same as the Archduke Albrecht. Rudolf, his brother, was Emperor Rudolf II (1576-1612).

The Jews of Verona lived dispersed in the community, one here, the other there. However, the Bishop and the city's inhabitants wished to designate a certain place for them, a street, in which they could live capsuled up just like the Jews of Venice. When they wrote about that to Venice, the Senate obliged them in all they desired. Hereafter, they designated a street for the Jews near the city's market-place, gave them houses to live in and also a beautiful synagogue. They dwelt there in much roomier quarters than heretofore and, with God's help, they multiplied, spread out far and were much respected.

Many people died in Savoy and Piedmont where the pest raged. In Turin and Asti also many died and God's hand was regrettably raised against the Jews. It was reported to the Duke that there were a people (i.e. the Jews!) in his land spreading this infectious disease to all places where the whim took them. After this matter had been thoroughly investigated, he had them apprehended alive and killed them with unheard of tortures and under horrible martyrdoms, so that the people seeing and hearing of this became fearful. In Trieste, at the border of Istria situated by the coast of the sea, this pestilence also raged, and many died of it. The Jews were accused with the words, "It was you who brought the plague here, for you buy and sell merchandise and you cover with it the entire city." But after this matter had been investigated and it was found out that the accusation was false, the murmuring against them halted primarily because the epidemic also raged amongst the Jews several of whom had already died. A man from Goertz ought to be especially remembered for his good: he had money distributed to the poor of the city, and they lacked nothing as long as the plague lasted. Remember him, Oh God, forever. Finally, after the course of two years, the pestilence stopped in all the regions of Italy.

In 5360 (1600), a great cold wave hit in the region of Genoa. All the trees froze and were beautiful to look at like the fruits from the Hadar tree.[409] In all of Italy no Etrogim[410] were available, one costing as much as ten Guilders – something unbelievable heretofore. Regardless, big-hearted people paid for them in order to fulfill the statutes.[411] Remember them for this, Oh God.

There was a major war raging in the land of Hungary; the Emperor's troops had penetrated to the outskirts of Buda(pest), had the surrounding territory under their control, and the Turks had retreated to the citadel. When the Jews there saw this, they reaffirmed their lives by saying, "Let us

---

[409] C.f., S. J. Rapoport in his *Erech Millin*, a Talmudic encyclopedia.
[410] A lemon or grapefruit-like citrus fruit used during Succoth Festivals.
[411] C.f., Leviticus 23:39-43.

fight bravely for our wives, children, and our belongings, and may God do as it is pleasant in His eyes." After that, they fought against the imperial troops with vigor and fortitude, defeated and totally destroyed them so that they had to withdraw with ignominy. This caused people to get up and smear the Jews before the Regent, saying, "Master and Emperor, the Jews have caused our defeat so that we could not conquer the city of Buda(pest). Therefore, there is only one judgment for them, namely, to expel all those Jews who now live in our land." But the Emperor replied like a sage and Angel of the Lord, "On the contrary; they are to be praised in that they fought with dedication to their Ruler, and I do not doubt that, if the day should come, those Jews who live amongst us would also fight for us with the same self-dedication. They have done no evil." Praised be He who inspired such in the Emperor.

After the course of one year, when the generals had gone to war, the imperial troops invaded the Turkish part of Hungary, carried the war to the Turks and made great booty. When the rich Jews of Buda(pest) noticed that the imperial armies did aim to conquer Buda(pest), they became very timid and thought of ways to escape. They therefore fled to Stuhlweissenburg, [412] a Ducal free-city. At one time, one of the Hungarians said to the im- perial Field Marshal, "Come to my side, and I shall hand over Stuhlweissen- burg to your power." He followed this fellow with his whole army, and after he had led the troops over the side roads, they reached the city and took it. But when the Turks in the city heard that, they marched toward them, fought with them and slew them. Many of the Jews were also slain and the remaining twenty-two persons were robbed and plundered. After ransom- money was put on their heads, they had to walk as captives before the enemy until they arrived in Vienna. Thereafter, these faltering people sent mes- sengers to all of the lands of Germany, Italy and Turkey, and when their ransom had been raised, they were released. Praised be He who frees the captives.

In Prague there lived a certain Jew, Mordechai Meisel by name, a very respected and generous man. He had access to the Regent and he also en- joyed the finest reputation among the Imperial Princes. He had a wife, but no children. When he had grown old and aged, his reputation of honesty was wide spread, he was respected in the Emperor's Court, and he was beloved by his fellow Jews; he annually distributed gifts to the needy, and his name was known throughout the land. When the day of his death came near he called his wife, Frommet, and said to her, "Go to my chest in which

[412] This Austrian city, also called Alba Regia or Regalis, was the coronation and burial place of Kings. From 1543 until 1601, it was occupied by the Turks.

I keep my golden coins, take out a considerable sum of money, and give it to the Gaon Rabbi Loewe[413] so that he may distribute it among the city's poor and learned, for it is written: 'Chartity saves from Death.'"[414] After she had promised him that she would act according to his wishes, she lied to him in her stinginess; she pretended to have done already what he had charged her to do. Yet he recognized her falsehood: "You faithless, stubborn woman; you were already obstinate during my lifetime, how will you behave now that I am close to death?" Thereupon this good man died, and was gathered to his fathers. And on this occasion all the princes of the Empire came to pay him their last respects, and even the Emperor sent his delegate to participate in the funeral. After the period of mourning was over for him, the Emperor had his entire fortune confiscated, all of his possessions, which he had earned and scraped together. More than six hundred thousand marks in silver were taken from his house. The Rabbis were also forced to put all those in ban who, in his name, held in their hands receipts of loans, silver and golden vessels or other written documents; and those who refused to hand them over to the over-seers they could be taken to the Imperial Treasury. For, the Emperor's experts had told him that he had a claim to this inheritance and that it was coming to him because Mordechai had left no heirs behind.

There was also a respected woman in Constantinople who had easy access to the Turkish Sultan, before whom all the nobles at the Court bowed down, and who channeled all matters to him when one wanted to see the Sultan. Once upon a time, a distinguished Prince arrived holding a sack full of money in his hand, and said to her, "Accept this money under the condition that you procure the management of a certain place." After she had accepted the money from his hand, she said to him: "It shall be as you have said, Prince. You can rely on me!" As another Prince heard this, he figured: I shall also go to her and offer her double the amount, on the condition, that she procure for me the management of a given place. He went to her and she permitted herself to be won over by the latter, for he had given her a far better present than the other.[415] When the first one got wind of this, he became very irate, gathered a few irrepressible people, entered the Jewish quarter in Constantinople in broad daylight, invaded the house of that woman, and butchered her and all the members of her family. Only her

---

[413] Rabbi Loewe ben Bezalel was a Rabbi in Moravia for twenty years, went to Prague in 1571 and founded there the so-called Klause. In 1592 he became the chief Rabbi of Posen (in Poland).

[414] Proverbs 10:2

[415] A similarly phrased sentence, repeated here, is omitted.

little boy remained alive. He then changed his religion and became a Moslem. The Sultan asked afterwards for the cause of this incident and then confiscated all of her possessions, more than nine hundred silver shekels, which this woman had scratched together. All of it was brought to the Royal Treasury and the news of this incident spread throughout the whole land.

In that same year of 5362 (1602), a monk by the name of Bartolomeo from Siena arose in Italy. He was so respected, because he spared neither Dukes nor Counsellors as he preached before the Christians and set them straight, that he was regarded as a saint. Incidentally, he also visited Modena where he preached before the Duke and put the Jews in a very bad light before him. The Duke then ordered them to wear special insignia, so that all who saw them would recognize them.

In the fifth month, Av, which had already brought us so much suffering,[416] the monk went from there to Mantua, where a multitude greeted him. He preached to them in the open street and said only bad things about the Jews so that, in consequence of his sermons, they were hated even the more. On a Holy Sabbath, a very hot day, some young children went out to play in the courtyard of the synagogue. One of the people passed by and saw them. He then said to the monk, "Do you know, these weakheaded Jews poke fun at you and your preachments?" The monk had them arrested immediately and thrown in the same prison where the common criminals were housed. During the following night, he had them brought before him and took them to account. They were tortured and their lives were embittered through cruel martyrdom; they were made to confess things which had never even entered into their minds. On the following Tuesday, [417] he had several of them assassinated in prison and they were throttled in the most brutal fashion. On Tuesday morning, they were dragged by the horses' tails to the market place, strung up high in the trees by their feet before the eyes of all simply in order to insult the People of the God of Israel. The rest of the Jews had locked themselves in their houses until the storm had blown over, for they feared for their lives. If the Duke had not sent his Princes and servants to the market-place, fully armed, to thrust down anyone who dared to lay hands on the Jews, not one single person would have escaped, and not one refugee kept alive. This is how badly this anti-Semite had deprecated them in the eyes of the people. Praised be He who saves and liberates. Despite all this, the monk's wrath was still not assuaged, and upon his order the wives, children, and relatives of the murdered were expelled with the warning, never to settle again in the territory of Mantua. Wagons and men were assigned

---

[416] E.g., the two destructions of the Temple in Jerusalem.
[417] Probably the night from Monday to Tuesday.

to them to accompany them to Verona, and from there they were sent to Venice where they were given permission to settle. The weak amongst them were given food and clothing. On Wednesday, the Duke informed the Jews that they should bury the martyred saints in the middle of the night, although they had done no evil. And thus it happened. After that, the anti-Semite desired to journey to Ferrara. The Duke let him have one of his ships, but ordered the captain and all his sailors not to permit him to disembark until they had taken him outside the borders of his country and dominion. This they did.

In those days, a poor Jew wanted to make a journey. But when he came to the main road, common and brutal folk fell upon him, gouged his eyes out, and killed him. Another one, also travelling peacefully on this road was assailed by these devils and killed. There was no safety for anyone who wished to travel to and fro. See this, Of God, and witness it, for they conspire against us day by day, and we are in their eyes like sheep on the slaughter bench.

Before this ensnaring sub-human person (the monk) reached Ferrara, the Jews living there threw themselves to the very feet of the Cardinal and said to him, "Sire, this anti-Semite has acted so and so, he has spilled the blood of the martyrs although they have done no injustice. But now, Sire, save us and avenge our faults for the sake of your own high station." And he responded, "Fear nothing, for I shall not permit that he afflicts you with any disadvantage." When this Haman appeared before the Cardinal, he set him straight and told him, "Watch your steps and do not say anything good or evil about the Jews. They are not even to be mentioned before the people." And he obeyed the Cardinal. The Jews of Venice also went to the nobles and Senators and told them what this man had caused in Mantua. They also showed to them the wives and children, the offspring of those martyrs, who had been murdered on the Day of Storm. This astounded the nobles and they released written decrees in all places where Jews lived and they forbade him to preach. And when this Haman arrived at Venice, he was not allowed to enter the city, and he had to remain in Murano, which is located near Venice. Once they went to him and conversed with him to see if he could really perform miracles. But later on they threw him in jail and sent him to Rome laden down with heavy chains. And it is not known what has become of him. Only the sentence over him, emanating from Rome, arrived saying that all pictures of him in Mantua were to be burnt on the threat of excommunication. After that, it became quiet in the land, and the Jews lived as heretofore.

Many of the Jews in Padua lived dispersed in different parts of the city

when the Bishop's order arrived to give them a domicile in a specially designated quarter of the city as in Verona. Thus the Jews were given a special
street, in which the synagogue stood, plus the adjacent part of the city.
Those houses which stood there were torn down, and each Jew built a new
one that year according to his means. But the Supervisors drove them on,
saying, "Hurry up and finish your work. Move into your homes which you
have just built." After that, they were chased out of the (old) houses in
which they had lived dispersed before; and they live until this day in their
new street which was assigned to them.[418]

The Turkish Sultan, Murat, ended his life in 5362 (1602)[419] and the
Princes chose his son, Sultan Mohammed, for a ruler when he was a mere
lad of seventeen years of age. He ascended the grand-ducal (i.e. Sultan's)
throne, and his dominion was grounded on a firm basis. One day he took ill
with samallpox. When he was near death, his servants said to him, "A
woman of sensible mind ought to be found for our Master who could wait
on him and cure him of his critical illness." At the same time she was to
prepare his food and wait on him. This pleased the Sultan much, and thus
it was done. A very respectable woman from the women of the sons of
the Gaonim lived in Constantinople, namely the widow of the eminent
Gaon Rabbi Solomon ben Nathan from Udine, of blessed memory,
who had been sent to Venice on orders of Sultan Selim II. And because she
was widely known for her expertise in the preparation of medications, she
was brought to the Sultan's Palace where she prepared for him a proper diet
which he liked and also her medications in order to heal him from his
sickness. After he had recovered, he showed himself most grateful to this
woman for all of her good deeds shown him; he gave her gifts according to
the wealth of a Sultan, and the other Princes also showered her with presents.

In 5365 (1605), her son, the generous Rabbi Nathan ben Solomon desired
to visit Venice. After he had found a suitable ship and had paid for the fare,
the Sultan gave him a letter addressed to the Council of Venice which was
headed by the Doge Grimani. Having arrived there, he presented the letter
to the Council, which honored him greatly. When he came to the Synagogue
of the Levantines,[420] he gave donations for holy works and for the poor of
Palestine – may it soon be rebuilt – and also presents for the city, for which
God may remember him forever.

---

[418] The following paragraph was put by this translator at the end of the book as a
proper and prayerful conclusion of this historic document.

[419] This is not correct: Sultan Murat III died on January 16, 1595 and his son Mohammed III died on December 22, 1603.

[420] There were also two more synagogues: one, the poorest, belonged to the Germans,
and the second, of the *Ponentini*, was supported by the Spanish Jews.

For all the lands of Italy this was a very dry year, for from the Day of Simchat Torah[421] the rains had ceased to fall, and before the month of Nissan when it rains only a little, no rain fell and throughout the winter snow did not come. The entire populace noticed this. Tell your children about it.

When, in the month of Adar, the Pope finished his life and died,[422] the Cardinals elected Cardinal Allessandro di Medici from the family of the Grand-Duke of Tuscany and placed him on the papal throne of the 13th of Nissan (April 11th). This made the whole people very happy. And the Jews also felt happy, for they thought: he will surely give us relief from our work and from the toil of our hands.[423] He was named Leo XI. However, he did not live a long time, for he died on April 27th, and all the people mourned his death sincerely, for he was a decent man.

About this time a son was born to King Philip III[424] of Spain which caused among the citizens of all the cities of his kingdom a great joy. This news was publicized in all of the provinces and in each one in the language of the particular country. All nations and princes were overjoyed. May it please our Father in Heaven to fill the King's heart, and the hearts of his entire nation so that it will be instilled in the hearts of his Princes of the Empire to be merciful to us and to all of Israel. Amen.

May it please you, Father in Heaven, to gather up the dispersed from amongst the nations, to lead us to Zion in Jubilation and to Jerusalem in Eternal Happiness, so that we, Judah and Israel, may serve You in unity as in the days of yore and in the years past. May Judah's and Jerusalem's sacrifice be pleasant in the eyes of God. Amen. May this be God's will.

Here ends the account of the unknown Corrector. (about 1605)

---

[421] The Rejoicing of the Law; this holiday marks the annual completion of the reading of the Torah. It is the merriest of all Jewish holidays next to Purim.

[422] Pope Clement VIII died March 5, 1605, i.e., the 15th of Adar, 5365.

[423] Genesis 5:29; i.e., he will ease our lives.

[424] Philip III reigned from 1598 until 1621.

BIBLIOGRAPHY

Abrahams, Lionel B., *"The Expulsion of the Jews from England in* 1290," *JQR*, VII, 1894-1895.

Adler, Michael, *Jews of Medieval England*, London, 1939.

Aescoly, A. Z., "David Reubeni in the Light of History", *JQR*, XXVIII, 1937.

Albornoz, Sanchez, "Itinerario de la conquista por los Musulames", *CHE*, X, 1948.

Allgemeine Encyclopädie. Ersch, J. S. and Gruber, J. B.

Anonymous, "Cronicas de los reyes de Castilla don Fernando y dona Isabel," *B.A.E.*, tomo 70.

Aronius, "Karl der Grosse und Kalonymus aus Lucca", in *ZGJD*, II, 1882.

Aronius, *Regesten zur Geschichte der Juden im Fraenkischen und Deutschen Reiche bis zum Jahre 1273*, Berlin, 1887-1902.

Asher, Abraham, *Benjamin de Tudela*, Itinerario, I, London, 1842.

Atiya, R. S., *Crusade of Nicopolis*, London, 1934.

Bacher, W., "Abraham ibn Ezra dans le nord de la France," *REJ*, XVII, 1888.

Bardinet, Leon, "Condition Cioile des Juifs du Comtat venaissin pendant la XVe, Ciecle", *REJ*, VI, 1883.

Beauvais, Vicente de, *Speculum Historiale*, Venice, 1591.

Benoit, P. R. "Akiba", in *Rev. Biblique*, 1947.

Benoit, P. Milik, J. T., and Vaux, R. de, *Discoveries in the Judean Desert*, II, *Les Grottes de Murabba'at*, Oxford, 1961.

Bialloblotzky, Christian Hermann, *The Chronicles of Joseph Hacohen. . . .*, London, 1834-1836.

Bosnage, Jacque, *L'Histoire et la Religion des Juifs*, ed. a la L. Haye Rotterdam, Reinier Leers, 1707.

Browe, "Die Hostienschändungen der Juden im Mittelalter," *Römische Quartalschrift*, XXXIV, 1926.

Calzas, Amor J. J., *Curiosidades historicas de la Cuidad de Huete*, Madrid, 1904.

Careras, Candi F., *La aljama de judios de Tortosa*.

Careras, Candi F., *Memoria de la Academia de Buenas Letras de Barcelona*, Vol IX.

Cardozo, Isaac., *Las excellencias de los Hebreos*, Amsterdam, 1679.

Cassel, D., *Manual of Jewish History*, McMillan, London, 1913.

Cheney, Edward., "The Execution of Cardinal Caraffa," in *Philobiblon Society*, VI, London, 1860.

Colombo, A., "L'ingresso di F. Sforza in Milano," in *Archivio Historico* Lombardo, 1905.

Dahmus, J., *Seven Medieval Kings*, Doubleday, N. Y., 1967.

David, Abraham ben., (ibn Daud) *Seder ha-Kabbalah Cracow 1820*, Jerusalem, 1956.

D'Azevedo, *Historia dos Christaos Novos Portogueses*, Lisbon, 1921.

Depping, C., *Les Juifs dans le Moyen Age*.

Dozy, Reinhart P. A., *Histoire des Musulmans d'Espagne*, Leyden, 1861.

Duruy, George, *Le Cardinal Carli Carafa*, Paris, 1882.

Eidelberg, Shlomo, "Jewish Life in Austria in the 15th Century," *JPS*, Philadelphia, 1962.

Espina, Alphonse de., *Fortalitium Fidei*, Lyons, 1511.

Finkelstein, Louis, *Akiba, Scholar, Saint, and Martyr*, New York, 1936.

Fita, P., "Templarios, Calatravos y Hebreos," in *Bol. Acad. H.*, XIV, 1889.

Fita, P., "La Inquisicion en Sevilla," in *Bol. Acad. de la Hist.*, XV, 1889.

Frankel, Z., "Monatschriften," Breslau, *JTS.*, 1851-1868.

Goldmann, Salomon, "Iggereth Teman," N.Y. *Histadr. of America*, Vol. XXXIV, 1950.

Galipapa, Hayim, *Emek Rephaim*, 1348.

Gans, David, *Tsemah David*, Offenbach, 1768, Libr. of Congr. Ds 114-G 3.

Gieseler, J. K. L., *Compendium of Ecclesiastical History*, Clark, Edinburgh, 1853.

Goni Gaztambide, Jose, "La matanza de judios en Navarra, en 1328", in *Hispania Sacra*, 1959.

Gomez, Moreno, "Las primeras cronicas de la reconquista," in *Bol. de la Academia de la Historia*, C. 1932.

Gottheil, R., "Columbus in Jewish Literature," in *American Jewish Historical Society*, II.

Graetz, Heinrich, "History of the Jews," *JPS*, Philadelphia, 1941.

Graetz, H., "Les monnais de Simon du temps de l'insurrection des juifs sous Adrien," *REJ*, XVI, 1888.

Gruenebaum, Paul, "Un episode de l'histoire des juifs d'Ancone," *REJ*, XXVIII, 1894.

Hacohen, Joseph, *Emek Habakha*, revised Hebrew ed. Epstein & Co., Jerusalem, 1956.

Hacohen, Joseph, *Emek Habakha*, with critical notes by S. D. Luzzatto and publication by M. Letteris, Vienna, J. P. Sollinger, 1852.

Hacohen, Joseph, *Emek Habacha*, translation into German, w. preface, notes and register by M. Wiener, Leipzig Oscar Leiner, 1858.

Hacohen, Joseph, *Emek Habacha* in Latin by Bibliotheca Caesareo-Regia Vindobonensi.

Hacohen, Joseph, ben Joshua, *Sepher Divrei ha-Yamim l'malke Zarfat u'malke Beth Otoman*, Sabionetta, Cornelio Adelkind, 1553.

Hacohen, Joseph, Amsterdam, *Salomo ben Joseph Proops 1733*.

Hacohen, Joseph, S. Bak & A. J. Menkes, Lemberg, 1859.

Hammer-Purgstall, J. de, *Histoire de L'Empire Ottoman*, 8 Vol., Paris, Bellizard, 1835.

Hammer-Purgstall, J. de, *History of the Ottoman Empire*, Budapest, 1827-35.

Hayyat, Yehuda, *Maarehet Ha-Elohut*, Ferrara, 1557.

Hitti, Philip, "The Origins of the Islamic State," *Columbia Studies*, N.Y., 1961.

Hitti, Philip, *The Arabs*, Chicago, H. Regnery, 1967.

Hyamson, Albert, *A History of the Jews in England*, London, 1928.

Illescas, Gonzalo de, *Jornada de Carlos V a Tunez*, Madrid, 1804.

Jellinet, A, *Zur Geschichte der Kreuzzüge nach handschriftlichen hebräischen Quellen*, Leipzig, 1854.

Jewish Encyclopedia, Funk & Wagnalls Co., N. Y., 1911.

Jost, I. M., *Geschichte der Israeliten*, Schlesinger, Berlin, 1820.

Jost, I. M., *Geschichte des Judentums und seiner Secten*, Leipzig, Doerffling and Franke, 1857.

Juster, *Les Juifs dans l'empire Romain*, Paris, 1914.

Juster, "La condition legale des Juifs sous les roi Wisigoths," in *Etudes d'histoire juridique*, P. F. Girard, 1912.

Kalonymus bar Kalonymus. Even Bohan, ed. Habermann, Tel Aviv, 1956.

Kalonymus bar Kalonymus. Published by Maestro Callo, Naples, 1489.

Kaufmann, David, "Contributions à l'histoire des juifs en Italie," *REJ*, XX, 1890.

Kaufmann, David, "Delivrance des juifs de Rome en l'année 1555," *REJ*, IV, 1882.

Kaufmann, David, "Une page de l'histoire de la Renaissance," *R. E. J.* XXVII, 1893.

Keyserling, C., *Geschichte der Juden in Portugal*, Leipzig, 1967.

Klausner, Joseph, *Historiah shel Hassifruth Ha-Ivrith Hahadashah*, Jerusalem, 1937, Vol. 1-3.

Kestenberg, R., "Hussitentum und Judentum," in *Jahrbuch der Gesellschaft für Geschichte der Juden in der Czechoslovakischen Republic*, VIII, Prague, 1936.

Kraus, Samuel, "Le roi de France Charles VIII et les espérances messianique," *REJ*, LI, 1906.

Kraus, Samuel, *Antoninus und Rabbi*, Vienna, 1910.

Lefevre, Cl. & F., *Miracle des Hosties poignard dées par les Juifs*, "Moyen Age," 1953.

Levy, A., "Don Joseph Nassi," *JQR*, II (1889).

Liebeschuetz, B., "The Crusading Movement in its Bearing on the Christian attitudes toward Jewry," *The Journal of Jewish Studies*, VOL X, 1959.

Loeb, Is., "Les expulsions des juifs de France au XIVe siècle," in *Jubelschrift, in honor of H. Graetz*, Breslau, 1887.

Loeb, Is., *Joseph Hacohen et les chroniquers juifs*, Paris, 1888.

Loeb, Is., "Les Exiles d'Espane en France," *REJ*, X.

Martin, Felipe Ruiz,. "La Expulsion de los judios del reino de Napoles," in *Hispania*, XXXIV, 1949.

Marx, A., "Texts by and about Maimonides," in *JQR*, N. S., XXV, 1935.

Max, A., "The Expulsion of the Jews from Spain," *JQR*, XX, 1908.

Meisel, W., *Eben Bochan* (in German), Budapest, 1878.

Miret y Sanz., "El asesinato de los Judios de Monclus en 1320. Episodio de los pastorells en Aragon," *REJ*, LIII, 1907.

Modona, Leonello., "Les Exiles d'Espagne a Ferrare," *REJ*, XX (1890).

Morais, S., *Italian Hebrew Literature*, N. Y. 1926 3 d. by Jul. H. Greenstone.

Muenz, J., *Moses ben Maimon. Sein Leben und seine Werke*, Frankfurt, 1912.

Muenster, Sebastian, *Cosmographia Universa*, Heidelberg, 1868., Paris, 1575.

Munk, Salomon, *Melanges de Philosophie Juive et Arabe*, Paris, A. Franck, 1859.

Neubauer, A., "Document sur David Alroi (de Isaac Sambari)," *REJ*, IV, 1882.

Neubauer, A., *Medieval Jewish Chonicles*, Clarendon Press, 1887 (Hebr).

Nostradamus, Cesar de, *Histoire et chronique de Province*, Lyon, 1614.

Pastor, Luis., *Historia de los Papas*, Barcelona, 1927.

Porges, "Les relations hebraiques des persecutions des juifs pendant la premiere croisade," *REJ*, XXV, 1893.

Prescott, Wm. Hickling, *History of the Reign of Ferdinand & Isabella, the Catholic in Spain*, 1837.

Ranke, Leop, *History of the Roman Popes*, Lea & Blanchard, Phila, 1884.

Rapoport, Sal. Yeh. Loeb, *Ereh Millin*, Landau, Prague, 1852.

Rassow, P., "Die Kanzlei St. Bernards von Clairvaux", in *Studien und Mitteilungen zur Geschichte des Benediktiner Ordens*, XXXIV, 1913.

Reusch, H., *Der Index der Verbotenen Buecher*, 2 Vol., Bonn, 1883-1885.

Rigg, J. M., "The Jews of England in the 13th Century," *JQR*, XV, 1903-1904.

Rodocanachi, Emmanuel, *Le Saint Siege et les juifs. Le gheto a Rome*, Paris, 1891.

Rosenberg, H., *Alcuni documenti reiguardanti in Marrani portogusi in Ancona*, Citta di Castelo, 1935.

Rossi, Azariah de, *Kol Elohim*.

Roth, Cecil., *Standard Jewish Encyclopedia*.

Runciman, S., *A History of the Crusades*, Cambridge University Press, 1951 (vol. I and II).

Sacerdos, Gustare, "Deux Index expurgatoires de livres hebreux," in *REJ*, XXX, 1895.

Sauval, Henri, *Histoire et antiquites de la ville de Paris*, 1724.

Schirmann, I., "Joseph ha-Naggid," in *Moznayim*, 1939.

Schudt, Joh. Jacob, *Juedische Merkwuerdigkeiten*, Frankfurt a/M, 1717.

Schuerer, O., *Geschichte des Juedischen Volkes im Zeitalter Jesu Christi*, I, 1898.

Sée, J., *Emek habacha*, transl. from French, Paris, 1881.

Steinhartz, S., "The Expulsion of the Jews from Bohemia in 1541," in *Zion*, XV, 1950.

Tello, Pilar Leon, "Emeq Ha-bakha de Yosef Hacohen," in *Instituto Arias Montano*, Madrid-Barcelona, 1964.

Tillemont, Sebastien Le Nain de, *Histoire des Empereurs*, II.

Torrutiel, "Abr. ben Shelomo de Sepher ha-Kabbalah," ed. Neubauer in *Med. Jew Chronicle*, I.

Treece, H., *The Crusades*, Random House, N. Y., 1963.

Universal Jewish Encyclopedia, N. Y., 1941.

Usque, Samuel, *Consolacam as Tribulacoes de Israel*, Ferrara, 1552.

Vajda, E., "Récentes publications sur Maimonide," in *Journal Asiatique*, CCXLI, 1953.

Verga, Salomon ibn, *Shevet Yehudah*, ed. Sohet. Jerusalem, 1947.

Villani, Giovanni, *Historie Fiorentine*, Milano, 1729.

Vogelstein, H. and Rieger, H., *Geschichte der Juden in Rom*, II, Berlin, 1895.

Waxman, M., *A History of Jewish Literature*, Vol. 2, Thomas Yoseloff, N. Y. and London, 1933 and 1960.

Wickersheimer, B., *Les accusations d'empoisonnements portées pendant la première moitié du XIVe siècle contre les lepreux et les juifs* (4. International Congress de la Historia de la Medicina, Brussels, 1932.

Wilken, A., *Geschichte der Kreuzzüge*, I.

Wolf, Gerson, *Geschichte der Juden in Wien*, Vienna, 1861.

Yachya, Joseph ibn, *Shalshelet ha-Kabbalah*, Venice, 1586, Jerusalem, 1962.

Zacuto, Abraham, *Sepher Yushasin*, edit, Filipowski, London, 1857.

Zeitlin, Solomon, "The Legend of the Ten Martyrs and its Apocalyptic Origins", *JQR*, XXXVI.

Zeitlin, Solomon, "The Fiction of the Bar Kokhba letters", *JQR*, LI, April 1961.

ibn Zerah, Menahem ben Aharon, *Tseda le-derekh*, edit. Sabionetta.

Zunz, Leop, *Gottesdienstliche Vorträge*, J. Kaufmann, Frankfort a/M, 1892.

Zunz, Leop, *Zeitschrift des wissenschaftlichen Judentums*, Berlin, 1823, Vol. I.

Zunz, Leop, *Zeitung des Judentums*, Berlin, 1857.

INDEX OF NAMES